CONGRESS AND NATIONAL
ENERGY POLICY

CONGRESS AND NATIONAL ENERGY POLICY

JAMES EVERETT KATZ

Transaction Books
New Brunswick (U.S.A.) and London (U.K.)

For

JURGEN SCHMANDT

Copyright © 1984 by Transaction, Inc.
New Brunswick, New Jersey 08903

All rights reserved under International and Pan-American Copyright Conventions. No part of this book may be reproduced or transmitted in any form or by any means, electronic or mechanical, including photocopy, recording, or any information storage and retrieval system, without prior permission in writing from the publisher. All inquiries should be addressed to Transaction Books, Rutgers—The State University, New Brunswick, New Jersey 08903.

Library of Congress Catalog Number: 83-17878
ISBN: 0-87855-486-6 (cloth)
Printed in the United States of America

Library of Congress Cataloging in Publication Data

Katz, James Everett.
  Congress and national energy policy.

  Includes index.
  1. Energy policy—United States.   2. United States.
Congress.   I. Title.
HD9502.U52K38 1984   333.79′0973   83-17878
ISBN 0-87855-486-6

Contents

Preface

Energy is commonly appreciated as a crucial issue and often considered, as by President Jimmy Carter, the greatest problem, short of war, that will be faced by the present generation. It is a primary cause of the current competition between the major world powers and indeed determines to a great extent the state of nations.

As the United States struggles to adjust to the new realities of an inimical energy regime, the perspectives of sociology and political science offer a new view of the dramatic events taking place. The clash of conflicting political, economic, and sociological forces can be seen at all levels of the United States government.

There is a general consensus that U.S. energy policy should be directed toward at least four fundamental goals:

1. Adequate or increased energy supplies.
2. Increased conservation and efficiency in end use.
3. Reduced U.S. dependency on (not necessarily use of) imported energy.
4. Protection against disruption of foreign energy supplies.

Despite consensus on these goals, the government's role in attaining them has been highly controversial. The federal government has used an array of programs, including price controls and supports, energy market regulation, and the allocation of energy supplies. An enduring point of contention in all such programs has been the extent to which various groups have or have not been served, be they citizens, businesses, energy producers, or energy consumers.

The main focus of this book is on the ideologies and policies that have driven the U.S. government in pursuit of the above goals. The search for specific programs that would fulfill the above goals, and the institutional mechanisms used to implement these programs once they were devised, are examined in detail. The leadership of the federal bureaucracy—the president, his top staff, advisors, and cabinet officials—are shown in their roles as energy policy makers and negotiators. The principal focus of the book, however, is on Congress's energy policy and the dramatic changes that have recently occurred in this area. Congress's organizational processes are examined in the light of an expanding understanding of what constitutes the energy problem, and what means must be adopted for its solution.

This book investigates the creation of new agencies in the federal bureaucracy, the assignment of authority as a response to energy problems, and Congress's utilization of its own administrative support units to control its policy environment.

Congress is a critical forum for the discussion and resolution of major national problems and makes major contributions to the creation of national policy. Also its role in policymaking is relatively open to assessment by the public. However, Congress has been increasingly criticized for its inability to effectively respond to the challenges of the modern world. It has been claimed that the legislative body is fractionated by regional and special interests, that a breakdown of party disciplines has led to chaos, and that its archaic structure obstructs rapid response to complex problems. Congress's handling of the energy problem is often cited as a graphic example of its inadequacies. This book assesses the validity of this accusation and other congressional weaknesses that may interfere with the U.S. policy process.

It is hoped that the conclusions reached through this analysis would be used to achieve a clearer understanding of governmental organization and power in the United States.

It is with immense pleasure that I can at last thank publicly those who have contributed to the successful completion of this book. Professor Irving Louis Horowitz played a crucial part in this project. He inspired me to undertake the research and encouraged me to persevere. I deeply appreciate his guidance and insights. Dr. Craig Shapiro gave me important help in the early stages of research. Mr. Robert Reynolds provided invaluable research assistance and contributed many helpful suggestions and critical comments, especially in chapters 12 and 13.

Ms. Laura Battey lent her superb intellectual and editorial skills to improving the manuscript. Her fine hand is evident throughout and I greatly benefitted from her efforts.

Being able to thank these talented individuals does not discharge my debt of gratitude to them, but I wish to recognize their work in print. They have my heartfelt and enduring thanks.

PART ONE
THE STRUGGLE

1
America's Horizon Darkens

The seemingly sudden emergence of the energy crisis in the early 1970s was actually the result of gradual and often dimly perceived changes in both the domestic and foreign situations.

The Domestic Scene

While the fact that the United States consumes 30 percent of the world's energy production is often cited as an example of American profligacy, it is less well known that in the early 1950s this country consumed an even larger percentage of the world's output. Most of the energy, however, was domestically produced. Over the past century the United States has been a net energy exporter and the average cost/unit of energy has declined in absolute terms. This history did not prepare the American public for the precipitous deterioration of the energy situation in the 1970s.

First, brown-outs occurred as electric generation failed to meet peak demand, gas utilities refused to make new connections, and heating oil supplies became scarce. The already diminishing supply of oil in 1973 was further decreased by an oil embargo which forced sacrifice on consumers and disrupted political and economic processes. Gas lines, lowered speed limits, and school and factory closings made real to the American people the dramatic reduction in energy supplies and a new dependence on foreign sources of oil. The possibility of a future massive societal disruption over energy supplies was foreshadowed in the civil disobedience and violence caused by fuel shortages during the summer of 1979.

Although the United States still possesses huge energy resources—its gigantic coal reserves, for example—and is the third largest oil producer in the world, the cost advantages it once had in finding and producing energy have now been lost. This highly industrialized country, built upon energy-intensive activities and low-cost energy sources, is adjusting to a new set of economic conditions. The shift to more expensive energy is altering national economic and social patterns. In the past, social and economic problems were ameliorated through the availability of low-cost energy, but for the foreseeable future this opportunity has been lost.[1]

As the American public was unprepared for the shortages of the 1970s, so

3

the federal government was organizationally ill-equipped for handling energy affairs. Congress in particular was called upon to resolve the energy problem, but it, like the executive branch, was too uncoordinated, fractured, and goal-conflicted to respond with specific programs or long-range policies that could effectively deal with the energy shortages of the early 1970s.

Congress was at the forefront of the search for a national energy policy, because of both public demand and its own self-perception as a vital national force. However, there were several factors that militated against Congress being successful in its search. First, there was no national consensus on either the nature of the energy problem or how to respond to it. Second, the history of American energy policy, and the evolution of policy structures to administer it, had not prepared Congress for dealing with energy in a direct way. Finally, changes in America's global standing and in international politics foreclosed options which had in the past been successfully exercised.

Consensus On Energy Policy Nonexistent

The American public's consensus on the major issues facing the government, and which had provided a base of support for the country in the period following World War II, gave way to the emergence of myriad issues dividing Americans along ethnic, class, regional, and occupational lines. Containing communism was no longer perceived as the dominant mission of America and no new unifying purpose has emerged in its place. Accompanying this erosion of consensus has been a decline in citizen faith in the government and the institutions controlling the society. One opinion poll after another has shown sharp drops in the public's confidence in Congress and the executive branch.

This fundamental shift has had radical consequences for the United States government as it struggles with the creation, direction, and oversight of American policies. Public problems created by accelerated change spill over from the area of policy to profoundly affect the government structures and processes themselves. This is particularly true of Congress as an organization which has had to adapt to changing conditions in its external political environment in order to remain a viable force.

In the 1970s Congress could no longer anticipate the attitudes of its constituents and supporters toward the novel and complex issues it was being forced to confront. At the same time, the prestige and support formerly given to government officials by the public, legitimizing new policies and approaches, were no longer offered. Yet, as its relationships to constituents have increased in complexity, and the environment itself has grown more complex, Congress, in its central position in the government policy process, has come under increasing pressure to deal with aspects of its environment over which it has diminishing control.

American Energy Policy History Contains Diverging Themes

For the past two centuries, until 1973, American energy policy, such as it was, was dominated by one assumption: there are bountiful and practically limitless energy supplies that should be exploited. However, who should benefit from this bounty, and who should control these vast resources, was more problematic. Three themes emerged sequentially to address this question, and new policies were established in turn which took up each theme.

Before the 1870s, a laissez-faire or "hands off," "first come, first serve" theme characterized the United States government's position in relation to energy resource use. The scant energy policy that had been formulated ad hoc responded to particular problems and private interests, and each energy source was perceived as an independent entity. Because public land distribution was used by the government as a source of revenue, resources rapidly became privately owned. Such action was justified on the basis of a national faith in unlimited growth and unlimited resources.[2]

By the beginning of the twentieth century, however, due to a dawning realization that energy sources were indeed finite, competing interests were demanding representation in the energy policymaking process. While the segmented patterns continued, the government increasingly was forced into performing the new function of allocating resources and making compromises among the increasing number of contestants demanding a piece of the energy pie. Policy formed on the basis of the nineteenth century belief in unlimited opportunity, an infinitely expandable frontier, and infinitely expendable resources had not, however, been replaced; decisions were still made on the basis of distributive procedures. A second theme thus appeared during the Progressive Era, which was that the government should be involved in assuring a stable and competitive market, especially in oil.[3]

In the 1910s there were demands for the resolution of oil industry problems, such as fluctuating or high prices, unstable supplies and monopolistic practices, and even calls for an extension of federal influence over the production and marketing of petroleum products.

With *Standard Oil v. U.S.* (1911), the United States government made its first real attempt to control oil policy by using the Sherman Anti-trust Act to break up Standard Oil. Under President Woodrow Wilson, the Petroleum Advisory Committee allocated American supplies. During World War I, the government discovered that the existence of a vertically integrated industry with centralized authority allowed more government control, since fewer people had to be consulted in decision making.

Even at this time, oil was creating problems for Americans and causing the public to question the probity, quality, and ability of its government. In 1912, President Taft set aside publicly owned lands to preserve oil for the navy, but in 1921 Interior Secretary Albert Fall persuaded President Harding and the Secretary of the Navy to transfer the reserves to the Interior Department. After the transfer was complete, Fall leased the land to oil companies in return for various bribes, instead of soliciting competitive bids.

The ensuing Teapot Dome scandal caused President Coolidge to establish the Federal Oil Conservation Board to oversee the oil industry. In a later development, the oil lobby displayed its impressive influence by winning congressional protection which was later parlayed into even greater influence. Two major tax subsidies for the oil and gas producers, established in 1926, provided for intangible drilling costs and a 27.5 percent wellhead depletion allowance. By increasing the rate of return from oil and gas exploration, development, and production, the capital flow to the oil industry was increased, relative to other investments, including those in other energy sources. As a result, domestic oil and gas production was artificially stimulated. This lowered their price (relative to other energy sources) for most of the past half century and caused them to attract greater user demand than other energy sources.[4]

In the 1930s the exploitation of large Texas fields caused a glut of oil and a sharp drop in oil prices. This brought havoc to the oil industry and led eventually in the late 1930s to prorationing the market to regulate demand and control prices, causing prices to rise to the satisfaction of producers, but resulting in domestic oil costing substantially more than it would have if it could have been freely produced domestically or delivered from abroad. (Low foreign oil prices led eventually to political pressure from major domestic oil companies and coal producers who obtained mandatory quotas on oil imports in 1958. In the name of national security high levels of costly domestic production would be protected to avoid foreign dependence and the possibility of supply interruption.[5])

Also during the 1930s a third theme emerged, which maintained that the federal government should represent the consumer and protect his interest in the marketplace. The Natural Gas Act of 1938, which extended federal control over interstate gas pipelines, and the establishment of the Tennessee Valley Authority, which provided low-cost power and rural development, were two examples. This redistributive theme was simply added to the other two—rapid exploitation of domestic resources and governmental manipulation to enhance market competitiveness—without any attempt to rationalize or coordinate policy across fuel and use areas. Each area of energy supply—coal, gas, hydro, oil (and eventually nuclear)—was handled separately, as was each consumption sector—utilities, transportation, industrial, and residential.

Energy policy actions in the 1950s aggravated this problem. Tax decisions made it more profitable to drill oil overseas while an oil import quota was levied to stimulate domestic production. The nation committed itself to a

42,000-mile interstate highway network while interurban rail and mass transit withered. The Supreme Court ratified the Federal Power Commission's powers to regulate natural gas prices, which held prices very low as gas consumption skyrocketed. The Eisenhower administration abandoned its investment in research aimed at advancing the gasoline-from-coal technology developed in Germany during the war, and other fuel conversion research was also dropped during the postwar years.

Thus, by the 1970s the low prices of oil and gas had been subsidized by the general taxpayer, to the detriment of other energy sources, while the actual cost of energy was held artificially high by restricting imports of foreign oil. The consequence of these policies was that America was more heavily dependent on gas, and especially on oil, than if there had been no governmental policies distorting the energy market.

Although the "public interest" is difficult to define, it is clear that the past half century of government policy has not always served the United States's general welfare. Since the 1920s there has been a record of conflicting and counterproductive government energy policies, initiated and supported by special interest groups. While the oil industry is largely responsible for creating criss-crossing policies of privilege and preference, the coal industry, consumer and environmental groups, and labor unions also won concessions and special benefits. In short, government policy was formed in response to the most dominant or organized group regardless of its impact on either the larger energy picture or the general public interest. This energy decision-making method caused a movement away from the market system toward increasing government intervention to correct and modify earlier decisions. It also contributed significantly to the energy shortages and perilous dependence on foreign oil in the early 1970s.

Segmented Policy

This method of accretion has been largely maintained until the present, and today's energy policy is still the result of competing and conflicting interests. However, since the 1960s this process has become more difficult and more complex because of the addition of strong new interests demanding participation in energy decision making. The involvement of environmentalists, new energy industries (such as those represented by the solar lobby), and public interest groups in energy policy, and an increasing recognition of resource scarcity, have weakened the accepted system of energy policymaking and obscured the boundaries between the public and private sectors in resource allocation. Besides the addition of new interest groups, the involvement of leadership at the highest levels in response to energy shortages and the international implications of energy crises have further complicated energy policy processes. At the same time, the clientelism, which is produced by pluralistic decision making, obstructs policy adjustments to meet energy challenges. Thus, while an innovative and comprehensive energy policy has become increasingly necessary, the means for its realization have become increasingly complicated and elusive.

Linkages among congressional committees and subcommittees, executive agencies, and outside interest groups have formed interlocked triangles of operation, referred to as "cozy triangles," "subgovernments," and "policy whirlpools." The energy policy system is especially illustrative of this fractionated and highly politicized method of decision making, because it is divided into subsystems formed around coal, oil, natural gas, electricity, and nuclear energy, each with its own problems and demands. The energy policy system is thus a collection of discrete decision-making structures, fragmented by clientelism, and lacking coordination, or even communication.

The 1973-74 Arab oil embargo destroyed what little potential this system had for effective energy policymaking. It scrambled the "cozy triangles" to the point of virtual ineffectualness or forced their readjustment. At the same time, the resource subsystems, that before the embargo maintained a fair degree of stability and self-containment through their individual methods of addressing problems, after 1973 grew increasingly incapable of producing policy that was relevant to the new realities of resource scarcity and the new demands for participation in policymaking. Energy policy could no longer be simply the sum of individual interests and decisions combined through small adjustments in operating techniques.

An increasing demand for comprehensive planning and program coordination to connect the resource-based subsystems has forced a general realization that change is urgent.

America's International Preeminence Has Been Reduced

Aggravating attempts to devise comprehensive solutions to complex, interrelated problems is the fact that the United States is much less a powerful free agent in the world community and much more a giant constrained by the interests and activities of other nations. While at the close of World War II the United States was in a position to impose many of its wishes on other countries, this is no longer the case. Congress, along with Americans in general, has had trouble adjusting to that fact.

The national economy is society's engine and the United States economy, which at an earlier period existed with a modicum of independence from the global situation, is now deeply enmeshed with that of the entire world. The United States economy requires imports in order to function and exports in order to remain viable. Labor policy, monetary actions, crop prices, steel production, and other influences that may emanate from the opposite side of the world influence directly and indirectly the daily life and economy of the United States. Economic interactions are now more direct, significant, and frequent.

Transnational corporations have become a force in world trade, now accounting for about 15 percent of the world's gross national product.[6] At the same time, transnational oil companies (most of them U.S.-based), which had long dominated international petroleum trade, do not have as strong a political backing from their home governments as they used to. Once power brokers, they have become mere oil brokers, while international oil trade itself has become unprecedentedly large.

These and related developments have become significant because the United States government is no longer able to exercise direction over the economy independently of other nations' economies to the extent it once could. This situation reinforces the importance of economics in politics and policy, diminishes the distinction between domestic and foreign economic issues, and makes a clear understanding of foreign developments imperative.

Nations have also become physically interdependent. Environmental destruction and pollution in one nation can affect its neighbors, and even countries on other continents. Nuclear weapons proliferation and easier methods of their delivery mean that events in distant countries can rapidly come to threaten the United States.

The change in the relative importance of America in the world constitutes another significant alteration in the global environment. While the United States is still one of the most powerful nations, its dominance has declined. Since the end of World War II the United States has lost its nuclear weapons monopoly and its strategic invulnerability. In 1950 the United States was responsible for half of the world's military expenditures; by 1983 this figure had been more than halved. In the same years, the U.S.'s proportion of the world's monetary reserves dropped from 59 percent to 6 percent; the percentage of world goods it manufactured over the same period declined from 60 percent to 28 percent.[7] While at one time United States power over other nations often made the expression of its will concomitant with its realization, today it must bargain and enlist other nations' support for policy coordination.

New coalitions have emerged which have further redistributed power. China and the Third World have emerged. Europe and Japan have recovered their industrial power. Along with the multiplications of actors, issues have become many-sided; the problems of food, energy, trade, economics, and natural resources now involve many nations and are addressed through many forums. Rather than two or even three blocs dividing the world, there are numerous and often conflicting regional, economic, and ideological interest groups.

The best recent illustration of the changed global situation is the 1973-74 Organization of Arab Petroleum Exporting Countries (OAPEC) oil embargo, levied by the Arab oil-exporting nations, some of which were considered by the United States to be friendly regimes. This natural resource embargo was designed to create an unacceptable economic hardship so that exporting nations could win politically what they could not achieve militarily. The result, which involved penalizing the American consumer for United States foreign policy, drove home a realization of the interrelatedness of the various policy positions. Yet despite the United States' reduced international economic power, why was it unable to use its still massive economic and military power to force the embargoing nations to comply with American wishes and ward off the threat to national survival? Why was the United States forced to handle an international resource problem domestically rather than by expropriating the needed resource from another country through coercion?

United States Options Foreclosed

In order to answer this question, it is necessary to look at the factors leading to the degeneration of the traditional power arrangements between nations. Political power in modern history results from a functional relationship between military and economic power, which is based on technological achievement. Thus the People's Republic of China is prevented from being a power equal to the United States and the Soviet Union by its technological backwardness. Similarly, Britain was only able to conquer India (which was more advanced than Britain in some respects and had considerably larger manpower resources) because of Britain's higher order of technological achievement, which was irresistible when transformed into military power.[8]

However, the functional relationship between technology and economic, military, and political power has been dramatically altered by the recent use of oil as a political weapon. The states levying the embargo weapon have none of the components which in the past have led to power. Suddenly, by the single fact of their possessing oil, these states have become a significant force in global politics and economics. The OAPEC nations were able to impose their will on Japan, causing her to reverse long-standing national policies toward the Middle East, and coerce many Western European nations to declare support for the Arab cause. To resist the political demands of OAPEC could have meant strangulation for Japan and stagnation for Europe— essentially, social and economic catastrophe.[9]

In the past, the technologically advanced nations have had counterweapons with which to balance any threat to a vital resource. The traditional answer to coercion has been economic sanctions. Thus, when the Iranians nationalized their oil fields in 1953, oil buyers, simply and in concert, bypassed the Iranian oil in favor of other resources. This quickly brought the revolting Iranians to their knees and the cooperative Shah back to power. However, by 1973 what had historically been a buyer's market in oil had shifted to a seller's market and several of the largest producers had joined the embargo, which left no alternative energy sources readily available.

Other types of economic counterweapons, such as a retaliatory embargo on spare parts, vital trade items, or food were simply not feasible. Unlike the need for oil in a large industrial nation, the need for food in a small nation, as, for example, Abu Dhabi with 200,000 citizens, could easily be met by a food-producing nation antagonistic to Western interests. In the global contest of power, the Western nations are counterbalanced by the Communist nations, especially the Soviet Union and People's Republic of China. These powers would offset any economic sanctions not totally supported by an air and naval blockade.

An embargo on spare parts would only prevent the production of oil, defeating the purpose of the retaliatory action. Further, the effects of such a counterembargo would only be felt after several months of continued oil field operation. The same factors that weaken a nation also make it insensitive to economic disruptions which could be levied by the Western nations. The facetious suggestion that the West can embargo only TV sets, air conditioners, and Hollywood movies, though an exaggeration, suggests the reality that low technology economies are not easily damaged by the withdrawal of modern amenities or even modern "necessities."

The traditional remedy to situations similar to the embargo, the solution which has worked effectively in the past, is the exercise of military force. A power that refused to supply a raw material considered necessary by a militarily stronger nation was either conquered and colonized by that power, or forced into a semicolonial position. Such solutions were not feasible during the 1973-74 embargo for three reasons. First, such action is now considered morally reprehensible. The postwar era is an age of decolonization.

Second, a nation resorting to military force would now find itself faced with a guerilla war in the occupied nation, and the experience of decolonization and the moral resistance to the restoration of a colonial or semicolonial relationship have resulted in a strong commitment to resist new attempts at subjugation by military expeditions. Moral and military factors empty the word "victory" of substantive significance, as has been amply demonstrated by the American experience in Vietnam. Short of physically destroying a guerilla force and the indigenous population which supports it, it is most difficult for an occupying force to win a guerilla war even with dramatic military superiority.

The third reason is the interpenetration of political and military factors as discussed earlier. A military expedition against an oil-producing nation fifty years ago would have been an isolated incident, a localized matter with few reverberations. Today, however, such an incursion would not be a narrowly delimited event but a cause of worldwide repercussions, perhaps drawing the Soviet Union into direct conflict with the United States. Such a possibility almost became reality during the 1973 Arab-Israeli war. Any attempt to re-align the situation through military force faces enormous problems. This does not mean that a military expedition to the Middle East is impossible. Nations pressed to the wall in their need for natural resources can be driven to war, despite the great national peril. This was demonstrated by the Japanese attack on the United States in 1941, which was precipitated to an extent by America's cutting off oil to Japan.

The problems and options facing the West that have been posed by oil supply disruptions are not separate from the larger confrontations and compe-tition in world politics. The United States and Soviet Union compete and struggle in the Middle East as they do elsewhere.[10]

The implications of the United States' external weakness in combatting OAPEC meant that the response would have to be largely internal. Thus the externally induced crisis permits an analysis of how an American institution—in this case the Congress—behaves in response to a severe crisis. To understand how severe, it would be useful to review the domestic events that made the United States particularly vulnerable to the OAPEC oil em-bargo.

Oil Dependency: A Perennial Concern

From the very beginning of America's dependence on oil, concern had been expressed about the consequences if the supply were interrupted. In 1866 the United States Revenue Commission wanted to insure that synthetic re-placements would be available when the then-known crude reserves were ex-hausted. In 1914 the Bureau of Mines warned that the total future production of the United States would be 6 billion barrels, about the amount now produced every two years.[11] In 1920 the United States Geological Survey admonished that "the position of the United States in regard to oil" was "precarious," and a few weeks later another Geological Survey official stated that "within perhaps three years, our domestic production will begin to fall off with in-creasing rapidity due to the exhaustion of our reserves."[12]

After World War II there were repeated warnings about dependence on foreign oil or the depletion of domestic reserves. The Payley Commission in the early 1950s, the Office of Science and Technology studies and the annual report of the Atlantic Richfield Company in the 1960s, and the National Intel-ligence Estimate in 1973 sounded warnings which were persistently ignored, largely because so often they had been without substance. Each time the question of energy dependence was raised, the failure of previous predictions was the response, and the low price of energy sustained a general lack of interest.

In 1956 M. King Hubbert, then a petroleum geologist with Shell, told petroleum engineers that United States oil production would reach its peak by 1971 at the latest. It was, in fact, reached in 1970. (Shell deleted this prediction in the published version of Hubbert's paper.)[13]

As the energy supply system became more taut and precarious, a few "voices in the wilderness," noticing that circumstances had changed, tried to incite government action, but to no avail. The core issue was that the oil supply was becoming more important, more imported, and more vulnerable to interruption; soon it was to be held hostage for America's foreign policy.

1973: Dire Predictions Materialize

A rare confluence of negative influences occurred in the United States energy picture in 1973. Historically self-reliant for its oil needs, the United States first became a net importer of oil in 1947; by 1973 the country was importing nearly 7 million barrels a day. Daily production from domestic sources doubled over this same period, peaking at 11.2 million in 1970 and declining to 10.8 million in 1973. Imported oil accounted for 30 percent of the total United States demand in 1973; oil imported directly from Arab sources accounted for over a million barrels a day, more than double the amount imported eighteen months earlier.

In spite of the increasing dependence on imported oil, the real prices for domestic oil had declined. The price of energy had risen less rapidly than that of other goods and services. Thus the United States and other countries, following the classic economic model, increased their demand. Yet by mid-1973, even before the embargo darkened its horizon, the United States was experiencing an unprecedented shortage of refined petroleum products, despite steadily rising oil imports. The shortage was due in part to insufficient domestic refining capacity and strong foreign demand for petroleum products. The West had become overwhelmingly dependent on insecure sources of oil, yet had no reasonable contingency plan in the event of a supply interruption.

In addition, the cost of discovering and recovering coal and oil in Europe and America increased during the 1950s and 1960s, while oil from the Middle East was remarkably inexpensive by comparison. (Extraction cost about 10¢ a barrel.) Because of the price disparity, domestic sources declined in importance and the Western economies became heavily dependent on imported oil. There had been enough unused capacity in the world system so that the earlier embargoes, during the 1958 Suez crisis and the 1967 Arab-Israeli war, went largely unnoticed. In fact, the United States was able to increase its own domestic production to meet the shortfalls facing Europe. However, 1972 - 1973 was an unusual period of marked economic expansion throughout the

West (Europe, the United States, and Japan), which sharply increased the demand for petroleum and strained the capacity of available tanker fleets. Natural gas supplies had fallen off due to price regulation imposed on interstate shipments, and, as a result, consumers switched to oil.

Simultaneously, environmental demands made the acquisition of alternative energy sources such as shale more difficult and expensive. Coal mine and strip mine legislation discouraged coal production. Air quality standards prompted many utilities to burn oil in place of coal. The slow pace of nuclear energy development and the accompanying legal, procedural, and environmental restrictions meant a greater-than-anticipated reliance on oil. Emission standards aimed at reducing auto pollution meant an all-time low gas mileage rate at the same time that Americans were driving more miles than ever before. All these factors added to the demand for petroleum and, with the artificially low prices of oil and gas, wasteful and inefficient uses went unnoticed—dangerously so, given the limits of both the energy supply and its security.

Environmental safeguards also hampered efforts to find sources of more domestic oil and gas. There were administrative postponements, procedural setbacks, and dilatory court cases until legal issues could be resolved and until data could be gathered and assessed on the environmental impact of various energy exploration and exploitation projects. Concern over environmental destruction delayed the construction of the Trans-Alaska Pipeline, designed to tap newly discovered oil and gas on Alaska's North Slope. In the wake of a highly publicized blow-out in the Santa Barbara Channel, a five-year moratorium on drilling was levied there. Sales of leases for oil exploration on the Outer Continental Shelf and federal lands were delayed, pending environmental impact assessments.

All these restrictions placed an increasing demand on the declining domestic oil resources. The situation in other countries, especially in regard to air pollution and delays in nuclear power station construction, was not markedly different. World demand for oil was at a record high.

Finally, the United States price controls, which had been applied to domestically produced oil that at one time was above world prices, remained unchanged as world prices rose, with the consequence that there was less profitability in, and therefore less production of, "old" United States oil.

Thus, within this framework of high demand and limited sources, the embargo hit home. Most threatened Western nations quickly conceded to OAPEC demands. Their surrender was complete and abject, with the exception of Holland and the United States. How the United States policy makers dealt with the domestic ramifications of the energy shortage and the 1973-74 crisis in particular is discussed next.

Notes

1. Frank Helmut and John Schanz, *The Economics of Energy Problems* (New York: Joint Council on Economic Education, 1975).
2. United States Congress, Interior and Insular Affairs Committee, "History of Federal Energy Organization: A Staff Analysis," committee print (Serial 93-19), 1973; David H. Davis, *Energy Politics*, 2nd ed. (New York: St. Martin's, 1978); George W. Pierson, "The M-factor in American History," *American Quarterly* 14 no. 2, part 2 (1962), pp. 275-89.
3. Robert Wiebe, *The Search for Order, 1877-1920* (New York: Hill and Wang, 1966); Richard Hofstadter, *Age of Reform: From Bryan to FDR* (New York: Knopf, 1955).
4. Walter J. Mead, "An Overview of Past United States Energy Policy," *Materials and Society* 2 (1978), pp. 109-11.
5. Ibid, p. 110; M. A. Adelman, "Efficiency of Resource Use in Crude Petroleum," *Southern Economics Journal* 31 (July 1964), pp. 101-22.
6. Robert O. Keohane and Joseph Nye, Jr., *Power and Interdependence: World Politics in Transition* (Boston: Little Brown, 1977); *Transnational Relations and World Politics* (Boston: Harvard University Press, 1972).
7. International Monetary Fund, *International Financial Statistics* 35 (August 1982), p. 41; *Handbook of Economic Statistics* (Washington, D.C.: National Foreign Assessment Center, 1980).
8. Hans Morgenthau, "World Politics and the Politics of Oil," in Gary D. Eppen, ed., *Energy: The Policy Issue* (Chicago: University of Chicago Press, 1975).
9. James E. Katz, "International Energy Agency: Processes and Prospects in an Age of Energy Interdependence," *Studies in Comparative International Development* 16 (Summer 1981), pp. 67-85; Henry Nau, "U.S. Foreign Policy and the Politics of Oil, "*Atlantic Community Quarterly* 12 (1975), pp. 426-39.
10. Irving L. Horowitz, *Three Worlds of Development*, rev. ed. (New York: Oxford University Press, 1972); "Death and Transfiguration in the Third World," *Worldview* (September 1977), pp. 20-25.
11. Edward J. Mitchell, *U.S. Energy Policy: A Primer* (Washington, D.C.: American Enterprise Institute, 1974).
12. Robert Sherrill, "The Case Against the Oil Companies," *New York Times Magazine*, October 14, 1979, sect. 6.
13. Linda Charlton, "Decades of Inaction Brought Energy Gap," *New York Times*, February 10, 1974, p. 42.

2
Oil and Turmoil:
Congress and the Nixon Administration

The Energy Situation 1973

In 1973 the halting and sometimes contradictory steps undertaken by the federal government in an attempt to offset the worsening energy crisis (see chapter 1) were further weakened and counteracted by congressional divisiveness, fluctuating administrative dictums, and the influences of powerful special interests. These impediments to policy formulation, and the legislative entanglements they caused, increased the United States' vulnerability to the Arab oil embargo and interfered with the implementation of appropriate energy programs.

During most of the Nixon administration, energy policymaking was subsumed under general economic policy and organizational planning. In 1971, however, his Economic Stabilization Program addressed itself directly to energy legislation. The first phase of this program, effective August 15, 1971, included a price freeze on crude oil and petroleum products for ninety days; this action, one of the most radical economic policy moves ever made by the United States, froze wages and prices throughout the economy. Phase two of the Economic Stabilization Program, which lasted from November 14, 1971, to January 10, 1973, controlled the trade and price of all newly produced crude oil and petroleum products. Phase three returned the oil industry to a free-enterprise structure, with an admonition to "exercise voluntary restraints on price increase."[1]

On January 17, 1973, Nixon restructured the country's mandatory oil import quota plan, a plan which had limited the amount of foreign-produced oil that could be brought into the United States, thereby protecting domestic producers of expensive oil from being undersold by oil importers. Nixon's changes allowed the unlimited purchase of home heating oil and diesel oil from foreign sources for the next four months. Oil import quotas were later relaxed, then ended, partly in response to pressure from a coalition of Northeastern and Midwestern congressmen.

As Congress, the administration, and special interest groups battled over the quota issue, a reshaping of high level federal energy policy structure began. In early February 1973, Nixon underlined the seriousness of the energy situation by choosing three "Administrative strongmen,"[2] John Ehrlichman, Henry Kissinger, and George Shultz, to head the Special Committee on Energy. However, the divergent concerns and distractions of the three appointees prevented the committee from functioning effectively: National Security Advisor Kissinger did not yet consider oil a central foreign policy issue; Treasury Secretary Shultz delegated authority for energy matters to Deputy Secretary William Simon; and Domestic Affairs Advisor Ehrlichman was preoccupied with Watergate.[3]

On February 7, William Simon was named chairman of the Oil Policy Committee and expected to revise the faltering mandatory oil import program. Charles J. DiBona, from a consulting firm, the Center for Naval Analysis, was selected as Nixon's energy advisor because the Department of Treasury, normally responsible for oil import policy, lacked energy experts. Thus, by the end of February, the Special Committee on Energy became largely inoperative, and primary responsibility for federal energy policymaking was split between Simon and DiBona, men of highly contrasting temperaments and ideologies.

Overall reaction to the worsening energy situation was varied, and nearly everyone lacked awareness both of the larger picture and of feasible plans for effective action. The oil companies themselves had difficulty understanding the flood of regulations and the administration's fluctuating positions. The oil shortage remained incomprehensible to most Americans who still believed in quick technological solutions.

Despite frenzied administration entreaties, fuel prices continued to climb under the voluntary restraint regime. Finally, on March 6, 1973, mandatory controls were reimposed on the nation's twenty-three largest manufacturers of crude oil, gasoline, heating oil, and other refinery products.

Petroleum prices remained under control during the rest of the Nixon administration. Price controls, imposed by authority of the Economic Stabilization Act of 1970 (and implemented on August 15, 1971), were continued in various forms until April 30, 1974. But even with their expiration, petroleum prices continued to be controlled under the provisions of the Emergency Petroleum Allocation Act (EPAA, PL 93-159), enacted in November 1973 (discussed later in the chapter). Price controls were further extended by the Energy Policy and Conservation Act (see chapter 5).

Presidential Concern

On March 23, Nixon removed the ceiling on the volume of oil imports to small, independent distributors facing "hardship." At the same time, the administration appealed to domestic refineries to step up gasoline production to deal with increases in consumption and rapid depletion of supplies.

In an April 18 message to Congress, the president outlined a comprehensive energy program to cope with shortages and price increases. Calling the situation an "energy challenge" rather than a "crisis," he suggested that while action was needed to protect consumers and oil companies, circumstances did not warrant extreme measures. He proposed increased domestic fuel production and advocated the following measures:

- Amending the Natural Gas Act to end the Federal Power Commission's price control authority.
- Restructuring the Mandatory Oil Import Program.
- Creating a federal energy policy agency.
- Speeding up the Alaska Oil Pipeline project.
- Revising environmental protection procedures.

His focus remained firmly on increasing energy supplies to satisfy America's ever-growing energy appetite. Only in a secondary way and in cautious terms did Nixon speak of modifying demand for energy and stressed only voluntary approaches to energy conservation. (The original emphasis on conservation included in the draft of Nixon's speech by White House energy specialists was eliminated by their superiors.) Implicit in the policy message was that energy production took precedence over environmental protection. Nixon attacked Congress for refusing to pass proposals that would end federal natural gas price regulation, extend a tax credit for exploratory oil and gas drilling, and license offshore terminals for supertankers. Some in Congress, responding to Nixon's accusations of inaction, called his plans inept and unworthy of legislation.

Meanwhile, the energy situation continued to deteriorate. By May, Nixon's high-level energy policy reorganization was in chaos. Concern was rising that the major oil companies were attempting to supplant independents. After battling with White House staff and congressional leaders over demands for assistance to independent oil companies, Deputy Treasury Secretary William Simon announced the administration's mandatory fuel allocation program on May 10. (Within weeks, however, a newly created White House Energy Policy Office overruled this decision, adding confusion about the administration energy policy.)

Independent gasoline stations were also severely affected by the shortages and by May, 562 had closed and 1,376 were threatened with closings.[4] President Nixon, persisting in his rejection of consumer rationing to solve crude oil and gasoline shortages, and still encouraging voluntary conservation, required that suppliers provide independent stations and other petroleum product users with the same percentage of refinery output as that sold between October 1, 1971 and September 30, 1972.

Then, in a sudden shift, the administration signaled that it would work on the consumption side, in addition to the supply side, of the energy equation. On May 29, Treasury Secretary Shultz revealed that the administration was considering an increase in the federal excise tax on gasoline in order to curb demand and increase federal revenues. High officials began alluding to fuel rationing if voluntary restraints failed.

In a June 29, 1973 speech, Nixon reviewed those measures he advocated in April which he claimed had already proven effective. The president then proposed an increase in energy research, promising to add another $100 million for fiscal year 1974. This step opposed diametrically the general attempt to discourage all federal spending. The policy reversal was prompted by the belief that the threat of a serious fuel crisis could be ameliorated by technological breakthroughs.

The president also used the speech as an opportunity to pursue much needed changes in the federal bureaucracy structure. He argued that the evolution of the energy situation had not been matched by appropriate organizational changes. Now he felt the fuel shortages were making these changes imperative. To accelerate research efforts, Nixon requested that Congress unify the various energy research and development units into an integrated Energy Research and Development Administration (ERDA). He asked Congress to create a Federal Energy Administration (FEA) authorized to take any necessary action to meet the nation's energy demands (about these agencies see chapter 3). In what became a standard attack on Congress, Nixon warned that unless it immediately acted on his proposals, it would cause an energy crisis that would place the nation "at the mercy of the producers of oil in the Mideast."[5]

Project Independence

Nixon's warning seemed justified when, on October 18, 1973, the Arab oil embargo was levied on a highly vulnerable United States, ending hopes that traditional U.S. suppliers could assist in averting a major shortage. In the past, the United States periodically avoided shortages by buying surpluses from Europe or Arab countries. On November 7, the president responded with his Project Independence, aimed at developing "the potential to meet our own energy needs without dependence on foreign energy sources."[6] The original target date to eliminate all oil imports, then accounting for about 30 percent of United States oil consumption, was set for 1980.

Project Independence was given political significance when Nixon called it "absolutely critical to the maintenance of our ability to play our independent role in international affairs." He then exhorted Americans to demonstrate the crash program spirit of the Apollo and Manhattan Projects. The Project's value-laden concept of self-sufficiency struck a responsive chord, but few Americans were aware of its monumental cost and difficulty. A survey showed the gap between perception and reality: the majority of Americans were unaware that the United States imported any oil. By contrast, nearly every energy specialist saw Nixon's Project Independence as totally impractical.

The day after his Project Independence speech, Nixon announced he would work with Congress to develop mutually acceptable proposals rather than present it with an administration bill. However, he also emphasized his desire for additional presidential power over energy resources and an elimination of existing hindrances on it. He proposed several energy measures of which the most controversial included:

- Authorizing full production in Naval Petroleum Reserve #1, (Elk Hills, Calif.).
- Exempting stationary pollution sources from federal and state air and water quality laws and regulations.
- Permitting the Atomic Energy Commission to grant a temporary operating license to nuclear power plants without holding a public hearing.

The president insisted that these provisions be enacted before December 1973 and requested that certain powers be added to them. He asked for increased presidential authority to allocate and ration energy supplies (most notably gasoline); suspension of the Federal Power Commission's price regulation of newly discovered natural gas; and presidential authority to exercise the far-reaching provisions contained in various acts (the Defense Production Act, the Economic Stabilization Act, and the Export Administration Act), regardless of their expiration dates.

Opposition sprung up to Nixon's "production" orientation to solving the crisis. Environmentalist Stewart L. Udall, former Secretary of the Interior, for example, believed the Arab oil embargo was less of a problem than America's "unsatiable appetite for energy and resources and its wasteful use of them."[7] Other critics said Nixon's energy program was "too-little, too-late." Assorted businessmen, oil company executives, utility operators, and analysts maintained that he was not responding quickly enough to a grave situation. A leading oil economist, Professor M.A. Adelman, alluded to Watergate when he accused Nixon of "dragging his feet because he knows the necessary measures will be unpopular. He is so unpopular now that he feels he cannot afford to do anything that will alienate more people."[8] Nonetheless, it remained for Congress to meet Nixon's challenge with a comprehensive national energy policy.

Congress Attacks the Energy Crisis

Despite Nixon's accusations, Congress had been far from idle as the 1973 energy crisis worsened. A major step was the Emergency Petroleum Allocation Act (PL 93-159) passed in November. This law, whose goal was to distribute scarce fuel supplies evenly, required that the president use mandatory allocations to distribute petroleum products equitably both in the oil industry and across the United States. Although Nixon originally opposed this bill, his position changed rapidly when voluntary allocations failed.

The EPAA gave priority to users involved in food production, public safety, fuel production, and mass transit, and eventually involved massive transfers of "rights" to acquire petroleum products at a specified price.

The act also protected independent retailers and refiners, in particular by requiring that they receive a specified proportion of available fuel supplies. While the major oil companies objected to the system, those who were protected by allocations became its strong supporters. This helped cement a coalition favoring a regulated petroleum market which affected Congress as it struggled toward a comprehensive energy policy. The first of several struggles is described next.

National Energy Emergency Act, 1973

In the fall of 1973, Congress began action on Nixon's far-reaching proposals and request for special powers. The National Energy Emergency Act (NEEA), which the administration had intended as the centerpiece of Project Independence, was never enacted, but caused some of the sharpest congressional debate of 1973. It was introduced in the Senate on October 18 by Senator Henry Jackson (D-Wash.), as S 2589, and in a later similar version in the House by Congressman Harley Staggers (D-W.Va.), as HR 11450. The Jackson-inspired bills were stronger and more extensive than the president had requested. The NEEA placed restrictions on advertising lighting, car speed limits, and indoor temperatures. The act also sought to ration gas, curb the energy consumption of public and commercial establishments, control fuel choices of utilities, and regulate refinery operations. Congress also sought to reserve veto power over presidential implementation of the above measures.

Senate. Both Houses went to work on the bills immediately. The Senate moved rapidly because Jackson's tight control of the legislation enabled him to resist pressures from special interest groups. So the Senate bill maintained its original language through the committee mark-up. White House attempts to change the bill were blocked by Jackson, who constantly claimed he was being assailed by special interests seeking preferential treatment.

The Senate passed S 2589 on November 19, with relatively few amendments. Two significant amendments were: (1) unemployment benefits for some who lost jobs due to energy shortages, and (2) antitrust law exemptions for oil companies cooperating in fuel conservation programs. Both these amendments, offered by Jackson himself, indicated the Senate's concern about equity, and its willingness to experiment with new private sector arrangements.

House. In contrast to the Senate's action, the House initiated major changes in the emergency energy bill. House Interstate and Foreign Commerce Committee members working on HR 11450 became increasingly aware of its controversial implications. Of primary concern was the delegation of excessive power to the president, the oil industry's immense windfall profits gained at the public's expense, and hardship and unemployment in areas hurt by fuel being allocated elsewhere. Intense industrial lobbying efforts contributed to the difficulty of decision making and added heat to the debate. And time was limited—because of the oil embargo, committee members, indeed much of the Congress, felt they could not adjourn for the Christmas holidays and face their constituents until emergency energy legislation was passed.

As a result, the House bill, reported out of committee on December 7, was a hodge-podge concocted, as Congressman Richard Hanna (D-Calif.) said, "by a bunch of blind men trying to put together a jigsaw puzzle."[9] It contained seventy-five amendments; sixty others were offered during floor action, and thirty-six were adopted. Another seventy-seven amendments had not yet been introduced when debate was cut off. Since the heavily amended bill bore so little resemblance to the original measure, Staggers introduced it on the floor as HR 11882, a clean bill.

Brock Adams (D-Wash.) found the bill had become a "Christmas tree," as special interests lobbied to protect themselves in the pending legislation. Other members called it a "can of worms," and a "monster."[10] The attempted resolution of important issues created a cross-hatching of uncomfortable compromises, and some representatives saw the bill merely as an opportunity to advance personal causes. This was exemplified by amendments forbidding integration-inspired busing and the export of petroleum products for the Vietnam war.

The House bill reserved a large role for Congress in energy emergencies. It would permit the president to establish fuel conservation measures (subject to congressional approval), place restrictions on windfall profits, and approve antitrust waivers for oil companies similar to those in the Senate energy bill. It would give the president less power than the Senate's legislation and establish a Federal Energy Administration with extensive powers to stimulate energy development, control excess profits, and impose conservation plans such as setting highway speed limits, encouraging car pools, and limiting business energy use.

During these December days of floor debates, the House voted thirty-six more amendments to the bill. These included amendments which permitted Congress to veto any gasoline rationing plan of the president, gave federal aid to those unemployed as a result of energy cutbacks, and required oil, coal, and natural gas companies to publicly announce their reserve and production levels.

The proposed weakening of environmental protection standards during the energy crisis caused particularly heated debate. Although the House refused to suspend the clean air requirements, it agreed to postpone the effective date for some of them; it rejected an amendment temporarily suspending auto emission controls during the fuel shortage. Finally, early on December 15, the House passed the bill, 265-112.

Conference. The Senate-House Conference Committee—which had the task of integrating the two versions of the bill—was composed of eleven senators and seven representatives. After three days, when the conferees had agreed on most of the bill's details, Nixon invited Jackson and Staggers to the White House to design a conference report compatible with administration objectives. Both refused to go. Then, the president sent William E. Simon, who was then the White House's energy director, to the conference. Two conferees objected strongly to the administration's presence and refused to attend: Congressman John Moss (D-Calif.) returned home and Senator Lee Metcalf (D-Mont.) simply boycotted the meeting, saying, "Such presentations must be in the open and away from the suspicion that a secret deal is being made in the 'other room'."[11]

Simon presented the committee with Nixon's three strongest objections: the congressional veto power, the windfall profits provision, and federal aid for people losing their jobs due to energy shortages. With Simon's support, Senator Paul Fannin (R-Ariz.) presented a list of twenty exemptions from congressional veto of presidential powers that Nixon urgently wanted. House Democrats, however, flatly rejected any changes in congressional veto powers, and conferees generally refused Simon's suggested changes.

The resultant conference bill, without concessions to the White House, was the focus of sharp debate on the floor the last two days before Congress's 1973 adjournment. The Senate was still stalled late on December 21. Earlier that day, the administration had proposed forty changes—mostly deletions—in the conference bill. As administration lobbyists met with senators throughout the afternoon, they gradually reduced the number of demands. Though some senators actively negotiated with the administration, Democratic leaders resisted its lobbying efforts, which they considered unwarranted interference, and the Senate ultimately rejected the administration's requests.

At the same time that the administration was applying pressure, senators from oil-producing states began filibustering against the conference committee bill. Russell B. Long (D-La.), Finance Committee chairman, claimed that since the windfall profits provision was a revenue measure, his committee should have held hearings on it. Fannin followed Long on the floor. Generally upholding the administration's position, Fannin called the bill "a blueprint for chronic energy crisis," and attacked Congress for not levying unpopular conservation measures and for preventing the president from doing so. He claimed that the windfall profits provisions and the congressional veto power over presidential rationing and emergency plans made the conference committee bill "absolutely impracticable, unworkable," and he vowed to kill it.[12]

Jackson, leader of the Senate conferees, realizing that the filibuster could not be ended before adjournment, met with Senate leaders in the chamber cloakroom to design a compromise measure. The resulting clumsy amalgamation of compromises on the six remaining administration objections were incorporated into the conference committee bill. Among the changes were eliminating the windfall profits provision and requiring oil, coal, and natural gas companies to report their data to the Interior and Justice Departments instead of to the public.

Jackson held that his compromise measure retained Congress's original intent but gave additional time to pass a more detailed and effective energy program. Meanwhile, the president would have interim power to impose rationing and conservation measures if deemed necessary.

The stratagem which Jackson and other Senate leaders had devised was to attach the newly revised version of the bill to another unrelated, noncontroversial, and House-passed bill to expand the Wild and Scenic Rivers System. The bill fell short of satisfying the administration's final demands, but the "yes" votes of Fanin and Hansen signaled tacit agreement from the White House. The compromise measure was passed by an overwhelming 52-8, and sent to the House.

House Response. A chaotic and unhappy House took up S 921 on the same day, December 21. Freshman Dale Milford (D-Tex.) reflected many House members' feelings when he voted against Jackson's compromise measure "because I simply do not know what is in the bill."[13] Jack Kemp (R-N.Y.) said the "bill constitutes a virtually unparalleled abrogation of constitutional power by the Congress, giving to the executive actual lawmaking power."[14] The Senate's elimination of the hard-fought windfall profits tax provision displeased many representatives. Staggers, especially upset, said: "The Senate considers the House . . . its doormat, and I for one am tired of their saying, 'You take this or else'."[15]

Despite his disagreement with the Senate's tactics, Staggers was in basic sympathy with the bill's substance, and began working hard for adoption of the Senate measure. On the final day of the session, he moved that the House suspend the rules and consider the Senate's compromise bill, but his motion was defeated. The emergency energy bill was dead for 1973.

The failure to pass NEEA left an aftermath of bitterness. Concerning the oil industry's agitation over the windfall profits issue, Senator Jackson stated:

"They ain't seen nothing yet. They're . . . inviting not just an excess profits tax, but punitive action as well."[16]

He also noted bitterly that he could not distinguish the White House position from the oil industry position, and condemned the president for failing to anticipate the impending energy crisis and for impeding necessary legislation.[17] Other Democrats joined in his condemnation of the president. House Speaker Carl Albert (D-Okla.) accused Nixon of attempting to "rewrite history" by shifting the responsibility for fuel shortages to Congress, and Senate Majority Leader Mike Mansfield (D-Mont.) found Nixon "great on messages . . . on rhetoric, but when it comes to legislation, he is wanting."[18]

The failure to pass the NEEA during the first session of the Ninety-third Congress can be attributed largely to three factors: (1) intensive lobbying from special interest groups and the public's ignorance about the causes and extent of fuel shortages; (2) lack of focus resulting from the plethora of proposed amendments and multitude of differing viewpoints received and held by congressmen; and (3) the administration's unwavering position of vetoing any energy legislation not in accord with its basic policies and ideology.

National Emergency Energy Act, 1974

Because there had never been a full congressional vote on the NEEA, it was technically still alive. (In the closing days of the first session, the Senate had voted only on a compromise measure, not on the House-Senate report and, therefore, was able to reconsider the bill in January 1974.) When the act S 2589 was taken up in January by the second session of the Ninety-third Congress, an "unholy alliance"[19] of senators moved to recommit it to a conference committee. The motion was passed because opposing interests wanted the act to be reconsidered.

The major issues debated during the second conference on the Emergency Energy Act were substituting an oil price ceiling for the windfall profits tax and weakening of clean air standards. Calling the "meteoric increases" in oil prices a most urgent problem, the conference replaced the windfall profits tax with a rollback provision setting a maximum price of $5.25 per barrel for all domestically produced oil, about 30 percent of which was then selling at the world price of $10.35 per barrel. Automobile pollution limits would be postponed, and standards controlling industrial and utility emissions would be relaxed. Unemployment benefits were to be extended to all workers losing jobs as a result of energy shortages, not merely those specified in the original provisions of S 2589.

The Senate finally accepted the conference report by a two-thirds majority on February 19, 1974, after defeating three attempts to send it back to the conference committee for stripping of the price rollback and ceiling provisions.

On February 27, the House adopted the conference report by almost a two-thirds majority (258-151), after rejecting several challenges. Since the bill's three controversial issues were voted on separately, minorities opposed to individual measures were defeated; no antagonistic majority emerged to kill the whole bill. Thus, attempts to eliminate the price ceiling, congressional veto of presidential conservation measures, and presidential rationing power were frustrated in turn. The latter provision was retained only because Republicans voted to preserve the conference language, despite opposition to it from the administration and the oil lobby.

After the vote, the act was sent to President Nixon, who vetoed it on March 6, 1974. He explained that despite lengthy efforts, including "investigations, accusations and recriminations," the legislation produced by Congress "solves none of the problems, threatens to undo the progress we have already made and creates a host of new problems." The president objected especially to the bill's price ceiling on domestic oil, since it would further limit production, and to the act's unemployment provisions as being unfair and unworkable.[20]

Senate attempts to override the veto on the same day failed. Six senators who had supported the conference language the previous month suddenly supported the president's veto. Nixon's defenders argued that every barrel of United States oil that the ceiling would eliminate would have to be imported, but Jackson attacked this assumption by pointing out that, between February 1973 and February 1974, the price of oil had doubled, rising from $3.40 to $6.95 per barrel, while over the same time period domestic production had decreased from 9.4 to 9.2 million barrels per day.

Senator Edmund Muskie (D-Maine), a staunch conservationist, attacked the veto as being a lever to eventually weaken environmental protection laws. Another Democrat, Senator Birch Bayh (D-Ind.), denounced the economic rationale used by Nixon to justify his veto:

> Rather than support the price rollback, which would provide desperately needed relief for American consumers, the President offers what he insists on calling a windfall profits tax. But . . . it is really an excise tax, the burden of which will be carried by consumers as the oil companies . . . continue to rake in record profits.[21]

Oil-state senators, on the other hand, worked to sustain Nixon's veto of S 2589 because of their unwavering opposition to price limitations on oil. Paul Fanin, who had filibustered against the Emergency Energy Act in late 1973, supported the veto because he felt that the price rollback would cut domestic oil production and increase imports. Senator Henry Bellmon (R-Okla.) held that price ceilings would be another step toward government control of private industry.

Congress was prevented from overriding Nixon's veto of S 2589 by the same factors that had held back the Emergency Energy Act in December 1973: regional, economic, and ideological disagreements over proposed solutions. The intense regional splits between energy-producing and energy-consuming states especially frustrated consensus seekers.

Ideological disagreements during debate on the National Energy Emergency Act concerned environmental as well as economic issues. Conservationists were concerned that, in the rush to develop new energy sources, environmental protection would be disregarded. But differences in economic philosophies were seemingly the most divisive factor preventing the achievement of a national energy policy, for they separated not only members of Congress, but also Congress and the White House.

The Last Hurrah for NEEA

On March 6, 1974, a revised Emergency Energy bill was introduced in the House as HR 13834 and in the Senate as S 3267. Like the vetoed bill, these bills would grant the president rationing authority and give the FEA jurisdiction over implementing conservation measures. The revised HR 13834 included the oil price rollback provision and instructed the president to set "equitable ceilings" on imported oil. The bill proposed ending oil companies' huge foreign tax write-offs and forcing imported oil prices down sharply. This attempt "to restore rationality to the pricing system of petroleum products"[22] seemed to many an economic impossibility; no one would import a product which could only be sold for less than the importer's acquisition price.

The bill's radical economic vision provoked a tough response from the Nixon administration. William Simon, the administrator of the recently created Federal Energy Office (FEO), informed the House Interstate and Foreign Affairs Committee on April 3, 1974, that, since the Arab oil embargo had ended, the nation no longer needed an omnibus emergency energy bill. Simon and Nixon preferred that Congress direct its "prompt attention" to the eighteen energy bills that the administration was supporting. Harley Staggers protested: "It's Congress that has the right to write the law of the land, not the President. The emergency is now and we think something should be done."[23] The FEO and various committee members countered with criticism of the House Democrats' handling of the revised energy legislation; testifying before the House and Senate, FEO officials began consistently accusing Democrats of making a scapegoat of the oil industry.

After acrimonious hearings, HR 13834 was brought to the House floor under suspension of the rules clause requiring a two-thirds vote to pass. On May 21, 1974 it was defeated (191-207): the first time legislation aimed at rolling back oil prices failed to obtain a majority in the House. The Senate subsequently discontinued consideration of the companion bill, S 3267, which omitted the price rollback provision that Nixon had criticized but retained other provisions which the president found objectionable.

Various factors had contributed to congressional reticence to attack the energy problem. While the government's momentum had been generally slowed by the Watergate scandal, congressional power was undermined by a haphazard overlapping of authority concerning the energy issue. In addition, perception of an energy shortage began to lose credibility when the oil embargo was lifted on March 18, 1974, so pressure on Congress to formulate a comprehensive energy plan was reduced. On the same day he vetoed the NEEA, Nixon had claimed in a news conference that "the back of the energy crisis has been broken" and that energy prices would begin "moving downward." Many expected the president to be right.

Once again ideological division over economic issues and government intervention in the free market had impeded the passage of national energy policy. Yet against the backdrop of the NEEA battle, a policy of price controls and government regulation had already taken hold, despite lip service to free enterprise.

Before examining additional steps in the search for a national energy policy, it is useful to assay the implications of the actions during the Nixon administration.

Conclusion

The lessons learned from early United States attempts to forge a national energy policy may seem so obvious as to need no belaboring here. Yet, it is of the utmost importance that they be clearly understood so that the energy policy process of the future stands a chance of being more effective.

In the political area, experience has taught that when warnings are received too early in the development of a dangerous situation, or are repeated too often, a cry-wolf syndrome sets in, and warnings lose credibility. Numerous predictions of an imminent energy shortage had been in error throughout modern history. Experience has also taught that, since we cannot react to every possible threat, some warnings must be ignored. Therefore, discounting signs of an impending energy crisis in 1972 and 1973 can be excused. However, these warnings were studiously ignored or became excuses for policies that eventually worsened the crisis.

Mismanaged Crisis Management

The crisis's reality was continually questioned. Americans, traditionally the "people of plenty," found it incredible that they were actually running short of a vital product, that the government could not simply order more oil to be produced, or that the most technically advanced nations in the world were dependent upon undeveloped ones for their economic survival. No consistent image of the energy problem was presented to the public, and skepticism in the media and among the public was uncountered. There were frequent accusations that the crisis was created for conspiratorial reasons—the oil companies wanted higher prices or the president wanted to distract the public from administration errors—explanations far more acceptable and comprehensible to the United States than a radically altered global situation. Mass manipulation, a tool that had effectively mobilized the public in the past, was neither systematically nor successfully attempted. Government officials alternately scolded Americans for their wasteful habits or reassured them that their energy-extravagant lifestyles could continue. However, the bland reassurances by government officials that the situation was under control were belied by oil shortages and lengthening gas lines.

Poor quality and misleading information about the shortage, its extent, or duration, prevented the development of appropriate policies, or even of a sense of the general direction to be taken. The clash of theories and ideologies contending to interpret the shortage and offer solutions merely increased dissension and dissensus. No satisfactory economic models existed to predict the consequences of policies. Adding to the confusion were administration predictions about the near future, which fluctuated wildly on an almost daily basis, and official explanations and interpretations of the crisis, which contradicted one another. Some, such as former Interior Secretary Udall, found the shortage beneficial because it provided Americans with a valuable lesson in conservation. Others, such as American Petroleum Institute's president Frank Ikard, maintained that the shortages would free the oil companies to tap domestic resources. Some even thought the crisis would strengthen national security by forcing the upgrading of the military and rationalizing the seizure of Persian Gulf oil.

The administration's response to the growing chaos was Project Independence, a catchy title for a disastrous approach. Nixon was practically alone in his administration in believing that the nation could realistically become independent of foreign energy sources by 1980. The cost of this achievement would be astronomical, and, in economic terms, suicidal. The administration chose to deal with the embargo and energy shortage initially with symbolic gestures rather than with a meaningful plan of action.

Any concerted action that was attempted was seriously hampered by the unfolding Watergate scandal, which weakened the president and diverted attention from the importance of building a sound energy policy. Presidential attempts to galvanize the country to action on energy were greeted skeptically as attempts to distract the nation from administration transgressions. The fragmentation of a once strongly centralized administration into smaller power centers further divided an already fractured Congress and encouraged strife within the bureaucracy. Weak attempts to build broad national consensus through speeches and pronouncements failed utterly.

Yet, it would be a mistake to assume that only Watergate prevented the federal government from mobilizing the national will toward effective energy policy. There was little that even a strong government could have done in 1973-74 to expand energy supplies in the short run—the few demand restraint mechanisms then available were hideously clumsy and inappropriate for the job. Because the government had never seriously coordinated energy policy but instead handled each fuel source and usage separately, there were sixty government agencies that dealt with some aspect of energy, each operating with little or no communication with the others. One agency's data and recommendations would be challenged by another's. The crucial management center—the White House—had, under Nixon, a consistent record for centralizing power and for viewing problems in political and public relations terms. However, by 1973 it was in no position to take the tough, effective but politically costly measures that would be necessary to deal with the rapidly unravelling energy situation. Neither the required information and knowledge nor the political power was available to presidential-level policy planners. The usual alternative, consensual policies based on shared ideologies, could not develop because too many diverse and competing groups from every sector of American life had joined the fray over energy policy.

The Effect of Controls

It is not without irony that the destruction of the public legitimacy of the free market approach to oil policy occurred under a president who strongly espoused the free market system. Between 1971 and 1974, Nixon continued to underscore his faith in the free enterprise system and his desire to remove petroleum products from price controls, yet he also continually expanded the range of petroleum products that were to be included under price controls and federal allocation processes. Although fuel allocations were adopted prior to the embargo, their continuation became certain once the embargo's pressures began affecting the economy.

The net effect of these controls and allocations was to decrease supplies and economic efficiency while increasing hostility toward the oil companies. Further, despite its short-term nature, the Emergency Petroleum Allocation Act of 1973 (EPAA) implemented far-reaching controls affecting energy supply and consumption patterns which reinforced and prolonged the distortions of the system.

Beyond the dislocations caused by domestic price controls and allocations, their accompanying regulations were often poorly conceived, causing endless confusion and complaints. Despite the problems with price controls they had strong support in Congress in 1973-75. Price controls were premised on the belief that reliance on private markets would *not* lead to lower costs and, in fact, the "free" market could be manipulated to benefit the powerful. A bitter conflict was waged in the Nixon administration over this issue, and the pro-control forces won, in large part, because of the fear that the public would perceive that market power (abetted by the government) was working to the advantage of the major oil companies and that independents would charge discrimination against themselves and the public. The administration's impression managers defeated its ideologues. While the entitlement program (a complex arrangement of transferring oil costs among refineries) did not result in exact equalization of product prices, it did eliminate gross disparities in crude oil costs. More significant, the entitlements program's fairness eliminated some industry pressure for abandoning the EPAA. The EPAA also hid many of the economic dislocations of the entitlement from the public. At the same time, it split the oil industry so that many refiners and marketers (who were protected by the act) became set in opposition to the producers, who were hurt financially by the controls.[24]

To the extent the national response to the 1973-74 oil embargo itself was "managed," it was through the mechanism of central allocation and both a Republican president and a Democratic Congress joined in this supporting approach. Nixon's January 19, 1974 speech reflected clearly the bifurcation between rhetoric and policy. While he advocated a market approach to long-run energy security and supply problems, this was only for the *future*, and he explicitly rejected such an approach in *principle* for the duration of the embargo and specifically ruled out any price-based system of allocation.

The extent to which the administration's response to the embargo was political (in contrast to a pure laissez-faire market approach) was the Nixon administration's sponsorship of the International Energy Agency (IEA). The IEA was designed to limit the impact of future embargoes and drive down the OPEC price, but oddly enough also to maintain international prices above a level to protect domestic energy producers. (The price floor was about the same as the ceiling over domestic prices.)

As the OAPEC embargo gradually wound down, the nation found itself with no effective response, either to immediate energy problems or to potential future energy emergencies. A precedent had been established, nonetheless, which was that supply reductions were treated as political issues with economic consequences rather than economic issues with political consequences. Further, the emphasis on rationing, combined with the past experience, indicated that in any future energy emergency, the government would "nationalize" the supplies and distribute them according to criteria determined by the federal government. Knowledge of this likelihood discouraged the private sector from preparing for an uncertain future. Any such preparation costs—such as individual stockpiling—would accrue to the individual undertaking the preparations, while the benefits of such actions would be shared collectively. This served as a disincentive to private efforts to prepare for future energy problems, while the government found itself unable to assume responsibility for contingencies. Such an environment—where rhetoric and policy conflicted, where energy policy was heavily and widely politicized, and where there was no mechanism, either private or public, that could handle an energy emergency effectively—remained in effect for the rest of Nixon's term in office and throughout that of Gerald Ford's.

Congressional Struggles Yield Little

Various groups tried to use the energy crisis to their own benefit. Moving companies and all-night convenience food stores wanted special considerations. Antibusing and antiwar forces in Congress also tried to advance their causes by attaching amendments to the energy bills. Industries advocated weakening environmental regulations. Labor and minority groups sought special aid. Nixon used energy legislation as a means of expanding presidential powers and Congress to add new oversight requirements to presidential actions. Each group wanted special exemptions or privileges for itself, all rationalized as being in the nation's best interests. By its unprecedented effects, the energy crisis created unusual and even unheard-of coalitions. Groups pursuing the new matrix of energy policy payoffs radically departed from their traditional alignments overnight, creating new political patterns. (The implications of these new coalitions are examined in chapter 10.)

On balance, the National Emergency Energy Act (NEEA) bill can be seen as the government's hasty response to the delegitimating consequences of the energy crisis, reflecting neither a coherent administration strategy nor careful consideration by congressional committees. Instead the bill was animated by competition to avoid public hostility resulting from the oil shortage and energy price spiral, and a desire to assign blame to other parties. The blatant distrust of the judgment, foresight, and competence of the president and his advisers threatened to paralyze the government. The White House was consequently anxious to avoid any further blame for mismanagement on energy. Congressional inaction on various energy proposals made Congress an inviting target for administration criticism.

Congress, of course, responded in kind. The combination of inflation, energy, war, and abuse of presidential power issues led Congress to reassert itself by reversing historical trends and curbing presidential powers. Its new stance was symbolized by the War Powers Act, which was passed in 1973 over a presidential veto, and by its new streamlined organizational form, resulting most notably from the Budget Reform and Impoundment Control Act of 1974. Through these and various other maneuvers, Congress was able to destroy Nixon's hegemony over policy, limit the "imperial presidency," and forcefully assert its own authority. But in terms of formulating energy policies, Congress was hardly more effective than the White House. All the efforts and rhetoric aimed at bolstering congressional responsibility seemed largely forgotten when the energy crisis struck. While blaming the administration for the 1973 energy crisis, one of Congress's first reactions was to assign great power to the president through the NEEA. Ironically, Congress proposed expanding presidential power at the same time that it was considering impeachment. By 1974, the pendulum swung back and Congress made the president's rationing power so limited as to be almost worthless.

In Congress's hurried attempt to develop energy legislation, it was whipsawed by regional concerns, conflicting special interests, and contradictory advice from various experts. The policies that were contained in the NEEA were imprecise and at some points even incoherent. The powers given to the president were hastily conceived (for one example, the presidential power to ban advertising of energy consuming products could include items ranging from cars to electric shavers, or even razors).

The characteristics of the energy crisis—simultaneously acute and diffuse, immediate and long-range, technically complex and painfully obvious, deeply interpenetrated with all other societal processes—typified the emerging problems resulting from fundamental shifts in the international and domestic socioeconomic structures (as outlined in chapter 1). The nation in general—and Congress in particular—had not addressed the politics of scarcity before and lacked the conceptual and organizational tools to deal with it. A government of specialized bureaucratic structures and detailed standard operating procedures has difficulty addressing a problem, like the energy crisis, that cuts across so many systems.

The next chapter focuses on the early development of the organizational mechanisms temporarily created to manage and regulate the production and consumption of energy.

Notes

1. Helmut A. Merkleim and W. Carey Hardy, *Energy Economics* (Houston, Tex.: Gulf Publishing, 1977), p. 182.
2. *United States News and World Report*, May 5, 1973, p. 55.
3. Robert J. Kalter and William A. Vogely, eds., *Energy Supply and Government Policy* (Ithaca, N.Y.: Cornell University Press, 1976), p. 284.
4. *New York Times*, May 7, 1973, p. 78.
5. Lester A. Sobel, ed., *Energy Crisis, Volume 1, 1969-1973* (New York: Facts on File, Inc., 1974), p. 161. In this same speech, President Nixon announced a reshuffling of the White House energy policy mechanism. He named Republican Colorado Governor John A. Love to head the newly established Energy Policy Office.

6. U.S. General Services Administration, *Public Papers of the Presidents of the United States: Richard Nixon, 1973* (Washington, D.C.: U.S. Government Printing Office, 1975), p. 269.
7. *New York Times*, November 27, 1973, p. 30.
8. Ibid., p. 57.
9. Congressional Quarterly, *Energy Politics* (Washington, D.C.: CQ Press, 1978), p. 14A.
10. *Congressional Quarterly Almanac* 29, p. 3251.
11. *National Journal Reports*, January 5, 1974, p. 28.
12. U.S. Congress, *Congressional Record*, December 21, 1973, p. 43172.
13. Ibid., p. 43281.
14. Ibid., p. 43289.
15. *Washington Post*, December 23, 1973, p. A4.
16. *New York Times*, December 22, 173, p. 10.
17. Ibid., November 19, 1973, p. 18.
18. U.S. Congress, *Congressional Record*, January 29, 1974, p. 1149.
19. Ibid., March 6, 1974, p. 5491.
20. Ibid., p. 5532.
21. U.S. Congress, House Report 93-1014, "Standby Energy Emergency Authorities Act," April 29, 1974.
22. U.S. Congress, House Interstate and Foreign Commerce Committee, "Standby Energy Emergency Authorities Act," hearings, April 2-4, 1974, pp. 131-97.
23. Douglas Bohi and Milton Russell, *Limiting Oil Imports* (Baltimore, Md.: Johns Hopkins University Press, 1978), p. 227.

3
Congress Reorganizes the Energy Bureaucracy

The struggle during 1973-74 to develop a comprehensive national energy policy was accompanied by increasing public demand for swift action and by increased congressional aggressiveness in learning about the energy crisis. Many citizens questioned the authenticity of the energy crisis; some believed that the oil companies and the administration were conspiring to defraud the public. Reports in 1973 and early 1974 of huge increases in oil company profits fueled congressional and public resentment over rapidly rising energy prices. This resentment was reinforced by statements of such former administration officials as S. David Freeman, who said that national energy policy was "formulated in Dallas and Houston and rubberstamped . . . in Washington"[1] and Congressman Les Aspin (D-Wis.), who charged that the administration would do nothing because oil and gas interests had contributed nearly $5 million to President Nixon's reelection campaign.[2]

Numerous congressional committees swung into action to investigate the government's handling of the energy problem and to find out why the executive branch could neither generate public confidence nor manage the growing energy shortages. For example, when new price increases were announced in mid-January 1974, the chairmen of four congressional subcommittees initiated hearings to determine whether the energy problem was fact or fiction. At one of these hearings, Senator William Proxmire (D-Wis.) intimated that the energy crisis was "a government-oil industry sponsored 'put-on' to raise prices and increase profits at the expense of the consumer."[3]

Many investigations called attention to the issue of energy data reliability. Federal Energy Office (FEO) director William Simon testified repeatedly that the data supplied by the oil industry to his office was insufficient to determine the extent of the fuel crisis. During a January 16 meeting of a House Select Committee on Small Business hearing, four energy policy experts stated that the oil industry, by keeping government uninformed about supplies and price, was able to reap exorbitant profits from the fuel shortage. Interior Department officials admitted the next day that government policy had been based upon oil and natural gas industry's statistics, and that the government had agreed to keep the records secret if industry would comply with the department's requests for information. Investigators charged that because there had been no means of checking the records or holding the industry accountable for its data, the companies' gas reserves had been grossly underestimated.[4]

Senate Permanent Investigations Subcommittee hearings, which opened on January 21, 1974, as Congress reconvened work on the stalemated emergency energy legislation, aired charges that the fuel shortage was contrived and that oil company profits were excessive. The subcommittee released affidavits from six oil policy officials in the Office of Economic Preparedness (OEP) and the Interior Department, indicating that the bureaucracy within the OEP was largely responsible for the administration's failure to anticipate the oil shortage and hence to plan for suitable action.[5]

In February 1974, the Subcommittee on Multinational Corporations of the Senate Foreign Relations Committee began explosive hearings on the relationship that had developed over the previous twenty years among the major oil companies, the U.S. government, and the Middle East oil countries.[6]

Congressional Concerns

The thrust and intent of these various hearings were different, but their conclusions generally pointed to the inadequacy of the energy policy bureaucracy that had developed in a haphazard fashion over the past century. By the early 1970s, it had become obvious that this decentralized bureaucracy was inadequate and inappropriate in a time of rapidly changing and growing energy needs. Reforms were needed.[7]

First, the data upon which energy policy had been established were incomplete, unreliable, and inaccurate. Knowledge about privately owned oil was a vital but missing component in any plans for dealing with shortages. Important information about the government's own resources and reserves and its activities in energy was fragmentary and sparse. Second, decentralization had resulted in the creation of numerous agency fiefdoms which, backed by special interest clienteles, could mobilize political resources to resist centralized coordination. The fifty-year evolution of regulatory agencies had resulted in a piecemeal structure with uneven coverage and dissimilar methods and approaches, as described in chapter 1. Each regulatory agency had a narrow mandate and compartmentalized responsibilities. While there was little duplication of authority, each agency tended to have tunnel vision and a preference for existing rather than new technologies and for proven but unimaginative approaches rather than experimental but possibly highly rewarding innovations.

The absence of a central leverage point hobbled congressional efforts to oversee or direct the executive branch's energy policy. Point-by-point coverage was cumbersome and exhausting and left important gaps. It was also difficult for Congress to obtain objective advice. Narrow, self-interested sources of advice and information from compartmentalized segments of the energy system predominated.

Finally, a permanent and systematic method for resolving disputes was lacking. Competition constantly surfaced among diverging energy technologies (e.g. coal vs. oil), conflicting orientations and interests (e.g. conservation vs. production), agencies with different priorities (e.g. Interior Department vs. Environmental Protection Agency), and between various levels of government (e.g. federal vs. state). Intergovernmental conflict over licensing of energy projects posed the most immediate obstacle to exploiting and delivering new energy resources.

Congress eventually set up the Federal Energy Administration (FEA) to manage energy problems, and the Energy Research and Development Administration (ERDA) to perform research and address long-term energy issues. The Atomic Energy Commission's regulatory and safety functions were split off as a separate agency—the Nuclear Regulatory Commission (NRC)—while the remaining bulk of the agency was folded into ERDA. Congress stipulated that FEA and ERDA were to serve as temporary, stopgap organizations until the energy problem could be more clearly assessed and agreement reached on a permanent bureaucratic solution.

FEA, originally to expire on June 30, 1976, was given a stay of execution until the end of 1977. By that time, it was correctly predicted, a single entity could be created to rationalize and organize the federal government's energy bureaucracy and provide Congress with the information required to oversee and give fundamental direction to national energy policy.

Atomic Energy: A Growing Problem

The lack of a strategic approach to energy policy and distorted energy research and development priorities were among the elements that led to rising congressional displeasure about the heavy stress the federal government had given to atomic energy. Atomic energy—because of its dramatic quality and importance to national security—had from its inception received concentrated attention and support from the federal government. The Congress's Joint Committee on Atomic Energy (JCAE), which became uniquely powerful and highly successful in encouraging the development of atomic energy, had its own fiefdom—the Atomic Energy Commission (AEC)—and was strongly bolstered by clients in the atomic industry; this resulted in the classic "cozy triangle" pattern.[8] One consequence of this arrangement was the promotion of nuclear energy rather than other fuel sources. The atomic energy sector's strong support enabled the nuclear industry to resist calls for accountability, and to promote atomic energy without exploring its costs, dangers, and risks. During the 1970s this independence was increasingly attacked, both from within the government and outside. During the 1973-74 energy shortages, criticism was augmented by supporters of competing energy sources and by public interest groups. While the nuclear industry had flourished under the old system, there was convincing evidence that nuclear power promotion had not been accompanied by the enforcement of strict safety standards or a concern for realistic and balanced appraisals.

Public interest advocate Ralph Nader, for example, charged that AEC and JCAE had colluded in covering up safety hazards in nuclear plants. Citing a secret AEC study group's report, which contradicted AEC assertions that nuclear power plants were safe, Nader accused the committee of sweeping safety problems "under the rug." He further noted that AEC acted in concert with the JCAE which, far from being a passive entity, had actively "condemned, bullied or ridiculed" anyone who tried to present opposing points of view or to express concern. He singled out Representatives Chet Holifield (D-Calif.) and Craig Hosmer (R-Calif.) for special criticism and obloquy.[9]

In hearings on the competitive aspects of the energy industry, Senator George D. Aikens (R-Vt.) described the AEC as an "agency of acquiescence" to energy industry interests.[10] Environmental groups' in-depth investigations of AEC activities found gross negligence and concealment of safety perils. Leaked AEC documents showed that for ten years the commission had suppressed studies of the dangers of nuclear reactors.[11]

The attacks weakened JCAE and AEC, while giving weight to arguments for rationalizing the energy structure and developing farseeing, balanced strategies. The intrusion of criticism into the once inviolate area of nuclear energy gave impetus to demands that the traditionally segmented and nuclear-dominated energy research structure be altered to correct past imbalances and biases.

However, the myriad proposals on how to accomplish this rationalization presented a major challenge for the White House and Congress as they attempted to choose the best form of reorganization that could be realistically achieved.

Restructuring Energy Organization

The need for a centralized federal energy organization emerged while the Nixon administration was having great difficulty in coordinating its own position on energy policy management. Constantly shifting White House arrangements and positions reflected the uncertainty of the nation as a whole. Four different people held the position of White House energy policy coordinator in 1973, and the White House consecutively submitted conflicting energy organization proposals to Congress. It appeared impossible to generate consensus either on the goals for an energy policy or the programs for their realization.

The Senate had signalled its dissatisfaction with executive disorganization by trying three times to create a permanent White House Council on Energy

Policy, comparable to the Council of Economic Advisers. For similar reasons, the Senate also endorsed the creation of a three-member council with responsibility for centralized energy data collection and analysis, coordination of federal energy programs, and operation of a long-term comprehensive energy conservation and development plan.[12] None of these senatorial plans were enacted, and federal energy agencies were not reorganized until 1974, when FEA and ERDA were established.

The steps leading to the emergence of federal agencies focused solely on energy are indicative of confusion about energy policy. It required more than a year to translate organizational desiderata into the organizational realities of FEA and ERDA, and this was done in the absence of any substantial decisions about energy policy direction. Managerial forms were created without a coherent energy policy.

Reorganizing Energy Policy Administration: The FEA

One of the administration's first reorganizational priorities was to increase its ability to handle short-term energy problems. Weaknesses in the White House energy crisis management arm, the Federal Energy Office (FEO—not to be confused with its successor agency, the Federal Energy Administration, FEA) demonstrated the need for expanded legislative authority, new powers to bring dispersed bureaucratic agencies under its supervision, and a clear mandate from the legislature to take action. It was in pointed awareness of these shortcomings that the Nixon administration approached Congress for additional powers to control and regulate energy policy.

On December 4, 1973, Nixon asked Congress to establish a strong Federal Energy Administration (FEA) to direct governmental programs related to the energy shortage. He proposed that FEA be given broad powers to act on national energy problems. There was sharp House/Senate disagreement about appropriate roles for the proposed agency. Should it be an enforcement agency, with power to limit oil profits and enforce conservation progress? Or should it be an information-gathering and analytic agency?

Because options about these issues differed, FEA's birth did not come easily. By late 1973, three different measures authorizing FEA were moving through Congress. One, part of the emergency energy bill (discussed in chapter 2) was bogged down in House/Senate disagreement. Another bill would give FEA wide-ranging power to limit oil company profits, create and enforce conservation programs, and encourage energy development; but the House Government Operations Committee reported on this bill only after Congress had adjourned for 1973. In the Senate, a third measure stipulated that FEA would oversee a massive energy information gathering and analysis program; it also provided for public disclosure of energy corporations' data. While this measure created an agency weaker than Nixon had requested, it overwhelmingly passed the Senate on December 19 but was not voted on by the House before its adjournment. Although the House Government Operations Committee had reported a similar bill, it was not considered because the House Democratic leadership wanted first to deal with the emergency energy legislation issue in the closing days of 1973.

When, on January 29, 1974, the FEA bill (HR 11793) again surfaced on the House floor, it was believed that the Senate would shortly pass the emergency energy legislation, but Staggers, floor leader of the emergency energy bill, cautioned the House that the administration planned to wait for the passage of the FEA bill and then kill the emergency bill. House Democrats therefore postponed passage of the FEA bill until the emergency bill passed, hoping that the latter's provision for a Federal Energy Emergency Administration, a skeleton of Nixon's proposed FEA, would encourage the administration to accept it. However, after Nixon vetoed the National Emergency Energy Act on March 6, and attempts to revise that legislation failed, the House again took up and passed the FEA bill. On May 7, President Nixon signed into law HR 11793, establishing a temporary FEA to deal with short-term fuel shortages.

Congress refused Nixon's request to give the new agency authority to "take all actions needed" to deal with energy shortages. Congress designed a weak, short-term FEA not only because of its desires to curtail expanding executive branch power and preserve its own policy prerogatives, but also because of its inability to develop meaningful long-range goals for the agency. There was no government policy around which to design a structure or organization. Nevertheless, the new FEA carried great responsibilities which it took on from the old FEO and the Interior Department's offices of petroleum allocation, energy conservation, energy data and analysis, and oil and gas, as well as the energy division of the Cost of Living Council. FEA's primary administrative missions were to develop energy shortage contingency plans, restrain oil companies from earning excess profits, and oversee the implementation of energy-conserving measures. Congress also ordered it to develop export and import policies for energy resources, and instructed that it deal only with short-term energy problems.

Congress also assigned FEA responsibility for developing national energy plans. Because of its own ineffectualness in this area, Congress turned to the executive branch for ideas, framework, analysis, and options—in essence, a new bureaucratic structure to handle the energy problem—yet limited the executive branch's power to implement new plans. FEA was mandated not only to report annually on the status and estimated quantity of the nation's oil and gas reserves and foreign ownership of domestic energy supplies and sources, it also was told to produce a comprehensive energy plan within six months of its establishment.

Reflecting greater emphasis by Congress on its own staff support, the General Accounting Office (GAO) was instructed to monitor and evaluate FEA's performance, which constituted a criticism of federal energy management as well as an endorsement of GAO's abilities. (GAO was also empowered to compel energy suppliers and large energy consumers to yield information upon request.) In sum, weighted with responsibilities, FEA was yet limited by a stricture which called for its dissolution two years after its creation.

FEA's Problems

FEA's life was short and extremely difficult. It lacked clear direction, and its leadership was fluctuating and uncertain, responding in an ad hoc, cumbersome way to each new contingency. The chain of command between FEA and other agencies was never clear or well established, resulting in constant conflict.

For example, by initiating its own study of federal government intervention in electricity rate-setting, FEA angered the Federal Power Commission; the Environmental Protection Agency (EPA) fought FEA and the Interior Department over strip mining. There was growing uneasiness among other government agencies over FEA's expanding role. Several critics maintained that its energy policy designs were too broad and long-range for an agency intended to be only temporary.[13]

The agency itself was an amalgam of antagonistic and disparate agencies, some of which had been in bitter conflict with one another prior to their incorporation together. Problems of coordination and control partly resulted from logistics: the FEA staff was dispersed throughout nine buildings. Commuting between offices took top officials' time. Testifying to Congress also absorbed a significant portion of FEA officials' efforts, especially after Congress discovered that energy-related hearings generated instant publicity. FEA also faced demands for special treatment from every conceivable group.

Placating the most powerful of these with favorable decisions alienated the others. FEA was required to direct the nationwide allocation of fuel products and determine the refineries' mix of production. (The final outcome was a nationwide surplus of heating oil supplies and a shortage of gas supplies.)

FEA attempted too much in too many areas, with too little knowledge. FEA's insufficient knowledge of the oil industry made effective regulations impossible. Once, to the horror of oil experts, FEA proposed that all gas stations post the lead content of diesel fuel, until it was informed that diesel contains no lead at all! These mistakes reduced FEA's effectiveness. In some cases, FEA's frenetic activity was actually counterproductive. Short lead times and increased workloads assigned by Congress compounded the problem. For example, FEA was required to determine how the nation should absorb the oil import reduction caused by the 1973-74 embargo, without knowing the reduction's magnitude. A workable strategy would have been to allow prices to increase and the market to allocate scarce supplies; the government could then have provided general programs to assist those who suffered as a result of the higher prices. However, the political climate was conducive to rolling back—not raising—prices. Consequently, FEA was forced to revert to procedures established by the traditional regulatory agencies and commissions, resulting in awkward and counterproductive pricing policies.

Ultimately these policies tried to protect "independent" refiners and retailers who purchased crude oil from major producers (in part to forestall even greater congressional protection of them). But their net effect was to discourage importation in violation of the Arab embargo. Thus, though it intended to be equitable to both large and small refiners, FEA regulations actually reduced small refiners' market shares instead of adding total supplies to the domestic market.

Lack of verifiable information also impeded FEA operations. Because official estimates of the embargo's size and its effect on the United States were inconsistent, FEA had to base its strategy on the "worst-case scenario," which assumed extremely serious disruptions. FEA's mission of necessity became how to minimize such a disaster. Once this negative goal definition was seized upon, programs were created which focused the agency's activities on it. Consequently, its approach depended upon highly inflexible procedures and operations that permitted only incremental change. Flexible schemes, such as those based on market pricing, were politically risky, and could have backfired.

However, though FEA's cautious strategy minimized the possibility of exhausting heating oil supplies during the winter and gas supplies during the summer (considered the worst possibilities under a highly effective embargo), it could not respond rapidly to new information that the embargo was ineffective. Operating on worst-case assumptions, FEA remained insensitive to the changing worldwide oil situation and domestic consumption patterns. FEA considered a narrow range of possible actions aimed at satisfying immediate objectives rather than undertaking an exhaustive search for the best possible solution.[14]

FEA itself was split between two competing objectives. The first—levied by Congress—was to act as a regulatory body, controlling prices and oil distribution while reporting industry transgressions to Congress. This led to antagonism between FEA and the energy industries. While FEA did have an effect in this area, it was, unfortunately, often negative, leaving a heritage which has continued to poison relations among public interest advocates, energy industries, and government. The adversarial nature of government energy policy administration is indicative of the myriad problems now facing the Energy Department.

The second objective—mandated by Presidents Nixon and Ford—was to help make the United States self-sufficient in energy resources, and expedite industrial and resource development. Yet FEA had neither the power nor the organization to undertake such a massive task. Although FEA had the higher public visibility, a much larger segment of federal energy activity was contained in the Atomic Energy Commission (AEC). AEC at one time held out the promise of energy self-sufficiency and during the energy crisis offered to expand its role to cover all types of energy. As FEA was being created, plans were also afoot to reorganize AEC into a broader energy research organization. Many of the issues discussed in the beginning of the chapter affected Congress as it undertook this reorganization task.

Evolution of Energy Research Organization

A confusing array of possible methods for remodeling the federal government's energy decision-making structure was placed before Congress—by the administration as well as by individual members of Congress—in response to the energy shortage of the early 1970s.

In his 1973 energy message to Congress, Nixon proposed a sweeping restructuring of federal energy and natural resource agencies. No parts of his proposals were adopted in 1973, but they set the stage for greater progress in 1974.

The most controversial element of Nixon's 1973 message was his call to establish a Department of Energy and Natural Resources to be drawn from eight different agencies which would manage programs in relevant areas. This proposal for a new department, whose core would be a reconstituted Interior Department, was a key component of Nixon's attempt to rationalize the federal bureaucracy along functional lines.[15] A similar department, which had been proposed in 1971 as the Department of Natural Resources, had stirred little enthusiasm and much opposition by special interests and by Congress, which refused to approve any measures furthering it.

Nixon also requested that a Nuclear Energy Commission, headed by five commissioners, be established to take over the licensing and regulatory, environmental, and safety functions of the AEC, which could then concentrate more on federal research and development (and eliminate the conflict between promotion and regulation of nuclear energy).

A third aspect of the Nixon proposal was unifying energy research and development (R&D) into one Energy Research and Development Administration (ERDA). ERDA would amalgamate the R&D components of the Atomic Energy Commission, the Environmental Protection Agency, the National Science Foundation, and the Interior Department.

No matter which method the administration chose for reorganizing its energy policy making structures, it risked opposition from one of the two intensely concerned, powerful members in Congress—Senator Jackson or Congressman Holifield. Jackson, influential because of his chairmanship of the Senate Interior and Insular Affairs Committee, favored pulling all resource programs, including energy, into one huge department. On the other hand, Holifield, chairman of the Joint Atomic Energy Committee and the House Government Operations Committee, did not want the AEC submerged within a massive Department of Energy and Natural Resources (DENR).

Early discussion within the administration over reorganization lent hope to the possibility of compromise. By mid-September 1973, however, this hope was gone. Key congressional committees were deadlocked over the basic question of whether there should be one conglomerate resource department, or a separate energy administration.

In reorganizing the federal government for the years ahead, Jackson maintained that energy was only one component of the larger process of managing all natural resources. Hence, he believed, one individual should oversee all national energy programs. A central agency, Jackson said, would place energy in proper relation to other natural resource issues such as public lands, the environment, and mineral exploitation. By separating these functions, and especially by splitting off the research coordination function, an energy secretary would be denied technical expertise and advice.

Those arguing for a separate R&D organization pointed to AEC's demonstrated competence. In contrast, they said, the Interior Department—which was to become the core of the new agency—had a dismal record of technological development, citing its inadequate coal program as an example. Holifield and others foresaw that the diverse missions of a new department, and the time it would require to meld cumbersome and disparate bureaucracies, would delay urgently needed energy technology development. Holifield himself saw that only a long-range but single-minded approach could solve the energy problem and advocated a single-purpose agency to pursue new sources that would make the U.S. energy independent. He saw NASA's race to the moon and the war-time atom bomb project as appropriate organizational models.

The 1973-74 oil embargo led the White House to redouble efforts to establish quickly an independent R&D agency. On December 10, 1973, Roy Ash, of the Office of Management and Budget, told the House Government Operations Committee that, while FEA would do short-term planning and involve itself in reducing energy demand, ERDA would deal with technology that can "yield new solutions to creating and using energy."[16] However, from the time that President Nixon gave Simon responsibility for Project Independence, early in 1974, disagreement between ERDA and FEA arose frequently.

Simon, anxious to expand his power over energy policy, and receiving the backing of Congressman Mike McCormack (D-Wash.), chairman of the House Science and Astronautics Committee's Energy Subcommittee, urged

Congress to fold R&D into FEA. When Simon stated that R&D could not be separated from energy policy implementation, he de facto contradicted the administration's position that FEA would not infringe on ERDA's independence.[17] The administration, on the other hand, not wanting to risk losing the powerful Holifield's support, had argued that ERDA should be independent.

The FEO director's overzealous power play indicated a lack of direction and coordination in the administration, and because Nixon's authority was being undermined by Watergate, the competing power centers had no leadership capable of disciplining them. Whatever the reasons, conflicting and changing positions of the White House toward reorganization proposals minimized their effect on Congress and on the content of the final reorganization bills.

ERDA

The passage of legislation creating an independent ERDA was a difficult and time-consuming process. Congressman Holifield and Senator Jackson led opposing sides in the ERDA debate, which focused on two key issues: (1) whether to create an independent ERDA or a larger DENR encompassing an ERDA, and (2) the relative priorities to be assigned nuclear versus nonnuclear energy development.

ERDA's creation involved power plays and tradeoffs that benefitted both Holifield and Jackson. Holifield succeeded in having the trade secrets and intervenors' provisions, which he claimed were antinuclear, dropped from the ERDA bill. Jackson had the president's tacit consent to sign his nonnuclear energy R&D policy bill. This act, PL 93-577, established a farseeing national policy stressing conservation, alternative energy, and environmental protection. (The law has been only partially implemented.)

With Holifield in the lead, the House readily adopted part of Nixon's reorganization plan. On December 19, 1973, it overwhelmingly approved the HR 11510, establishing an independent ERDA, based on AEC, and which would include energy research units from other agencies. However, part of AEC would remain in existence, reconstituted as the Nuclear Energy Commission, and would house AEC's units for licensing and regulating nuclear power plants. Amendments were rejected that would have directed the agency to support energy sources other than nuclear.

The Senate was slower to act. In 1974, it enmeshed its ERDA bill, S 2774, with Jackson's nonnuclear energy R&D bill, which had already passed in December 1973, and called for a ten-year $20 billion alternative energy program. While the House bill sat, the Senate gradually emerged with a vision of ERDA that stressed its nonnuclear activities. The Senate version was finally approved on August 15, 1974.

At the beginning of 1974, Jackson and the administration had still hoped for an all-encompassing Energy and Natural Resource Department, but both discovered that opposition (led by Holifield) was so strong in the House that if they had pushed for it, there would be no reorganization bill at all. When Jackson and Nixon finally realized that political obstacles to the massive Energy and Natural Resources Department concept were insurmountable, they settled for the achievement of smaller, first steps at reorganization. But even a compromise measure had to be pounded out in a bitter conference committee to resolve the differences between the House and the Senate versions.

Conflict in Conference Committee

The major differences in the House and Senate conference reports on the bill indicate disparate underlying philosophies with regard to nuclear power: the House wanted to protect nuclear development from critics and competing technologies, while the Senate wanted safeguards against the dangers of nuclear power and assurance that ERDA would not be dominated by nuclear concerns. The four sources of conflict in conference were the Kennedy amendment, a technical assistance clause, the regulatory commission, and a White House energy policy council.

The most troublesome of the four—an amendment added by Senator Edward Kennedy (D-Mass.) on the Senate floor—would have provided government financial assistance to citizen intervenors against nuclear power plants' licensing or rule-making procedures. He argued that citizen groups were increasingly failing to participate in the decision-making process, not because the AEC undervalued their contribution, but rather because they lacked money to hire attorneys and prepare their cases. Ralph Nader-style groups and the antinuclear lobby strongly supported Kennedy's amendment before the Senate conference, and it passed by a voice vote with no opposition.

On the other hand, Holifield was violently opposed to the amendment, as were most AEC commissioners. Holifield questioned intervenors' true motives, whom he blamed for delays in licensing and building nuclear power plants, and cautioned against what he viewed as the Kennedy amendment's destructive new concept. Although admitting that the government provides the poor criminal offender with a free lawyer, he claimed that this was quite different from financing opposition to programs formulated by federal agencies acting on the people's behalf.

AEC Commissioner William Kreigsman shared Holifield's disdain for the Kennedy amendment, believing it would set a dangerous precedent and could only make sense if all regulatory agencies financed intervenors on every major issue. Moreover, this costly step would bring the regulatory process to a halt.

Senator Lee Metcalf (D-Mont.) had introduced an amendment similar to Kennedy's requiring government agencies to provide technical assistance for intervenors in nuclear licensing or rule-making cases. Holifield strongly opposed this amendment also as an infringement on businesses' trade secrets, claiming that competent companies would withdraw from programs rather than risk disclosing their trade secrets. Thus the amendment's net effect would be to slow technological progress and attract only the poorest quality companies to nuclear programs.

The House also disagreed with the Senate's provision establishing a separate safety research capability for the Nuclear Regulatory Commission (NRC). Under the House bill the nuclear regulatory unit would be limited to using ERDA personnel or outside contractors, a procedure similar to the AEC's practice at the time. In contrast, the Senate Government Operations Committee reported that "to complete the separation of nuclear regulation from development it is essential that the (NRC) have its own research capability and staff."[18] Holifield, however, contended that such a separation would be ineffective because safety is inherent in every aspect of technological development and could not be arbitrarily compartmentalized. To do so would harm both endeavors.

The final important cause of contention between the House and Senate concerned a provision, proposed by Senator Ernest Hollings (D-S.C.), to establish a three-member White House Council on Energy Policy to develop and implement a comprehensive national energy plan. The administration and Holifield feared that such a council would interfere with the daily workings of other energy-related agencies. The conference settled on a temporary White House level coordinating council.

Staffs of the House and Senate Government Operations Committees struggled over the trade secrets and intervenors' provisions for two weeks without approaching an agreement. Congressman Frank Horton (R-N.Y.) offered a compromise providing intervenors with government studies and technical assistance only, but he immediately withdrew it when Holifield and other House conferees expressed their opposition. The conference then broke up in confusion and indecision, leaving the problem for staff to resolve. But, when the Senate staff met with their House counterparts, it was immediately obvious that there was in fact no real compromise. Faced with the impasse, Senate conferees and staff acquiesced to Holifield rather than lose the entire reorganization bill.

An interesting facet of the ERDA bill's development was that the House and Senate Government Operations Committee staff worked out many compromises between the House and Senate bills, leaving conferees to concentrate on the tougher issues separating the two chambers. The staff were given authority to make "certain tentative agreements" so that the bill would not be put aside until the next session in a rush to adjourn.[19]

Agreement

A compromise was finally forged in conference committee which was adopted by both houses and then forwarded to the White House. On October 11, 1974, President Ford signed legislation authorizing ERDA, which he called his "top priority" energy issue. Although a Nuclear Regulatory Commission was also created, the bulk of AEC's responsibilities—including nuclear weapons—was added to ERDA's work in nonnuclear areas of energy research. The new agency received fossil fuel programs from Interior's Office of Coal Research and Bureau of Mines, and exotic solar and geothermal energy programs from the National Science Foundation, though the latter retained control of basic energy research. R&D on alternative automobile power systems was transferred from the Environmental Protection Agency to ERDA. The new agency was tilted more toward conservation, alternative energy, environmental protection, and nuclear safety, and covered a broader energy spectrum than the agency originally proposed by Nixon. In fact, the Senate and conference had to override bureaucratic opposition when, with Ford's support, they expanded ERDA's function to include all energy research. In its actual programming, however, ERDA retained its pronuclear slant, ignoring the social aspects of the energy problem.

ERDA was organized into six program areas, each headed by an assistant administrator:

• Fossil energy
• Nuclear energy
• Environment and safety
• Energy conservation
• Solar, geothermal, and advanced energy systems
• Nuclear weapons programs

While there was no termination clause attached to ERDA, the president was directed to submit his recommendations for further reorganizations of federal energy activities to Congress by June 30, 1975.

Reflecting Congress's heightened sense of the need for control, the legislation also ordered ERDA's administrator to submit a detailed report on the previous year's R&D activities with each new budget. Another part of the ERDA legislation—which created the White House Energy Resources Council—reflected a desire for presidential level coordination. The Council included the heads of Interior, State, ERDA, and FEA, and was to harmonize federal energy agencies and advise the president and Congress on energy.

Curbing Nuclear Energy

Congress had led the White House into reorganizing the government's energy research and development responsibilities by replacing the "anachronistic''[20] AEC with the broad-based energy research agency. The new agency's degree of commitment to nuclear power, as opposed to other energy sources, was hotly contested, but the basic concept of reordering the energy structure met with little resistance. The overall goal of consolidating authority was to eliminate interagency squabbles that had interfered with energy policy formulation.

Before ERDA could be properly established, it had been necessary first to disarm the JCAE, which had traditionally hampered reorganization efforts that might slow atomic energy development or diminish its fiefdom—the AEC. Partly because of congressional concerns about overemphasis on nuclear energy, the JCAE began to lose its once awesome influence. Holifield himself relented to increasing pressure for energy reorganization, applied by Jackson and current and former AEC commissioners who agreed that the AEC had outlived its usefulness.

Virulent public attacks had also weakened the JCAE which was seen as being "outmoded," forcing an "overconcentration," and fostering "proprietary interest" in nuclear energy at the expense of other "more promising" sources of power.[21] The JCAE soon lost much of its influence over energy matters as a result of ERDA reorganization and in 1977 its responsibilities were split among several committees, putting the committee out of existence and weakening the nuclear energy lobby. (This process is described in detail in chapter 13.)

Because much of the effort to overcome the nuclear lobby would have been wasted if it were allowed to dominate the newly formed ERDA, the Senate included safeguards to assure that all energy technologies would receive ample consideration. The Senate report on the ERDA bill sought "balance and meaningful priority-setting among the competing energy technologies," by organizing ERDA along lines of energy sources. The House, however, with its many nuclear energy supporters, quashed moves to insert similar balancing provisions in its own legislative version.

ERDA was also aimed at resolving the biases inherent in the AEC. The latter's continual attempts, abetted by the JCAE, to justify nuclear energy regardless of the specifics of the situation, aggravated many members of Congress who preferred realistic and independent appraisals. To this end, the Senate carefully inserted provisions requiring detailed balanced planning and reporting procedures, which reemerged in Jackson's Federal Nonnuclear Energy Research and Development Act of 1974, mentioned earlier.

Much of the battle over creating ERDA (and also the Nuclear Regulatory Commission) had really been about breaking open the stranglehold which nuclear power interests had on federal energy spending, even though this stranglehold was originally self-imposed by Congress. The bureaucratic restructuring and committee reorganization were alone insufficient. ERDA's ability to function without bias was questioned because, although it contained people from the Office of Coal Research and the National Science Foundation, it was comprised primarily of the staffs of the nuclear-oriented AEC (all but 1,000 of ERDA's 92,000 employees). Although ERDA was immediately seen as antinuclear by the nuclear establishment, it is clear that it was heavily weighted toward atomic energy. The largest ERDA budget component was for nuclear weapons production and development; the next largest was for the civilian nuclear program, including a breeder reactor. Although ERDA would also be absorbing the major functions of the Bureau of Mines, only 10 percent of its budget was devoted to coal research and development, while 3 percent went to conservation and 1 percent to geothermal and solar energy. The legislation's stated intent that no energy technology be given an unwarranted priority was obviously not carried out in the budgeting.

ERDA's Short Life

ERDA was an awkward conglomerate of competing interests in possession of a nebulous mandate and diffuse goals and faced with an antagonistic combination of clients. Its unique set of responsibilities is suggested by the directives it received from Congress to make atomic bombs and develop solar panels, to foster exotic nuclear technology, and to look for better ways to insulate homes.

Such eclecticism resulted from ERDA's need to satisfy four constituencies. The atomic establishment wanted to push for nuclear energy development in every available format. Those generally interested in energy policy wanted a central mechanism that could rationalize and plan energy research, develop long-range objectives, and oversee the pursuit of these ends. Nuclear power opponents wanted a new nuclear safety agency (NRC) split off from energy development, because AEC could not realistically be expected to both promote nuclear energy and be circumspect about controlling, regulating, and evaluating it. Finally, proponents of other energy forms—such as coal, solar, and oil—sought an institutional structure that would promote development of their favored energy form. To continue with only a pronuclear government establishment, these latter three constituencies argued, would result in an imbalance of government R&D efforts.

In sum, the organizational premise of ERDA was balance between:

• long-range goals versus daily program development;
• possible directions for future energy development;
• supplying energy versus safety and environmental considerations;
• nuclear versus nonnuclear energy sources; and
• a massive energy department versus energy research, policy, and administration units scattered throughout the government.

Centralization versus Decentralization

ERDA was one manifestation of the drive within the government to centralize energy administration and research. Yet the conflict over centralization entailed more than simple disagreement over management styles; it involved various social and organizational processes as well. The impulse toward centralization is motivated by a desire for power or for improved administrative procedures. However, the inclination of many politically sensitive organizations is toward decentralization in order to protect their interests more effectively. The fragmentation that results from decentralization permits more in-depth control to be exercised over the policy area, and more insulation from competing policy areas. There is also increased power available resulting from specialization, particularly if a monopoly on knowledge can be obtained. On the other hand there is a point of diminishing returns where breadth begins to erode power.

Since political systems tend toward segmentation, differentiation, and decentralization, great effort and leadership is required to counteract these trends. However, while subdivision and devolution into bureaucratic fiefdoms is the general flow of government in ordinary times, a crisis creates an unusual opportunity to overcome these dispersionary forces. Outside pressure, generated by crises, give political leadership the authority it requires to overcome divisiveness. External pressure or crises become the driving forces toward new centralizing reorganizations. The government's lack of success in creating an Energy and Natural Resources Department under Nixon (or later under Carter) illustrates the difficulty of overcoming segmented fiefdoms. However, the relative success of energy reorganization during a crisis situation shows that unusual changes and threats emanating from the external environment are sufficiently strong motives to overcome much resistance and inertia. The example of ERDA (and FEA) show the usefulness of capitalizing on outside pressure or crises as rationales for centralization.

There is much validity in former AEC chairman Dixie Lee Ray's observation that *energy* was added to the title of the Natural Resources Department in an attempt to enlist the support of those in Congress who were concerned about energy shortages. Ray quipped that if that addition failed to persuade Congress to support it, "next year we'll call it the Department of Sex, Energy, and Natural Resources."[22]

Fading Glory

In retrospect, it appears that ERDA ultimately failed because it did not consider the social values and public processes acceptance involved in energy policy. It also ignored economic aspects (i.e. impact on capital markets) and environmental development, especially when contemplating elaborate projects.[23] The excitement of engineering overcame a balanced perspective of what actually was needed.

The space program did not provide an appropriate model for an energy program. ERDA succumbed to the same problems that have faced the space program as a result of its heavy emphasis on technologial accomplishment rather than social utility. The solution of the energy problem involves far more complex and wide-ranging problems than simply bringing expensive, exotic, and centralized power stations on line. While an oversimplification, it is nevertheless true that the basic ERDA approach was to project a high energy growth future, then seek nuclear and high-technology means of filling the anticipated gap.

In sum, though ERDA was a step away from the energy monoculture of the past, it was only an intermediate one. Many of the same questions that plagued the ERDA decision and its implementation would return when Congress and a new administration attempted the ultimate rationalization of energy research and administration by creating a Department of Energy (see chapter 6).

Notes

1. Linda Charlton, "Decades of Inaction Brought Energy Gap," *New York Times*, February 10, 1974, p. 1.
2. Lester Sobel, ed., *Energy Crisis, Vol. 2, 1974-75* (New York: Facts on File, 1975), p. 50.
3. U.S. Congress, Joint Economic Committee, "Energy Statistics," hearings, January 14, 1974.
4. U.S. Congress, House Select Small Business Committee, "Energy Data Requirements of the Federal Government, part I," hearings, January 16-18, 1974.
5. U.S. Congress, Senate Government Operations Committee, "Oversight Series, part 2: The Major Oil Companies," hearings, January 21, 1974.
6. U.S. Congress, Senate Foreign Relations Committee, "Multinational Oil Companies and U.S. Foreign Policy, part 5," hearings, October 11, November 27, 1973; "The International Petroleum Cartel, the Iranian Consortium, and U.S. National Security," committee print, February 21, 1974.
7. The following discussion is drawn from three reorganization studies: President's Advisory Council on Executive (chaired by Roy L. Ash), "Establishment of a Department of Natural Resources Organization for Social and Economic Programs" (Washington, D.C.: The White House, February 5, 1971); U.S. Congress, Senate Interior and Insular Affairs Committee, "Federal Energy Regulation: A Staff Analysis," prepared by Daniel A. Dreyfus. Serial 93-6 (92-41); and Federal Energy Regulation Study Team (William O. Dobb, chairman) *Federal Energy Regulation: An Organizational Study* (Washington, D.C.: U.S. Government Printing Office, 1974).
8. For a detailed discussion, see D. Brady and P. Althoff, "The Politics of Regulation: The Case of the Atomic Energy Commission and the Nuclear Industry, *American Politics Quarterly* 1 (July 1973: 361-83); and Steven Del Sesto, *Sci-*

ence Politics and Controversy: Civilian Nuclear Power in the United States, 1946-1974 (Boulder, Colo.: Westview, 1979).

9. *New York Times*, January 29, 1974, p. 38.
10. U.S. Congress, Senate Judiciary Committee, "Competitive Aspects of the Energy Industry, part 1," hearings, May 5, 1970, pp. 3-10.
11. *New York Times*, November 10, 1974, p.1. Criticism of nuclear energy since the early 1970s has become nearly a cottage industry among some journalistic, academic, and public interest circles, so no attempt to recapitulate the literature will be undertaken here.
12. U.S. Congress, Senate Commerce Committee, "Council on Energy Policy," hearings, August 10, 1972, February 7-8, 1973; and a report (93-114) on the measure, "Energy Policy Act of 1973."
13. *New York Times*, March 9, 1975, p. D3.
14. In general, FEA functioned similarly to other regulatory bureaucracies and organizations. Confronted with narrowly delimited objectives and possible methods to attain them, the organization developed a set of standard procedures that could operate almost independently of the objectives, and, at the minimum, avoid default or obvious failure. This is one variety of "satisficing" (see chapter 14).
15. The plan was designed by Roy Ash's commission (see note 7).
16. U.S. Congress, House Government Operations Committee, "Federal Energy Administration," hearings, December 10-11, 1973, pp. 59-73.
17. U.S. Congress, Senate Appropriations Committee, "Supplemental Appropriations, FY 74, part 2," hearings, December 6, 1973, pp. 1823-47.
18. U.S. Congress, Senate Government Operations Committee, "Energy Reorganization Act of 1974," House Report 93-1445 (October 8, 1974).
19. *National Journal Reports*, September 28, 1974, p. 1468.
20. *New York Times*, October 21, 1974, p.32.
21. Congressional reports cited, ibid.
22. A. R. Smith, "ERDA: Glamour Agency," *Bulletin of the Atomic Scientists*, January, 1975, p. 29.
23. U.S. Congress, Office of Technology Assessment, "Critique of ERDA," October 29, 1975.

4
A First Step: Congress and the Ford Administration

A brief overview of the awkward birth of the Energy Policy and Conservation Act (PL 94-163) may serve as a preparation for understanding the complex events which follow. Describing its genesis may result in some loss of suspense since the administration and both houses of Congress went through a complex process, weighing many details before agreement was reached on the act. Like the genesis of many acts, these were events that, in the telling, sound primarily like the drudgery they were—a drudgery of details, procedures, and negotiations that lie at the heart of national decision making. Finally signed into law in 1975, the bill was a remarkable compromise between two conflicting positions concerning energy pricing: it included provisions both to reduce and to raise the price of oil. That year, based on information from the Project Independence Study, President Ford requested an end to price controls on domestic oil and the imposition of a $3-per-barrel fee on imported crude oil. Ford, like Nixon, sought economic incentives to increase domestic production, and turned away from trying to reduce world oil-prices and exclusively relying on voluntary conservation and moral suasion to cut energy use. He also sought energy security by creating a strategic petroleum reserve and establishing presidential authority to ration supplies and control prices.

Congress's mood, however, was clearly against permitting private markets to control petroleum prices and supplies. Revelations and allegations about petroleum industry misbehavior caused the traditional free-market conception of petroleum supply to be seriously, if temporarily, questioned. The moderate initial support for raising oil price ceilings rapidly disappeared. Congress rejected Ford's proposals and sought to hold oil prices in check while simultaneously beginning action to eliminate the import levy. However, when Congress responded to Ford's threatened oil import fee by rescinding his power to levy such fees, Ford vetoed the bill.

The Democratic leadership also made several attempts to devise an alternative to Ford's program, finally agreeing on a plan which countered his move to decontrol crude oil prices. Their plan to maintain price controls to protect the consumer also included a stiff gasoline tax to reduce wasteful consumption, a utility-rate reform measure to encourage conservation, and oil-import quotas. The plan's supporters rejected decontrol on the grounds that it would permit OPEC rather than Congress to set U.S. energy prices.

The House Ways and Means Committee, under the chairmanship of Al Ullman (D-Oreg.), soon assembled its own plan, which approximated a compromise between the Democrats' and the president's plans. It proposed a gasoline tax tied to oil imports and a "gas-guzzler" tax to encourage high-mileage car purchases. While it seemed for a time that the Ullman plan might be adopted, the centerpiece of the program—the gasoline tax provision—was decisively defeated in June in the House, and several other provisions were weakened. With the Ullman plan's demise, attention shifted to omnibus energy legislation that had been drafted in the Senate Interior and House Commerce Committees, and which was gradually shaped into what became the Energy Policy and Conservation Act of 1975 (EPCA).

The battle between Capitol Hill and the White House resulted in a mid-year stalemate, which Ford attempted to break on July 14, 1975, when he announced a compromise oil decontrol plan. This plan included a windfall profits tax. The congressional response was to pass the Petroleum Price Review Act, which rolled back oil prices and extended them to "stripper well" oil which had previously been exempt. Ford vetoed the measure on the grounds that it would increase consumption and decrease production. Although the Democratically controlled Congress was continually able to block Ford's initiatives, it was seldom in agreement concerning its own program. Moreover, there was enough support for the administration position to sustain Ford's vetoes, which he used more liberally than any other president.

In a final compromise, Ford retracted his demand that oil be immediately decontrolled in favor of gradual decontrol. In turn, Congress said it would allow decontrol to occur after a forty-month period. It withdrew its demand for permanent controls or an oil-price rollback, which to Ford was the most objectionable alternative. In a conciliatory gesture, Ford eliminated the import fees he had levied ($2 per barrel), although the legislation, S 622, did not require him to do so. After much wavering, Ford signed EPCA on December 22, 1975. Besides the important pricing aspects, other topics were included in EPCA, which was actually an amalgamation of five other bills:

1. S 622, the Standby Energy Authorization Act, approved by the Senate on April 10, gave the president power to ration gas in an emergency and participate in the International Energy Agency.
2. S 349, the Energy Labeling and Disclosure Act, approved by the Senate on July 11, set appliance standards and efficiency targets.
3. S 1883, the Automobile Fuel Economy Act of 1975, approved by the Senate on July 15, required improved auto mileage standards.
4. S 667, the Strategic Energy Reserve Act, approved by the Senate on July 8, authorized petroleum stockpiling.

5. HR 7014, the Energy Conservation and Oil Policy Act of 1975, approved by the House on September 23, was far more inclusive than any of the Senate bills. The House debated over it intermittently for two months before passing it (by 255-148). It contained most elements of the preceding four Senate measures, as well as the controversial oil-pricing provisions.

Each of these measures is discussed in some detail below, with special attention given to its genesis and the administration's response to measures. The Ford program is examined first, followed by an analysis of the various Democratic plans. The House and Senate battles over the EPCA are discussed independently, followed by an overall assessment of the 1975 law.

President Ford's Initiative, 1975

When the Ninety-fourth Congress convened in January 1975, energy was rivaling the economy as the major national concern. That year, more than 1,000 energy-related bills overwhelmed legislative channels, making some concerted action imperative. Yet, no national consensus emerged to guide and coordinate energy policy formulation. Ford responded to the mounting pressure with his own solution to the nation's energy dilemma—a multifaceted program of thirteen interlocking titles, an ambitious and far-reaching program in terms of the issues addressed, and in its potential effect on American society. His proposed Energy Independence Act of 1975, sent to Capitol Hill on January 31, was guided by a conservation-by-price philosophy. It attempted to stimulate domestic production by increasing import fees on oil and thus its relative cost (see Table 4.1).

Ford's program contained several relatively innocuous proposals, such as establishing a strategic petroleum reserve and using governmental funds to improve the energy efficiency of low-income people's homes and thermal-efficiency building standards. It also contained some controversial proposals, such as an expanded role for the Federal Energy Administration (FEA) in locating and constructing energy facilities and in forcing utilities to convert from gas and oil to coal-burning generators. Some parts of Ford's program were highly controversial, such as the deregulation of all "new" natural gas, the levying of a 37¢ tax per every 1,000 cubic feet of gas (which was the equivalent of his separately proposed $2 tax on each barrel of domestically produced crude oil), and the weakening of clean air standards. Ford's plan relied on free markets to implement conservation and spur production, but governmental supervision and intervention would also play a considerable role.

Though Ford defended his highly controversial approach with a strong warning—"We face a future of shortages and dependency which the nation cannot tolerate and the American people will not accept"[1]—the predominantly

TABLE 4.1
Selected Proposal for a Comprehensive National Energy Policy, 1975

Issue	Ford Administration 1/15/75	Proposed Policy		
		Democratic Leadership 2/27/75	Ulman & Ways & Means 3/3/75	Senate Committee Report (dates as indicated)
1. Oil decontrol	End controls on 4/1/75	Reject decontrol	Gradual decontrol	Prohibited "old oil" to increase in price 3/5/75
2. Gas rationing	Authority to act only in grave crisis	Extend allocation and rationing authority	Standby end-use rationing in an emergency	Rationing for alleviating shortages or fulfilling international commitments, with congressional veto 2/25/75
3. Fuel efficiency standards	Freeze auto emission standards in return for voluntary mileage improvements	Tough mandatory standards	"Gas guzzler" tax rebated to high mileage car purchasers	Tough standards with penalty 5/15/75
4. Appliance labeling	New appliances and cars required to have energy consumption labels	Broad labeling including homes and cars	No proposal	Car and major appliance labeling 6/24/75

Democratic Congress launched an attack on the plan that delayed the passage of any comprehensive energy program for nearly a year. The record of this attack and the controversies and frustrated legislative attempts it produced offer a unique insight into the question of whether the U.S. political system is equipped to deal with the increasingly complex and divisive issues that lie ahead for this country. The question is addressed in the conclusion of chapter 4.

The Reception

Immediately after Ford announced his plan, oil producers, environmentalists, and Congress reacted with alarm and hostility, citing numerous economic and political realities which it appeared to neglect. Oil producers feared that taxation would prevent a balance between supply and demand and would eliminate the economic incentives for crude oil and natural gas production that free markets provide. Environmentalists feared the relaxation of regulations protecting the physical quality of life; the defense establishment was against

TABLE 4.1 (Continued)

Senate Floor (dates as indicated)	House Committee 7/9/75	House Floor 9/23/75	Conference Committee 12/15-17/75
Same as committee but allowed higher prices for hard-to-recover oil 4/10/75	Rolled-back "new oil" prices	3-tier pricing (adopted 7/30/75)	Gradually rising ceiling for next 39 months
Presidential energy allocation authority with congressional veto over action 4/10/75	Presidential emergency gas rationing and conservation power with congressional review	Same as committee	Limited presidential energy conservation and gas rationing powers, but either House could block plan
Same as committee 7/15/75	Moderate standards with penalty	Same as committee	Moderate standards with penalty
Same as committee 7/11/75	Required labeling for all major appliances except autos	Same as committee	FEA labeling of all major appliances except autos. (Auto labeling requirements mandated by other legislation.)

opening naval reserves; and conservationists threatened to fight drilling in frontier regions, increased strip mining of coal, and the opening of shale projects. The public also lacked faith in the president's ability to formulate energy policy. Al Ullman maintained that if the American people could have confidence in a "leadership that lays out a program that leads to a solution," they would be willing to confront the energy crisis with the necessary self-denial.[2] Under the circumstances, however, they were being asked to pay too high a price for something they were not sure was necessary. The administration admitted that Ford's plan would cost the American family up to $95 more a year than FEA had originally predicted. More alarming, and of intense concern to the Democrats, was the plan's national economic impact. Former treasury undersecretary Paul A. Volcker and economist Joseph A. Pechman testified that energy taxes and costs imposed by Ford's plan would total $30 billion, worsening the 1975 recession.[3] Nonetheless, Ford would have to confront the opposition in Congress and across the nation if he was to have an energy bill.

The Democratic Alternatives

As Ford was preparing his program, the Democrats, attempting to control the direction of policy development and to capitalize on the extensive hearings that had been held by various Democratically controlled congressional committees in the 1971-74 period, released an alternative plan developed by a special House group, the Speaker's Task Force on Energy and Economic Policy. The task force, appointed by the Democratic House leadership and headed by Congressman Jim Wright (D-Tex.), viewed recession and inflation as the greatest threats posed by the energy problem and energy conservation as the solution.[4] The task force plan, however, was an awkward mixture of mandatory controls, petroleum allocation schemes, higher taxes on gasoline and large cars, gasless days, subsidies for home insulation, and new utility rates designed to lower electricity consumption. Disagreement among the task force members and the need to satisfy divergent concerns had resulted in a jury-rigged set of inconsistencies and unexamined assumptions, which prevented the task force from garnering necessary support in Congress. House Speaker Carl Albert (D-Okla.) requested that another plan be developed in close cooperation with an existing Senate task force, chaired by John Pastore (D-R.I.). Pastore, who had served in the Senate since 1950 representing a frost-belt state, had emerged as one of the leading critics of the oil industry. He and Wright pledged themselves and their task forces to the creation of policy that would unite the Democrats and developed a plan which was introduced on February 27, 1975.[5]

The Wright-Pastore plan reflected the Democrats' philosophical commitment to easing economic recession caused by high world oil prices; however, it did not further Ford's goal to end American dependence on foreign oil by providing economic incentives to spur domestic energy production. The plan reflected doubts concerning the adequacy of market mechanisms and of higher prices to increase oil and gas supplies. It included a proposal, strongly supported by Senator Henry Jackson (D-Wash.), to establish a National Energy Production Board modeled after the War Production Board of World War II. The board would break bottlenecks to energy production, allocate energy when necessary, and wield various emergency and rationing powers. However, partly due to ineffective leadership in Congress, the plan failed to win broad support; it was especially opposed by the freshman Democrats in the House, many of whom wanted to see oil prices rolled back. Taking advantage of the new freedom of expression which had resulted from the increased democratization of the Congress, over half of the seventy-five Democratic freshmen in the House voiced their opposition to the Wright-Pastore plan, and one group of freshmen went so far as to develop its own energy plan.[6]

Al Ullman, in his role as chairman of the House Ways and Means Committee, attempted to develop an alternative to the Wright-Pastore and the Ford administration plans which would bridge the philosophical gap between them. Ullman sought to achieve a balance between the Democrats' proposal, which he felt did not increase oil prices enough to curb energy waste, and the president's plan, which he felt raised prices too much, hurting consumers and workers.

The heart of Ullman's program was a gradual gasoline tax increase to 50¢ per gallon. His plan encouraged energy conservation through measures such as a stiff excise tax on gas-guzzling automobiles. It also called for a gradual decontrolling of oil and natural gas prices in combination with a windfall profits tax, and the use of import quotas if necessary.[7] It also would eliminate major oil producers' percentage depletion tax allowance for oil and gas, increasing their federal taxes by an estimated $2 billion.

The administration reacted to the bill with praise for the House Ways and Means Committee's attempt to reduce dependence on imports and return to "free comprehensive pricing," but criticized the proposed import quota system and the gas tax on excess use. Oil industry leaders and economists also supported the committee's proposal to gradually decontrol oil and gas prices but vehemently opposed a proposed windfall profits tax; independents sought reinstatement of the depletion allowance and major oil companies argued against eliminating existing tax benefits on foreign production. Thirty-nine freshman Congressmen, on the other hand, announced their opposition to increases in the gasoline tax and to higher oil prices resulting from decontrol, charging that the committee's plan ignored consumer's interests.[8]

Early Hopes Dashed

Almost six months after Ford introduced his energy plan, only two bills were close to floor vote, and neither were seen as highly desirable by the administration. The Ways and Means bill fell short of Ford's proposal for cutting consumption through the price mechanism, and chances for its success during a House floor vote appeared slight. The Senate Commerce Committee's measure, the Standby Energy Authorities Act, which dealt with control of new natural gas prices, ran counter to administration desire to end price controls.

Finally, in June the Ways and Means proposal was gutted when the House—in a surprise move—rejected any increase in gasoline taxes. While this action considerably reduced the possibility of arriving at a consistent energy policy, it did permit the bill to be passed by both the Senate and the House. On July 17, Congress sent the president HR 4035, extending oil price controls to December 31, 1975, and directing Ford to set a ceiling of $11.28 per barrel for new oil.[9]

The issue of oil price controls remained the principal point of dissension. Ford, claiming that HR 4035 allowed a "drift into greater energy dependence,"[10] vetoed it on July 21. Lacking sufficient votes to override the veto, congressional leaders shelved the measure. A day later, the House responded with its own veto, voting to adopt a resolution to block Ford's proposed thirty-month oil decontrol plan.

On July 25, Ford proposed a compromise decontrol plan, under which oil prices would be allowed to rise over a thirty-nine-month period, until a ceiling of $11.50 per barrel on domestic oil was reached. This move by the administration indicated that it was willing—for the first time—to accept the idea of limiting rising oil prices and to agree to a longer phase-in period.

Although Ullman had predicted its probable success in the House, Ford's new decontrol plan was quashed by the House adopting a resolution of disapproval (HR Res. 641). The next day, July 31, Congress, under the Emergency Petroleum Allocation Act, extended the price control authority beyond its original expiration date, August 31, 1975, until March 1, 1976. The Senate approved this measure without change, but on September 9, Ford vetoed it, agreeing, however, to accept a temporary forty-five-day extension of controls if his veto was sustained, which it was the next day.

House Action

At this point, the focus of the policy debate shifted to an omnibus bill in the House Interior and Insular Affairs Committee. During September, the Energy and Environment Subcommittee held hearings on the president's proposals and then issued a clean bill (HR 7014, the Energy Conservation and Oil Policy Act; see Table 4.1). The bill contained eight major, controversial titles. An examination of these suggests the difficulties involved in its consideration by Congress and the administration as they gathered supporting and opposing comments, discussed amendments, and negotiated its final passage.

Bills are usually divided into "titles," each representing a major provision. HR 7014's Title II, concerning standby energy authorities and the national civilian petroleum reserve, granted standby power to the president to impose rationing, require international oil allocation, authorize oil company cooperation without fear of antitrust action, provide information to other international energy program participatory nations, and prescribe energy conservation plans.[11]

Title II also required the president to submit to Congress contingency plans for conservation or rationing, which would then have to be approved by both chambers before they could be adopted. The second part of HR 7014's Title II called for a civilian strategic energy oil reserve of up to 1 billion barrels, with an early shortage reserve of up to 150 million barrels.

The most controversial part of the House plan, Title III, allowed a gradual decontrol of domestic prices, providing there was an excess profits tax which would give to the government 90 percent of the difference between the purchaser price and the base price. This title also authorized the president to require more than the maximum efficient rate of production from some oil fields in the event of an emergency, allocate materials, and restrict exports. Small refiners were exempted from the full requirements of the entitlement program (which had FEA equalize the cost of crude oil to all refiners).

Title IV, also quite controversial, empowered the president to require from refineries an adjustment of their output in accord with the mandatory gas savings program and mandated a three-year freeze on gasoline consumption at the 1973-74 level. It also empowered the president to order a 2-4 percent cut in the amounts of gasoline which could be made available for purchase, classifying him in this transaction as the exclusive agent of U.S. energy products. Finally, this title encouraged a voluntary industrial energy conservation program.

Title V, Improving Energy Efficiency of Consumer Products, was divided into two sections. The first, parallel to S 1883, required a car fuel efficiency standard of 18.5 mpg by 1978, all the way up to 28 mpg by 1985, with stiff fines on cars that exceeded the limits. The second part concerned official energy labeling and efficiency standards for consumer products other than automobiles, parallel to S 349.

Title VI, Conversion from Oil and Gas to Other Fuels, extended the FEA's coal conversion authority for two years and provided loan guarantees for opening new underground mines to produce low sulphur coal.

Title VII was so controversial that its constitutionality was eventually challenged in court. It gave Congress the authority to accept or reject certain administration measures. Congress had fifteen days to veto an action, and if it failed to approve a regulation within sixty days of continuous sessions, the regulation would not go into effect. However, an approved contingency plan could be used without a fifteen-day review period if there was a shortfall in supplies to the International Energy Program (IEP) participatory nations which activated the emergency allocation system.

The final title of HR 7014, the Emergency Data Base, provided for an Office of Petroleum Auditing and Accounting within the General Accounting Office, which would audit companies in energy-related fields and make energy-related data available to the public, Congress, and the executive branch. A $10,000 daily fine could be levied on those firms not complying with a request to disclose the information described in the bill. This title, therefore, provided the plan, funding, and penalties necessary for the creation of an information system which would help Congress and the executive branch make more rational and informed decisions.

The HR 7014 House omnibus plan would avoid massive price hikes and at the same time provide a conservation program. It combined the mandatory gas allocation savings program with the mandatory import quota system contained in HR 6860, an appliance labeling section, better use of coal resources, and a better information base for problem solving.

House Omnibus Plan Sharply Criticized

The executive branch reacted negatively to the proposal. The Department of Transportation pointed out that the mandatory automobile fuel efficiency standards were only slightly higher than those in the president's voluntary program yet required unnecessary administrative costs and regulations. The Commerce Department found the industrial energy conservation program superfluous and costly, since energy price increases would force industry to reduce its use or find more efficient machinery.

FEA vehemently objected to four major aspects of HR 7014: (1) it would take at least two years to implement; (2) the windfall tax might prevent total decontrol from ever taking place; (3) the sixty-day congressional veto procedure gave Congress too much power; (4) the strictly delimited antitrust immunity for companies participating in the IEP did not allow them to participate fully in its various programs.

FEA also had several additional complaints. It maintained that there was too much congressional review power over the national petroleum reserve and too many penalties in the automobile efficiency program, and that the authority for production above maximum efficient rates was too broad. FEA also believed that the retroactive small refiners' exemption from the entitlements program benefited too few people; the coal production subsidies would benefit small, inefficient operators; and the performance standards for appliances were unnecessary. Finally, FEA found that it would be too deeply involved in decision-making processes through the bill's proposed industry energy conservation program.

Objections within the House Interstate and Foreign Commerce Committee, which finally approved the bill 26-17, followed the lines of the FEA critique. There was also concern that the fuel efficiency measure not only exceeded present technological capability, but also did not take into account the problem of new automobile emission standards, which could greatly affect mileage. Congressman Robert Krueger (D-Tex.) argued that the two-tiered price system (for old and new oil) eliminated the possibility of true "end-use efficiency" by setting two prices for the same commodity and concluded that it was more "abdication than alternative."

A Conference Is Called

Nevertheless, on September 23, the House approved HR 7014, substituted its provisions for those of S 622, and called for a conference. The Senate, concurring in the House amendment with an amendment substituting the texts of its versions of these bills (discussed in the next section), also called for a conference. Problems arose when the House rejected the Senate amendments on October 1. The bill was then sent back to the conferees and, one month later, after redrafting the language of the final provisions, Congress reached agreement. Yet, when the conference report was filed on December 9 (HR 94-100, SR 94-516), none of the Republican conferees nor three of the Democratic senators—J. Bennet Johnston, Jr. (D-La.), James Abourezk (D-S.Dak.), and Ernest F. Hollings (D-S.C.)—signed it.

Conferees reacted to the controversial oil-pricing issue by rejecting both House and Senate proposals to set up tiers of prices, opting instead to give the president flexibility in adjusting prices for various categories of oil. The average price per gallon for domestic oil was not to exceed $7.66, although this average could be adjusted to allow for inflation and to encourage production from certain areas. The combined increase in one year could be no more than 10 percent.

The House-approved gasoline allocation program, requiring a 2 percent reduction in gas consumption from 1973-74, was dropped by conferees. The antibusing provision was also rejected, and the House ban on joint ventures using federal resources was only to be applied to leases for gas or oil development on the outer continental shelf.

Ultimately, five bills which had been under consideration during the Ninety-fourth Congress were combined to constitute the Energy Policy and Conservation Act (EPCA). The most controversial aspect of the final act was the extension of price controls to new oil not previously subject to federal controls. The House was generally not as amenable to this measure as was the Senate, delaying the bill for months with a tug-of-war over price controls.

Senate Action

When the Senate attempted to develop its energy policy bill, Henry Jackson took the lead. He used his various committee assignments to affect almost all Senate actions that created the Energy Policy and Conservation Act of 1975, which he sponsored. During the Ninety-fourth Congress, Jackson served as chairman of the Interior and Insular Affairs Committee, and was on the Armed Services Committee (which had jurisdiction over the naval petroleum reserves), the Government Operations Committee, and the Joint Committee on Atomic Energy. Since Jackson, at this time, was preparing to seek the 1976 Democratic nomination for president, he used his prominence and committee membership to further his political ambitions. For example, in a dramatic political gesture, he summoned seven major oil company executives to a committee hearing and, with full media coverage, accused them of having withheld oil during the energy crisis to drive prices up.[12] The substance and controversy surrounding the bills which comprise the EPCA follows. Jackson, of course, played a role in each of them.

Presidential Powers

In February 1975, Jackson and several cosponsors introduced S 622 at almost the same time that Ford had his proposals introduced (S 594). After hearings and markup, S 622 resembled Title XIII of the administration proposal, which gave the president power to ration gas, implement energy conservation programs, allocate energy-related supplies and material, move to increase domestic supplies of petroleum, restrict exports of energy resources, and direct the implementation of the International Energy Program. Many of these powers had been issues of contention during the Nixon administration. There were, however, major differences between Title XIII and S 622. The latter, for example, provided for legislative review of executive decisions and a congressional right to veto rationing or conservation plans. S 622 also provided for an extension of the Emergency Petroleum Allocation Act, a larger role for states in formulating energy policy, limited presidential authority to raise "old" oil prices, and, according to its sponsors, an alternative to massive price hikes. It did not give the president control over privately held oil stocks.

In a minority report, Senators Fannin, Hansen, McClure, and Bartlett gave their primary reasons for opposition to the bill: its partisan tendencies, congressional review provisions, unnecessary extension of the Emergency Petroleum Allocation Act, the "inappropriate" conservation program, inadequate provision for U.S. participation in the International Energy Program, and authorization of production beyond the the maximum efficient rate, which they deemed an unconstitutional seizure of private property because it allowed the president to force companies to produce beyond their normal, or even most profitable, levels.

The Senate Interior Committee reported S 622 on March 5, 1975. In the ensuing Senate debate many of its amendments were rejected, such as limiting the president's power to demand oil production beyond the maximum efficient rate, preventing the extension of emergency allocation, and allowing the higher "new oil" price. After Jackson requested that a ceiling of $7.50 on the price of new oil be specified in this proposal, it was accepted. Amendments which were adopted included extending the deadline for states to submit energy proposals, extending the FEA coal conversion authority for six months, and cutting back the extension of the emergency allocation act for three months. The Senate approved S 622 on April 10.

Energy Labeling and Disclosure Act

The early history of this act is simply a record of uncompleted legislative action. Since 1973, Senator John Tunney (D-Calif.) had been seeking legislation ordering comparative efficiency ratings for major appliances. In January 1975, he introduced S 349, a bill requiring manufacturers to label large household appliances and automobiles with estimated energy costs for operation. Within two weeks, Ford had introduced his omnibus energy proposal, S 594, of which Title XII authorized the president to create energy efficiency labeling.

S 349 had been stronger than the president's bill because it ordered labeling rather than leaving the program's implementation to the president's discretion. FEA expressed minor reservations about the congressional bill because, although about 8 percent of the electricity used annually is for lighting and miscellaneous purposes, these could not be included in the labeling. Nevertheless, because the presidential and congressional proposals had similar objectives, S 349 passed the Senate on July 11, 1975, by a vote of 77-0.

This bill was simply aimed at assuring an informed choice in a free market economy, not at any predetermined final effect on consumer purchasing habits. Its far from prohibitive costs were to be borne by the government and consumers, rather than by industry. In short, S 349 was a relatively innocuous bill.

Mileage Standards

The Automobile Fuel Economy Act, on the other hand, was controversial. An earlier, similar measure was introduced by Senator Tunney in 1973 but never passed the House. The new bill authorized the Transportation Department to set annual mileage standards designed to raise average auto fuel economy to 21 miles per gallon by 1980 and 28 miles per gallon by 1985. The Transportation Secretary was authorized to adjust the standards, if not precluded by House or Senate action, and to levy fines for infractions. The bill also established a Department of Transportation prototype program to develop safe, fuel-efficient transportation forms.

At the start of the Ninety-fourth Congress, five different bills and one amendment concerning fuel economy were immediately introduced and, after committee hearings in March and May, were combined in a single piece of legislation. With some amendments from the committee, the bill was favorably reported out of committee on May 15, 1975, as S 1883.

Because the Automobile Fuel Economy Act would necessitate large research expenditures by automakers, it was strongly opposed by them. Moreover, since the bill contravened Ford's voluntary fuel efficiency standards proposal, resistance from the administration began while the measure was still in committee. Ford had sought to freeze emission standards until 1982, because of an agreement by U.S. automakers to increase average fuel economy by 1980.

Opposition to the bill from within the committee was not strong. In a key vote, only three senators supported Senator Robert Griffin's (R-Mich.) motion to substitute a voluntary fuel efficiency program for the standards mandated by the bill. However, Griffin and James Buckley (R-N.Y.) filed additional views with the committee report, calling the bill unnecessary at best, and at worst, a disaster. The problems they cited included the harsh civil penalties for noncompliance, which would impose great hardship on car manufacturers. They criticized Congress's failure to set car emission standards (which by default were 25 percent above that recommended by President Ford). Finally, they also faulted the bill's emphasis on the shift toward the manufacturing of small cars, which they claimed would penalize large families who needed correspondingly large cars.

After the bill reached the floor, Griffin proposed that it be recommitted to committee, but the Senate rejected the motion, preferring to establish the mandatory standards itself rather than allow the president to carry out his agreement with the auto manufacturers. Therefore, despite opposition from both the industry and the president, the Automobile Fuel Economy Act was passed in July 1975. In the following months it was to be incorporated into HR 7014 and finally signed into law as part of S 622.

The administration's opposition was partly based on a belief that the bill would increase foreign car sales, hurt U.S. automakers' competitive position, and weaken further an already damaged economy. The administration also feared that the new clean-air standards, by affecting car mileage, could make the efficiency standards set by Congress impossible to reach.

The history of the Automobile Fuel Economy Act affords a clear example of legislative success when congressional priorities differ from those of the chief executive. President Ford's motives related to the bill were not clear. However, the testimony and the committee reports suggest that he made a strong effort to block it. His choice of auto manufacturers as allies and of his close friend, Senator Griffin, to lead the opposition supports this conclusion. It seems unlikely that he would risk Griffin's prestige as an important minority leader for a cause he was not committed to defend. Most senators, however, openly supported the mandatory program. They efficiently assembled and organized the alternative proposals, constructed a committee draft, protected it on the floor, and overcame Ford's opposition.

Strategic Petroleum Reserves

Another issue related to the Energy Policy and Conservation Act, and one that had been occupying Congress for some time, was a strategic energy reserve. The first presidential commitment to such a reserve was made in Ford's January 5, 1975 State of the Union Address, which proposed a separate military and civilian oil reserve. However, similar proposals had already been under consideration by Congress since early 1973, when the Senate Interior Committee held hearings on oil and gas importation issues. Senators Jackson, Magnusson, Randolph, and Ribicoff had then introduced a bill creating a ninety-day oil reserve. The Nixon administration objected that it was unnecessary and inordinately expensive, and the bill never reached the president—partly because the oil embargo overshadowed all long-range energy planning.

Despite these early setbacks during the Ninety-fourth Congress, several bills, including an administration proposal, were introduced to establish a strategic energy reserve. In March 1975, after joint Interior-Armed Services Committee meetings reviewed these proposals, S 677 was produced—the Strategic Energy Reserve Act—which authorized the storing of energy supplies to cushion the impact of future import reductions. The reserves would be of oil and coal for the national, industrial, and utility sectors. Later in July, provisions of S 677 were added as a second title to the Senate's version of HR 49, which opened up production from the naval petroleum reserves. Although the vote for the plan was unanimous, Senator Edmund Muskie (D-Maine) warned of the prohibitive costs of building the reserves.

Despite Ford's favoring a reserve, there were concerns about the plan in his administration. FEA administrator Frank Zarb criticized the plan for forcing companies to pay for separate utility and coal reserves, which he considered an unjust burden. Zarb was also unhappy about the program's costs and noted that requiring that the reserves be filled within five years prevented benefits from international oil price fluctuations. He also noted that S 677 conflicted with the requirements of the International Energy Program (IEP) in allowing use of the reserves only after imports dropped 10 percent or more. (The IEP would go into effect after imports dropped 7 percent.) In partial response to Zarb's criticism, it was pointed out that the congressional proposal did not require the creation of the coal, utility, and regional reserves. It included a regional reserve system and a national reserve, granting Congress the authority to establish the others at its discretion.

Doubts about the reserve proposal were also expressed by the Office of Management and Budget and Commerce Department. In addition, a jurisdictional dispute broke out between FEA and the Department of Defense over control of the reserves in case of war. The Strategic Energy Reserve Act clearly caused disunity within the executive branch, although it may not have been obvious because agency comments on legislation must be negotiated within the administration before they are presented to Congress. Though Congress once again seemed reluctant to accept the administration's plan and substituted its own, apparently the issue was not considered sufficiently im-

portant to justify a major administration attack; nor was there enough disagreement in Congress to make administration opposition plausible.

By the time the Strategic Energy Reserve Act was incorporated into the
Energy Policy and Conservation Act, its separate end-use system had been
discarded, and it provided for storage of up to 1 billion barrels of oil in a
national reserve. In addition, the legislation required that at least 150 million
barrels be stored in the reserve within three years.

Culmination of Maneuvers

The final House and Senate action on S 622 reflected the divisiveness over
energy which had plagued Congress over the year. On December 15, the
House altered provisions concerning the granting of loans, omitting from the
conference version reference to the accommodation for loans and grants to
stimulate research in advanced automotive technology. These provisions were
originally part of the Senate fuel efficiency measure, S 1883, and in changing
them, the House essentially rejected the conference report.

By a vote of 215-179, the House then blocked any further attempts to
change the oil price provision and adopted a motion approving and returning
to the Senate a clean bill, S 622, containing all the language approved by the
conferees, except for the proposals for an automotive technology program and
loan guarantees for coal mines.

Protesting the oil price system, Senate opponents of the bill delayed sending
it to the president. Jackson warned that the deadlock over formulation of a
national energy policy "has resulted in a dangerous game of 'economic brink-
manship'" and urged clearance of the bill. A motion made by Jackson for
Senate-House agreement was thwarted by efforts to have the bill read in its
entirety and to postpone a decision concerning when voting would occur.
When the Senate cleared S 622 on December 17, opposition was still vehe-
ment. Lowell P. Weicker (R-Conn.) expressed the attitude of the opposing
senators: "When he needed a national energy policy, we got a political energy
cop-out. . . . Congress decided upon the carrot-and-the-stick approach. It decided to clobber the oil companies with the carrot, and after 1976, stick it to
the unsuspecting citizen."[13]

A year of regional, special interest, and political controversy finally resulted in the Energy Policy and Conservation Act (EPCA), (PL 94-162),
which established a national energy policy designed to maximize domestic
production, provide for strategic storage reserves, minimize the impact of
future disruptions in energy supplies, set domestic oil price levels, and reduce
domestic energy consumption through both voluntary and mandatory conservation programs. It also provided for stringent congressional scrutiny by the
General Accounting Office of oil industry activities. In the face of intense
opposition from oil-industry leaders, conservative Republicans, and oil-state

representatives, Ford signed the bill, acknowledging the defeat of his attempt to reduce oil consumption and increase production through higher fuel prices. The Act is "by no means perfect," he concluded, but it provides a "foundation upon which we can build a more comprehensive program."[14]

Ford's decision to sign the legislation came at the last minute. His resolve at the beginning of 1975 to support immediate oil price decontrol had steadily deteriorated as the months of debate wore on. Yet, at the end of the year he could still have achieved his objective if he had vetoed the EPCA, for the Emergency Petroleum Allocation Act (EPAA) would have expired on December 15, ending all petroleum price controls. However, Ford wanted the majority of Congress to share the responsibility for decontrol, for he feared its repercussions without the softening effect of a windfall profits measure, especially before an election year. High administration officials—Federal Reserve chairman Arthur Burns, Secretary of State Henry Kissinger, and especially FEA administrator Frank Zarb—pressed Ford to sign the legislation, which FEA itself strongly supported, in part because it would expand its bureaucratic powers and control. On the other hand, the Council of Economic Advisors and several Republican congressmen urged Ford to veto the measure.[15]

Ford ultimately felt he must end national uncertainty over energy policy and demonstrate that he was not a puppet of "big oil." At the same time, he needed some means of nipping in the bud Ronald Reagan's soon-to-blossom campaign (and strengthening his own) for the Republican presidential nomination. In his decision he was also forced to consider growing public concern over galloping inflation and skyrocketing oil companies' profits. Moreover, after a year of criticizing Congress for not passing an energy bill, his veto would certainly draw criticism, for the act did represent a policy, ungainly though it might be.

Conclusion

Despite the passage of EPCA, few thought the United States had acquired a realistic, comprehensive, and workable energy policy. Oil companies and conservative Republicans adamantly opposed it, while its supporters, including FEA administrator Zarb, argued only that it was the best that could be passed at the time. It was apparent to everyone that there was a wide gulf between the bill's stated purpose and its actual content. Developed to mollify interested groups, EPCA seemed like a national energy policy with conservation as its goal, but failed to translate this into programmatic realities. It simply endorsed the status quo by offering an immediate, slight reduction in oil prices, followed by gradual increments for the next four years, while postponing the difficult decisions involved in energy pricing. The modest and dilatory action embodied in EPCA was offered by the administration and Congress partly to offset accusations that nothing at all was being done about the energy crisis. One factor leading to this result was Ford's passive stance, which was "unprecedented since the New Deal."[16] For example, in his January 1975 energy initiatives, he merely listed the thirteen points he wanted addressed and allowed Congress the initiative in drafting a comprehensive, complex bill. By doing so, Ford violated a long tradition of presidential leadership. The move was especially ill-advised, considering the divisiveness which characterized the legislative body on energy issues.

It has been suggested that this shift of responsibility occurred because the administration was unable to develop a unified program of its own. FEA's attempt to create a plan for energy self-sufficiency nearly tore the agency apart and the hurried result—Project Independence Blueprint—far from being a design for energy autarky, simply predicted possible outcomes of various scenarios. It caused internal dissension in the administration, which may have feared losing face on energy or forfeiting tactical advantages on other issues if this disunity was brought to Congress's attention.[17] In any event, there was no mechanism for the recently installed president to either generate a comprehensive and widely endorsed plan from the bureaucracy or to impose one upon it.

Another possible reason for giving Congress the responsibility for a plan was Ford's lack of familiarity with the leadership role, a result of being in the minority party in the House of Representatives for nearly twenty-five years. His accustomed role as critic and refiner of proposals initiated by others, as well as his status as the first nonelected president in U.S. history, contributed to his passive stance. Finally, the Ford administration may have assumed that energy policy could not satisfy any constituency, and that creating a comprehensive policy would only serve to make enemies. Therefore, the administration chose to let the Democrats take the blame for whatever program was devised, rather than attempt mastering what has been called "an inherently insoluble problem."[18]

Whatever the reasons for Ford's reticence, the White House failed to take the lead in developing energy policy. Congress was severely divided along regional, ideological, and party lines. Therefore, the final energy bill could hardly be expected to be a coherent piece of legislation. It could provide few incentives for conservation and only disincentives for production.

The New Legislation's Contradictory Nature

Some problems resulting from EPCA could not have been anticipated due to inadequate information and models, but its major provision, Title IV (setting oil price ceilings and controlling refinery operations), blatantly challenges economic logic.[19] While EPCA's expressed purpose was to curtail oil imports, the specific actions it required increased U.S. dependence on imported oil. This ideological and substantive inconsistency resulted from an attempt to reconcile two diametrically opposed perceptions of the underlying causes of the energy crisis confronting the United States. The bill tried to satisfy both those who favored greater governmental involvement in meeting the country's energy needs by stabilizing or lowering energy prices, and those who wanted less governmental involvement, letting prices rise to world market levels. As Congressman Michael Harrington (D-Mass.) pointed out, these two schools of thought were incompatible, yet after three years of work, "Congress has devised a piece of legislation which embodies both views."[20]

EPCA's contradictory aspects have had numerous ramifications, some of which have been appreciated only recently.[21] For example, the bill badly damaged the U.S. auto industry. While the industry had moved toward decreasing the size of some of its models after the Arab oil embargo, the public, convinced by the promise of continued price controls on oil that the gasoline shortage was either concocted or had ended, began buying large cars again. While stimulating the demand for larger cars, EPCA also mandated new fuel economy standards, thus requiring automakers to develop technology for larger fuel-efficient cars in order to satisfy consumer demand and meet mileage standards. These factors aggravated the investment and capital problems of the industry during 1980, one of the worst years it ever faced, when it laid off 300,000 workers.

Nevertheless, EPCA marked the first successful effort by Congress to develop a comprehensive energy policy, a policy by which the government could intervene in various societal concerns which had previously been either considered in isolation by the government or had been left to the private sector to resolve. EPCA also attempted to deal at once with the intermeshed issues of the environment, energy, unemployment, recession, national security, and foreign policy; it mobilized political institutions to address energy needs and their concomitant economic aspects in an integrated fashion.

It must be emphasized, however, that EPCA constituted an extremely modest start. While it attempted to be comprehensive, if not organized and logical, and to initiate action, if not necessarily effective action, energy problems continued. Some, such as imported oil dependency, were aggravated by the legislation; others, such as those surrounding mileage and efficiency standards, seemed ameliorated. Still other provisions of the act, such as the strategic reserve, remained to be implemented years after the bill's passage. President Ford pointed out that the American public had become, or had remained, unconvinced of the reality of the dangers posed by the energy situation. He warned against what he considered to be the facile assumption of the Democratic Congress that the crisis could be resolved simply by more governmental involvement in energy policy.[22]

Congress and the nation's sense of crisis and unity of purpose, if not of approach, created by the Arab oil boycott, dissipated as Ford's term neared its end. The world was experiencing an oil glut, and it seemed for a time that market forces would destroy the OPEC cartel. And still American leaders could not agree on the reality of an energy crisis or on what should be done about it.

Yet, the EPCA's enactment signified above all the ongoing involvement of the federal government in determining long-range energy policy and all aspects of energy decision making. The act forced the Republican Ford administration and the Democratic Congress to agree that the federal government would have to assume a major role in setting energy production and conservation goals—a role that until then had been the responsibility of private consumers and producers. The specific direction and content of the laws that would realize these goals remained to be decided.[23] This was the situation Jimmy Carter inherited when he took office in January 1977.

Notes

1. U.S. General Services Administration, *Public Papers of the Presidents of the United States: Gerald Ford, 1975* (Washington, D.C.: U.S. Government Printing Office, 1977), pp. 60-61.
2. *Washington Post*, January 28, 1975, p. A1.
3. U.S. Congress, Senate Government Operations Committee, "Economic Impact of President Ford's Energy Program," hearings, January 31, February 6, 12, 1975; U.S. Congress, House Ways and Means Committee, "President's Authority to Adjust Imports of Petroleum," hearings, January 27, 1975, pp. 470-590.
4. The plan is presented on pp. 78-132 in U.S. Congress, House Interstate and Foreign Commerce Committee, "Energy Conservation and Oil Policy, pt.I," hearings, March 10-14, 1973.
5. U.S. Congress, *The Congressional Program of Economic Recovery and Energy Sufficiency* (Washington, D.C.: U.S. Government Printing Office, 1975).
6. Thomas Tietenberg, *Energy Planning and Policy: The Political Economy of Project Independence* (Lexington, Mass.: D.C. Heath, 1976).
7. U.S. Congress, House Ways and Means Committee, "Alternatives for Consideration in an Energy Program," Committee Print, March 3, 1975. See also, *Oil and Gas Journal*, March 10, 1975, pp. 26-27.
8. *Oil and Gas Journal*, March 17, 1975, pp. 84-85; May 19, 1975, pp. 54-55.
9. "New oil" was defined as oil newly discovered or pumped from oil wells in amounts greater than 1972 levels, the full year before the 1973 Emergency Petroleum Allocation Act was passed. This act superseded the Economic Stabilization Act's price controls.
10. *Public Papers*, p. 418.
11. These processes are described in James E. Katz, "Congress and the International Energy Agency," *Energy Communications* 7, no. 2, 1982, pp. 69-103. See also, U.S. Congress, House Interior and Insular Affairs Committee, "Presidential Energy Program," hearings, February 17-21, 1975.
12. His attack on oil companies may be found in U.S. Congress, Senate Interior and Insular Affairs Committee, "Current Energy Shortages, Oversight Series: The Major Oil Companies," hearings, January 22-23, 1974. See *New York Times*,

February 8, 1974, p. 8; *Washington Post*, December 21, 1975, pp. A1, A6, for a description of Jackson's presidential ambitions.

13. Congressional Quarterly, *Energy Policy* (Washington, D.C.: CQ Press, 1979), p. 41-A.
14. *Public Papers*, p. 1992.
15. Craufurd Goodwin, ed., *Energy Policy in Perspective* (Washington, D.C.: Brookings, 1982), pp. 503-7.
16. David H. Davis, "America's Nonpolicy for Energy," in *Nationalizing Government*, ed. Theodore Lowi and Alan Stone (Beverly Hills, Calif.: Sage, 1978), pp. 211-34.
17. John P. Weyant, "Quantitative Models in Energy Policy," *Policy Analysis* 6 (Spring 1980): 211-34.
18. Davis, p. 106.
19. New oil production was added to the other petroleum that had been under federal price controls since 1971. The price set by Title IV, the most hotly contested of all EPCA's sections, was significantly below the world price, a fact that would discourage domestic production, increase oil imports, and encourage consumption through low prices.
20. *National Journal*, December 27, 1975, p. 1735.
21. The conflicting motives of free market versus government control and lower oil prices versus adequate supplies through higher prices were reflected in the energy security aspects of EPCA. To some extent, the strategic reserve program represented a degree of compromise between governmental and private control. Nevertheless, EPCA allowed maximum governmental control and a minimum of interference with the market mechanism (although obviously the massive purchases of oil to fill the reserve would affect oil markets). Ford's energy security program demonstrated some of the cross-pressures which characterized the early Nixon attempts to devise a similar program. Like Nixon, Ford gave verbal support to the free market approach to long-term problems, and attempted to move future policy in that direction, but pursued an administered approach as the immediate solution to energy security. However, Congress consistently opposed any program which would rely on the private market, even when such opposition involved the sacrifice of significant amounts of authority to the president, although those in Congress might disagree among themselves on the appropriate action. Here again, EPCA converged conflicting forces.
22. *Public Papers . . . , 1976-77* (1979), pp. 2922-23.
23. In 1976, little was accomplished in energy policy terms, partly because it was an election year. However, a major policy development was the passage of the Energy Conservation and Production Act. Although the Ford administration had originally simply asked that FEA be extended, the Senate dramatically expanded the legislation to include a large program of energy conservation. Under Senator Edward Kennedy's leadership, the Senate added federal financial incentives for building weatherization, expanded data collection and analysis duties of FEA, and authorized FEA to guarantee up to $2 billion in various energy conservation loans. It also deregulated stripper oil wells and costly oil produced through technically sophisticated means, although oil prices in general were held in line with the EPCA commitment. The act further instructed the White House-level Energy Resources Council to develop a plan to reorganize federal government energy and natural resources activities.

5
Establishing the Department of Energy

One of President Carter's first major actions was the creation of the Department of Energy (DOE). The crucial issues surrounding its creation, as well as energy reorganization in general, were (1) jurisdiction and regulatory authority, (2) the effect of centralization on decision making and policy implementation, and (3) the changes in the power structure that result from consolidation.

Background

In 1971, President Nixon sent Congress a proposal to create a Department of Energy and Natural Resources by combining the Department of Interior (DOI), the civil functions of the Atomic Energy Commission, and several other agencies. Nixon's proposal was part of a larger plan to consolidate all domestic agencies into four super-agencies: Human Resources, Community Development, Natural Resources, and Economic Affairs. Senator Abraham Ribicoff, chairman of the Government Operations Committee and a supporter of the plan, complained at the time that the nearly complete lack of congressional interest in or action concerning Nixon's proposal was the administration's fault, because the administration had not consulted enough with Congress and relevant interest groups. In 1973 Nixon resubmitted his Energy and Natural Resources Department proposals, which Congress rejected. Still, it did create the Federal Energy Administration (FEA) in response to the Arab oil embargo (see chapter 3).

A 1976 Congressional Research Service Energy Organization study found energy interest organizations characterized by fragmentation, conflict, and duplicated effort. It recommended centralization, but only if a clear plan or broad consensus could be developed. The report argued that diverse approaches and policies would more adequately meet the nation's energy needs than a centralized plan pushed through legislative channels without attaining consensus among divergent interests.[1]

President Ford preferred a centralized approach and, in January 1977, submitted an energy reorganization plan to Congress. This action was mandated by the Energy Conservation and Policy Act (PL 94-385) discussed in the previous chapter. In 1976 it had extended FEA's life and directed that the president submit an energy reorganization proposal by the end of l976. One of Ford's last official acts was to propose a unified cabinet-level energy department which would include the FEA; the Energy Research and Development Administration (ERDA); both the Interior Department's Bureau of Mines and its public power marketing staff; the Agricultural Department's Rural Electrification Administration; and the cabinet-level committee, the Energy Resources Council. The new department would assume the Federal Power Commission's (FPC) authority to regulate natural gas prices but leave intact the Interior Department's custody over the use of public lands. The Nuclear Regulatory Commission (NRC) would remain independent, as would other functions of the DOI, to reduce conflicts between energy promotion and environmental considerations.

Ford's plan was supported by key Democratic senators—as well as by aides of President-elect Carter—giving a bipartisan cast to energy reorganization. While such presidential initiative could presumably facilitate enactment of the legislation, Congress's sensitivity to reorganization schemes that could alter its legislative committees' jurisdictions caused early resistance to the plan in the House and the Senate. Congressional committee staff and utility groups objected to the inclusion of regulatory functions such as those of the FPC into a cabinet department, on the basis that it would disturb the close relationships that had been developed there between the regulators and the regulated.

Several influences prevented energy reorganization during Ford's tenure: Ford's status as unelected Republican president; the Democrats' desire to compose their own energy legislation; unresolved conflicts among Democrats; and Ford's emphasis on higher prices (linked to decontrol of energy prices), which came at a time of recession and inflation. Although several important measures were passed during Ford's term, the oil and natural gas issue—which was inextricably bound with organization plans—seriously divided congressmen of oil-producing states (Texas, Oklahoma, Louisiana, New Mexico, Wyoming, California) from those of oil-consuming states. This conflict gave initial momentum to the search for a compromise. Later it became a problem for Carter as it separated him from many of his Democratic allies.

While the Nixon and Ford administrations' efforts to thoroughly rationalize and centralize the energy bureaucracy failed, they had laid important groundwork. There was widespread and, to a great extent, public recognition that some organizational changes were needed beyond the stopgap measures that had been thus far adopted. The constant shifts in energy organization beginning in l973 (see chapter 3) prevented the formation of strong institutional identities or mutually supportive alliances with constituent groups, both of which would have worked against centralization. FEA was criticized by the oil industry and consumer groups and even by Congress, which found ERDA's ambit too narrow. These factors helped form a favorable environment for Carter's attempts to create an energy department.

President Carter's Proposal

Governmental reorganization—particularly energy reorganization—was Carter's major campaign issue. On September 21, 1976, he proposed the creation of the Department of Energy (DOE), which would incorporate FEA, FPC, ERDA, and the energy regulatory functions of other departments and agencies. To insulate regulatory decisions from political pressure, internal regulatory boards were also proposed. Carter had attacked Ford for lacking a comprehensive energy policy and for allowing uncoordinated special agencies to proliferate. But his own proposal was so haphazard as to be called "bizarre" by one Senate staffer.[2] Congress's initial reaction to the proposal was the fear that by giving responsibility for energy regulation to a cabinet officer, the quasi-judicial functions of independent commissions would become politicized.

Shortly after his election, Carter began discussing reorganization plans and soliciting views from opinion leaders. On December 9, he asked Congress, public interest groups, and lobbyists to comment on ways of combining energy agencies to create a new department. At the time, proposals to combine ERDA and FEA into an Energy Department were being considered by Congress, along with Nixon's original idea of creating a Department of Energy and Natural Resources. There was also thought of including regulatory functions in a National Energy Regulatory Agency which would combine the functions of FPC, FEA, and possibly NRC, within a new department.

By December 15, when Carter met with Senator Henry Jackson, he had already decided not to merge the DOI with the new DOE. Jackson had favored a combined energy and natural resources agency (to be included within the soon-to-be-expanded jurisdiction of his committee). He maintained that conflicts between the two interests could be resolved best by creating a single department (see chapter 3). As a result of this meeting, however, Jackson accepted Carter's decision, recognizing that plans for a combined department would have been met with overwhelming protest from environmental groups. Carter's decision left DOI, EPA, and the Council on Environmental Quality (CEQ) free to focus on environmental protection. Elevating the status of environmental issues to cabinet-level softened opposition to DOE and to James Schlesinger, both being perceived as antienvironmental at that time. Schlesinger, who was slated to be secretary of the new department, was designated special presidential assistant on energy matters on December 23.

The next controversy was over which functions would be transferred to the new DOE; in particular, the management of public lands resources development was especially problematical. In his confirmation hearings in January 1977, Interior Secretary-designate Cecil Andrus stated that the DOI should maintain control over surface and subsurface mineral rights on federal lands, while Schlesinger was telling environmentalists that DOE should have control over them. Apparently, during the period from February to March 1977, Carter, Andrus, and Schlesinger, behind the scenes, sorted out the functions of DOI and DOE.

According to Schlesinger, drafting authority over the leasing of public lands "was the most difficult item we had to grapple with."[3] The result, as noted by Carter in his March 1, 1977, message to Congress, proposing creation of the new DOE, was that the legislation left DOI still in charge of leasing energy resources under federal control while the Energy Department would set long-term production goals and control the leases' economic aspects. Specifically, the energy secretary would regulate lease eligibility, bidding systems for leases, rates of production, and disposition of royalties, while the interior secretary would regulate land management, conservation, and the preparation of environmental impact reports.

The plan Carter presented to Congress on March 1 was remarkably similar to Ford's plan. The new DOE would include:

- Federal Energy Administration (FEA)
- Energy Research and Development Administration
- Federal Power Commission (FPC)
- from Department of the Interior (DOI)
  –the Bureau of Reclamation's power marketing functions
  –the four regional power administrations
  –public land leasing responsibilities (described above)
- from Department of Housing and Urban Development (HUD)
  –energy efficiency standards development
- from Department of Commerce (DOC)
  –the Industrial Energy Conservation Program
- from Department of Defense (DOD)
  –jurisdiction over and administration of certain naval petroleum and shale reserves
- from Securities and Exchange Commission (SEC)
  –power to regulate electric utility company mergers
- from Interstate Commerce Commission (ICC)
  –authority to regulate (including rate making) oil and coal-slurry pipelines

The Energy Resources Council would be abolished and the NRC and the EPA would remain independent.

Like Ford, Carter and Schlesinger hoped to create a comprehensive policy dealing with energy production and use. They saw a centralized organization as the best means to carry it out, but because their original commitments to environmental protection and resource conservation were endorsed by environmental lobbyists, their plan had a better chance for success than had Ford's. However, liberals and environmentalists expressed concern over Schlesinger's appointment, noting that, as AEC chairman (1971-72), he was lax on environmental protection, a criticism Schlesinger disputed. Opponents to Schlesinger's nomination cited his support for the breeder reactor, federal subsidies to utilities, and using plutonium in the nation's future energy system.

In sum, the early maneuvering over the DOE demonstrated that Carter was committed to keeping his promise to reorganize energy administration and was willing to exercise strong leadership to see that this commitment was fulfilled. Schlesinger had a background and reputation that made him well suited for the job of selling Carter's plans; his technical and economic orientations, forceful self-expression, governmental experience, and lack of party loyalty were, at least initially, powerful assets which won the confidence of many in Congress.

A prime advantage of Carter's proposal was that it tended to leave undisturbed the traditional power alliances that had been built up between federal agencies and their constituencies in the energy-policy arena. His plan was played down as a mere "box-shuffling exercise"[4] to avoid arousing opposition from entrenched interests.

While Carter was quite clear about what would be included in the new department, the administration remained noncommittal about specific details, in part because it expected each interest group to make some special organizational demands—such as requests for special bureaus or assistant secretaries—to protect its area. Therefore, as is typical of the technocratic approach, administration planners sought to discourage the marshalling of interest groups that could affect their plans for reorganization. They also tried to prevent the rallying of various interests and their allies within the executive bureaucracy and the formation of power centers in the new department, which would weaken the new secretary and reduce the department's responsiveness to the president.

The Senate Responds

Senator Ribicoff introduced an energy department bill in the Senate as S 826 on March 1, 1977, giving it his unqualified support and obtaining the bipartisan cosponsorship of, among others, Majority Leader Robert Byrd (D-W.Va.) and Senator Jackson, who predicted Congress would approve the plan before May. On March 2, Jack Brooks (D-TX) introduced the bill (HR 4263) in the House. At that time, Speaker Thomas P. O'Neill (D-Mass.) noted unanimous support for an energy department. The major reservation expressed among members concerned the division of leasing and management authority of public lands and offshore gas and oil areas. The continued authority of the Interior Department over public land use was a point of contention among senators, who called the proposed division of authority between the Interior and Energy Departments "a shaky kind of arrangement."[5] According to Carter's plan, the energy secretary would assume existing authority to prohibit joint bidding for leases by large oil companies, set oil- and gas-producing rates on federal leases, and determine the rates of development leaseholders must achieve or the conditions for granting waivers from such requirements. While this control would seem to represent an important transfer of responsibility, the plan actually gave Schlesinger less power than he wanted and preserved the Interior Department's jurisdiction over public lands.

An impressive array of industry groups opposed Carter's proposal to divide leasing authorities. The American Coal Association, the American Petroleum Institute, and the American Gas Association—all giant combines of industry interests—testified that the sharing of authority would hinder the process of energy development by causing needlessly long and expensive delays. They called for arrangements that would speed and economize the search for and recovery of energy resources.

Friends of the Earth, the National Wildlife Federation, and the Sierra Club opposed the administration's proposal for different reasons. These environmental groups feared that the split in leasing authority would allow reckless exploitation of public land in the pursuit of energy resources.

The leasing provision designed by the Senate to replace the administration's plan followed its same general lines but carefully and specifically detailed the responsibilities and obligations of both departments (retaining a strong hand for the Interior Department) and an orderly procedure for interdepartmental conflict resolution.

Controversy over Price-Setting Authority

Carter suggested that DOE include an Energy Regulatory Administration possessing rule-making authority over pricing and allocation of oil products (held by FEA) and pricing of interstate natural gas (held by the FPC), with final authority resting with the secretary. This plan to absorb the FPC and various power marketing authorities into a centralized structure became the most controversial aspect of Carter's plan. The White House pointed out the difficulties in coordinating the use of interchangeable propane and natural gas fuels—each of which was handled by a separate agency—and the need for centralized crisis management. However, although the administration was correct in its assumption that the FPC itself would have little political support in either Congress or industry, neither of these groups wanted to end the FPC's independence and collegial decision making. Thus, a variety of organizations, believing that the absorption of power marketing functions into the department would end their special access to the regulatory process, testified against the Carter proposal.

For example, two former FPC chairmen (who were also Democrats), Joseph Swidler (1961-65) and Lee White (1966-69), criticized the plan as "too vague" and "not showing an understanding of how the FPC functions." They held that an incorporation of the independent agency into a cabinet department would weaken the power of Congress. They also claimed that this centralization would hurt consumers, and that environmental protection would not be coordinated with energy development. In sum, they felt the administration's plan was "not carefully thought through."[6]

Consumer groups joined industry in attacking Carter's regulatory reform proposal. The Public Interest Research Group, Common Cause, and the Energy Action Committee testified to their concern about the political independence of the regulatory board and its relationship to the energy secretary. They also asserted that reorganization would ease Carter's bid to raise energy prices and taxes.

To a large extent, the controversy surrounding the price-setting mechanisms was generated because it was the key to a range of economic regulatory activities of the new department. Major energy-related trade associations resisted the absorption of energy regulation into "presidential government." Rather than evincing any enthusiasm for the FPC, slated for absorption under the new proposal, the trade associations objected to the procedural implications of the changes. For example, the National Coal Association saw in Carter's plan a deliberate attempt to politicize rule making. Similarly, public utility associations opposed the plan because it would give too much authority to a political appointee—the secretary—weakening the influence of both the power industry and Congress. The American Public Power Association was one of many utility groups that asked Congress to limit the secretary's pricing powers, while strengthening those of a quasi-independent regulatory board.

In sum, it was not the support garnered by the FPC that caused trouble for Carter's proposal; rather, trouble derived from the attempt to alter established, predictable, and comfortable relationships between regulators and the regulated and the ties of political support linking Congress to various interdependent energy industries. Entrenched interests much preferred the establishment of a quasi-independent board that would enable at least a modicum of the old special relationships to be preserved. Thus, it was primarily procedural rather than substantive and organizational issues that motivated energy industry and utility groups to attempt to alter Carter's plan.

Therefore, the major issue both in committee and during floor debate was the secretary's power to set oil and natural gas prices relative to that of a proposed three-member Energy Regulatory Administration. During the mark-up, Ribicoff, Charles Percy (R-Ill.), Edmund Muskie (D-Maine), and Jacob Javits (R-N.Y.) proposed an amendment giving oil and natural gas pricing authorities to an independent three-member regulatory board. This amendment, formulated by Senate aides and the White House, responded to senators' concerns about the administration's proposal to give the secretary final pricing authority not appealable in the courts. The committee report asserted that because energy prices were so critical to "the prosperity and living habits of every American, no single official should have sole responsibility for both proposing and setting such prices."[7] By the Ribicoff amendment, the secretary would make proposals to the board, and the board's decisions would be appealable in the courts (at that time FPC's were appealable; FEA's were not). As a concession to the administration, Ribicoff agreed to allow presidential vetoes over the board's decisions.

Information Gathering and Planning Emphasized

Because acquiring energy information had been a constant problem for Congress and the executive branch, Carter's original proposal included an Energy Information Administration (EIA) in the new department to centralize data collection and analysis.

A major function of the proposed EIA was to create a statistical "energy industry profile," a mandatory system of data reporting by energy-producing firms in order to determine economic conditions in the energy industry. This system would form the basis for analyses of industry profits, cash flows, investments, competitiveness, and costs for exploration, production and distribution.

Previously there had been more than 100 energy data programs in four federal agencies, and program reports were often either unavailable in a publicly usable form or conflicted with one another because their statistics were based on different assumptions. Projections and forecasts were often inaccurate and misleading. The data collection effort's fragmented quality meant that attempts to gather additional statistics burdened energy companies but did not necessarily improve the government's or public's understanding of the energy situation.

The Senate Governmental Affairs (formerly Operations) Committee, therefore, was enthusiastic about Carter's proposal to centralize and improve data collection and analysis.[8] The committee added provisions to ensure the professional quality of the data collection and analysis, insulate the data agency from political manipulation, and strengthen both its independence and credibility.

Underscoring the Senate's long-standing concern over the planning of energy policy, the Governmental Affairs Committee added provisions mandating a detailed outline of the nation's energy production and conservation goals for five- and ten-year periods. These reports—which were to be updated every two years—would identify strategies and objectives for action, including production goals for each major energy source (e.g. coal, uranium, oil) and time frames for their development, as well as set conservation goals. These reports would be used by Congress to formulate its own plan, which, in the form of a joint resolution, would constitute an approved national energy plan. While much of this planning required presidential action in its support, and a reporting requirement was eventually included in the final bill, the requirements for congressional action were deleted, leaving individual committees free to propose action or energy planning. The bill also required that the General Accounting Office audit a wide range of DOE activities, including ongoing internal projects, internal program management, and information collection.

Battle over Amendments

After the committee reported its findings to the Senate, there were several attempts to add amendments by senators who wanted their particular concerns addressed in the bill. Kennedy, for example, proposed that public interest advocates be reimbursed for the costs of legal battles over energy regulations or projects, while Thomas McIntyre (D-N.H.) sought to establish a special bureau for small business affairs in DOE. Committee chairman Ribicoff remarked, "We have been inundated during the hearings and markup by every group and special interest wanting an assistant secretary or a special office to take care of their affairs."[9] Demonstrating congressional unhappiness with perceived overregulation, Richard Schweiker (R-Pa.) proposed that every DOE regulation be subject to veto by Congress. Ribicoff, however, maintained that this amendment not only raised serious constitutional questions but would inappropriately and unproductively inject Congress into the department's daily operations. These more notable amendments were rejected by the Senate, although several minor ones were adopted.

With the proposed amendments and other issues taken care of in less than one day's debate, the Senate quickly and easily passed the bill (S 826), on May 18, 1977, with a vote of 74 to 10. For some time, there was fear that the legislation would become enmeshed with Carter's controversial energy plan (see chapter 6) or that it would be blocked because it gave too much power to the DOE secretary—a concern often expressed in the wake of past executive branch abuses of congressional prerogatives. Although the Senate measure gave less power to the energy secretary in price setting, he still retained a wide latitude in other areas, especially in decision making about the organization of his own department.

Commenting on the "checks and balances on the secretary," Senator Percy observed, "No one could say we're creating a czar of energy,"[10] and noted that the majority of the changes made in Carter's proposal were achieved by Senator Ribicoff, chairman of the Governmental Affairs Committee and the Democratic floor manager. Senator John Durkin (D-N.H.), the only Democrat to vote against the bill, complained that although the DOE bill had been discussed in the committee, there had been so little floor discussion of it "that 75 percent of the membership does not know whether it is the best or worst . . . possible proposal."[11]

The House Tackles Energy Organization

The reorganization plan was referred to the House Government Operations Committee; six days of hearings were held in March and April. The bill, passed by the full committee (37 to 2) on May 16, essentially conformed with the administration's original plan, including the controversial energy-pricing authority for the secretary.

During the committee's markup of the bill, Congressman John Conyers (D-Mich.) offered a novel amendment, giving the new department oil and natural gas import authority; it would then sell the imported energy to domestic oil companies. The reasoning behind this amendment was twofold. First, it would increase domestic competition by enabling all domestic firms to compete for available imports, thereby creating the most favorable price for consumers. If there was truth in the accusation that oil companies purchasing foreign oil had been keeping prices high at the consumer's expense, a government monopoly on oil purchases would result in better bargains and might even "bust" OPEC. Second, the amendment enabled the secretary to directly control the amount of imports, permitting him to indirectly affect the domestic oil exploitation rate and thus the total energy supply picture. It was passed by 18-16 on May 5, but on May 6, after heavy lobbying by the oil industry and the White House, the committee rescinded the initiative.

In keeping with the House's traditional proclivity for protecting special interests and for skepticism about the probity of federal programs, the Government Operations Committee made two innovations that went beyond Carter's original request. It created nine assistant secretaries of energy (outlining their areas of responsibility along special-interest lines) and an Office of Inspector General to investigate fraud and the quality of DOE program management and to uncover abuses in DOE operations. The office would also inform Congress about abuses and management deficiencies within the department.

An essential difference between the bill's House and Senate versions was that the House granted the secretary wide latitude in setting natural gas and oil prices, while the Senate gave this power to a three-member board. Although the House committee leadership responded to the Carter administration's pressure for a powerful energy secretary, many committee members did not. John Moss (D-Calif.), in particular, pointed out that the issue transcended the particular personalities involved in energy price setting and dealt with fundamental procedural issues. Several representatives joined Moss in viewing the president's plan as one of "the broadest delegations of legislative authority ever granted" to government agencies, giving substantial discretion in the vital area of pricing, and thereby opening it to the possibility of political abuse.[12] While these dissenters were defeated in the committee, their cause turned out to be the main issue in House floor debate on DOE.

Offered Amendments Widen the Policy Debate

Debate over DOE was much more prolonged in the House than in the Senate. However, while the principal topic of discussion in the Senate committee was the secretary's pricing authority, the debate on the House floor focused on an amendment cosponsored by Congressmen Clarence Brown (R-Ohio) and Moss which sought to establish an independent five-member Federal Energy Regulatory Commission within the department to set wellhead prices of natural gas and thereby circumscribe the secretary's pricing powers. While Moss strongly favored strict government regulation of natural gas prices, and Brown supported price decontrol, they joined forces in favor of a semiautonomous board. Viewing the FPC as inefficient, they nevertheless supported its open procedures, collegial decision making, judicial review of decisions, relative independence from the White House, and insulation from political pressures. Although apparently indifferent to the specific institution of the FPC, they wanted to see its qualities preserved in a new quasi-independent form in the new department and feared concentrating too much in the secretary's hands. Jack Brooks, the Government Operations Committee chairman, loyally supported the administration position on the House floor, as he had in his committee. He argued that a strong secretary needed two essential tools—price setting and control of utilities—to fight the energy crisis. However, despite opposition from the administration and Brooks, the Brown-Moss amendment was passed by a roll call vote of 236-119, with both Democratic and Republican majorities, supported by many public interest groups, energy companies, and utilities.

Other amendments considered include a proposal by Congressman Elliot Levitas (D-Ga.) giving Congress the power to veto any rules or regulations issued by the new department. Moss and Commerce Committee chairman John Dingell (D-Mich.) argued that such wide-ranging oversight jurisdiction could not be handled competently by Congress and opposed Levitas's amendment, but it was adopted by a vote of 200-125. Interior Committee chairman Morris Udall (D-Ariz.) proposed strengthening the interior secretary's authority to manage the leasing of public lands by removing the energy secretary's veto power over economic terms of leases; this amendment was rejected by 170-180.

House approval on June 2, 1977 to create an energy department specified a time delimitation of five years; under the terms of a "sunset" amendment designed to ensure congressional review of the department's work before authorizing its continuation, the legislation would expire December 31, 1982. Although the Senate version, passed on May 18, did not include such a clause, the Senate Governmental Affairs Committee had supported general sunset legislation the year before and some of its members would be in conference on the bill.

Senate and House versions differed further in the price-setting mechanism for oil, natural gas, and wholesale electricity. According to the Senate terms, jurisdiction over all three would be given to a three-member board whose decision would be subject to presidential veto. The House gave the secretary oil-pricing authority, but an independent commission—the Federal Energy Regulatory Commission—would control natural gas and electricity pricing. The Carter administration wanted power for the setting of these three prices to be given to the secretary of energy rather than divided. Consequently it sought adoption of the Senate version in conference.

Conference Committee

Senate and House versions of the bill entering conference committee were in general agreement over the need for an energy department and over its functions and powers. The House passage of the bill on June 3 allowed the time necessary to resolve House-Senate differences before the August recess, but the conferees were slow to start. Therefore, as Senator Jackson cautioned, many conflicts had to be dealt with expeditiously during July to ensure passage and signing of the bill before the August recess.

The major issue concerned balancing the authority over pricing and regulation of energy resources between the secretary and the independent regulatory commission that each of the houses had proposed. The conference committee agreement essentially combined the features of both plans and spelled out in detail the exact duties of both the secretary and the commission. A five-member commission—the Federal Energy Regulatory Commission (FERC)—independent but within the Energy Department, would be responsible for controlling interstate sales of natural gas, while the Energy Department would have authority over proposals for importing natural gas. Oil pricing and allocation responsibilities would be delegated to the Economic Regulatory Administration within the department, with FERC having veto power over changes in oil price controls and hearing appeals on individual oil-pricing cases, which had been handled by the Economic Regulatory Administration. The secretary would be given the authority to propose commission action, intervene in commission proceedings, and set time limits for decisions.

Another issue which received considerable attention in conference was a sunset provision in the House version calling for DOE's abolition in 1982, unless Congress renewed it. This provision resulted from an amendment offered by Congressman James Broyhill (R-N.C.) during House debate and, despite opposition by White House lobbyists, was adopted by 202-126. Brooks, chairman of House conferees, termed this move "one of the most difficult to deal with" since, although the amendment had passed by substantial margin in the House, "the Senate conferees were adamantly against it . . . including some leading proponents of sunset legislation."[13] Senate opposition was based partly on the fact that DOE would be engaging in long-term research and development contracts which extended beyond five years. Defending his proposition, Broyhill argued that Congress did a very poor job of reviewing the activities of the federal agencies it set up. Thus an enforced review of DOE was essential, he maintained, and would not necessarily mean its end but perhaps merely its revision. Moss warned that the amendment would cause uncertainty among the 20,000 department employees.

In conference the sunset provision was deleted, but the requirement for the president to submit in 1982 a review of the department was adopted. Despite this compromise, however, House approval of the conference report came only after defeating a Republican motion to recommit the bill to conference for reconsideration of the sunset provision.

The House provision, giving Congress power to veto DOE's rules and regulations, was also deleted by conferees; a House proposal creating an Office of Inspector General within the department was adopted.

Conference Report Filed, Bill Signed

The conference report was filed on June 26. On August 2, 1977, both the House and Senate approved the bill. Senator Ted Stevens (R-Alaska) opposed it, because it might hurt his state's interests. In particular he feared that DOE's regulatory consolidation would lead to extended litigation over the Alaska oil pipeline's pricing tariffs and valuations. Senator John Tower (R-Tex.) voted against the bill because of his objection to oil and gas price controls, and Senator Dewey Bartlett (R-Okla.) on grounds of preventing excessive government expenditure of the estimated $10.6 billion budgeted to DOE. These, and many other objections, were defused long enough to get the DOE conference report passed, and Carter signed in into law on August 4, 1977. Yet DOE's critics, far from being muffled by their defeat, ever more shrilly called for its dismantlement. Their partial success is another story (see chapter 9).

Conclusion

The political reaction to a presidential reorganization of the bureaucracy is multilayered, because leadership and patterns of authority are affected at every level of government. Congress, often establishing its hierarchy to parallel that of the bureaucracy, does not easily absorb the shock. Connections between specialized congressional bodies and their equivalents in the executive branch become attenuated. Abolishing or combining governmental agencies further increases the chances of disrupting committee's alignments and jurisdictions, affecting members who have been gaining seniority and hoping for chairmanship.

In January 1977, the jurisdiction of the Interior Committee of Senator Jackson, who also sat on the Governmental Affairs Committee and the conference committee for the DOE bill, was changed to encompass all energy oversight, which facilitated passage of the DOE bill through the Senate. The fact that the creation of DOE was Carter's first main presidential action presented to Congress during the postelection "honeymoon" also helped to secure passage. However, the most essential factor in the easy passage of the DOE bill was an almost universal, nonpartisan agreement on the urgency of the energy issue and the need for an energy department to develop and implement a comprehensive national energy policy.

But disagreement did arise over whether an organization or a policy should come first. Before Carter's energy plan was submitted to Congress, several senators complained that it was impossible to evaluate the proposed DOE without specific programs and policies to look at. Some senators proposed delaying decisions on a DOE until Congress had made a decision on Carter's energy policy proposals (discussed in the next chapter). During Senate hearings, however, Common Cause, a "good government" lobbying group, strongly opposed such delay, as did Senator Percy, who stated: "In order to have an energy policy that works, you have to have a framework. Organization is policy."[14]

Brooks's and Ribicoff's support of the administration's proposals were instrumental in overcoming opposition based on the lack of a policy framework. Although special interest groups, due to their connections within the bureaucracy, might have impeded governmental reorganization, lobbyists generally tended to support the reorganization because of its promise of greater efficiency. Industry-based coalitions, in particular, lack power if governmental authority is too diffused and fragmented. Forrest Rettgers, a National Association of Manufacturers official, noted before passage of the bill: "Business would be gratified to find all energy offices pulled into a single department," since fragmentation of government can make it more difficult to obtain government action in its interests.[15] In addition, the Energy Information Administration, established within the department, would relieve industry of a largely duplicative reporting burden and lessen government reliance on industry's data in planning energy policy and programs.

An Easy Legislative Journey

The reasons the DOE legislation passed so easily transcend the bill's specifics and involve changes underlying energy policy organization and processes. The first (called in another context, "public satisfying speculative augmentation"[16]) occurs when politicians detect a strong public demand for change and thus are not only willing to support, but in fact, compete to devise, changes that will meet this demand. This is usually done on a visceral level with little knowledge of whether the proposed reform will actually solve the problem. Widespread recognition of the need for energy legislation is demonstrated by the frequent calls for action and the large number of proposals to address problems of energy organization problems that have been introduced since 1973.

Second, the area of energy organization was in a state of nearly constant flux, as described in chapter 3. This meant that bureaucratic routines and stable power clusters had not been able to accrue around such newly created institutions as ERDA and FEA, which made them easy targets for administration reorganizers.

The most critical factor was the relative lack of bureaucratic power of the agencies picked out for inclusion in the new department. They had neither the expertise that could command deference nor a loyal constituency upon which they could depend for political support. Further, the agency personnel had low morale and lacked a strong leadership.[17] Faced with powerful forces demanding reorganization, especially from the White House, these agencies had little leverage with which to resist absorption.

Still, there was opposition to reorganization from specialized energy interests who had enjoyed access to decision makers under the traditional organizational arrangements. As pointed out in chapter 1, U.S. energy policy has historically been dominated by power clusters which had been operating homeostatically but independently of one another. The federal bureaucracy had been organized around these interests with the result that they maintained vigorous control over processes in their specific domains. To the extent that the energy department reorganization violated these "turfs," it was resisted.

Whenever possible, the administration planners sought to head off inroads by special interests, and while the administration remained as vague as possible about the department's structure, Schlesinger resisted demands that specific functions be included in specific bureaus. To do so would have weakened the secretary's power and militated against the technocractic and anti–interest group approach Carter and his staff wanted.

Nevertheless, the administration planners were not unrealistic in what they hoped to accomplish. They avoided attacking agencies, such as the Tennessee

Valley Authority, which were capable of marshalling strong interests for their protection. Whenever the administration's actions challenged traditional power clusters, as in the plan to absorb the FPC and other power marketing organizations, special interest groups and their congressional allies vociferously resisted the actions. Thus a quasi-independent agency, FERC, was created, which preserved most of the old relationships between the FPC and its clients.

DOE's Unresolved Organizational Dilemmas

The main motivation behind the Energy Department reorganization was the elevation of rationalism and technocratic functionalism over the traditional pragmatism of interest group politics and inefficient compromise. Yet, at least insofar as the Energy Department proposal was concerned, this elevation of utility over tradition was based on a realistic assessment of what should be passed. Thus, although the administration sought the strongest bill possible, its realistic approach dictated that what the proposal actually sought to accomplish be somewhat limited. Rather than bringing all federal energy responsibilities into one logical, integrated framework, it actually left many vital functions residing in the traditional interest-dominated power clusters.

Consequently, while the energy secretary has direct responsibility for energy supply planning, data gathering, and encouraging others to conserve energy, the real governmental decisions about energy conservation remain integrated with the power clusters that consume energy, such as the Departments of Transportation, Agriculture, and Housing and Urban Development, which are more oriented toward their respective clients than toward an energy bureaucracy. Even in the energy supply areas, DOE's authority is limited to research, regulation, and part of power marketing, while a significant portion of the production authority is ultimately controlled by the Interior Department. Moreover, it has little authority to govern the essential water and fossil fuel energy sources, nor does it regulate nuclear power.[18]

To many, then, the Energy Department seems a paper tiger, given the responsibility but not the tools to attack a far-reaching and fundamental societal problem. A substantial tension had been consciously established between the energy secretary and various other energy/environment power centers such as the Interior secretary, the Environmental Protection Agency, the Nuclear Regulatory Commission, industry, and state and local governments. Even the quasi-independent FERC could overrule some DOE decisions.

This realization of the theory of institutionalized "creative tension" means constant court challenges and continual appeals to the president to resolve policy disputes. It also means that effective and diligent presidential leadership will be necessary to overcome the inherent division of authority and conflicting goals that is the operational consequence of this divided organizational structure. Presidential leadership becomes a key variable in energy policy and, while the structural aspects of energy policy have evolved considerably between Nixon's 1971 proposals and Carter's 1977 legislation, they are yet far from ideal. The unrelenting criticism constantly directed at DOE since its inception left little doubt that a satisfactory alternative to the pre–1973 energy policy regime and power cluster processes had yet to be worked out.

The absence of major opposition from special interests was apparent when, early in congressional DOE hearings, both industry groups and environmentalists endorsed the plan. There was opposition to arrangements for the leasing of public lands, but this was set aside by committee members who preferred to focus on the pricing authority of the secretary. Some groups who raised the issue of public participation pointed out the failure of the administration's bill to mention citizen access to departmental decision making. Many of these latter proposals, such as Kennedy's amendment discussed earlier, were considered too controversial and too substantive for what was purely a structural reorganization bill, and were subsequently tabled.

During the 1960s, Congress labored for four years to pass legislation establishing HUD and two years to create the DOT. Nixon failed twice to have Congress consider a cabinet agency dealing with energy. In contrast, Carter presented the legislation for the DOE in March 1977, and five months later, after moving through Congress largely unchanged, it was signed into law. The most significant modification to the administration's proposal was the removal of energy pricing authority from the secretary and its allocation to the Federal Energy Regulatory Commission. This move reflected congressional fear of creating an "energy czar" with too much power, and became more controversial than the distribution of authority between the DOI and DOE.

The general consensus over the need for an energy department, congressional cooperation, and quick action during the immediate postpresidential election period, enabled President Carter to easily achieve a major reorganization of the bureaucracy—his administration's first significant achievement and legislative victory in a year otherwise marked by delay and defeat.

Notes

1. U.S. Congress, Senate Government Operations Committee, "Federal Energy Reorganization: Issues and Options," Committee print (September 1976).
2. *Congressional Quarterly Weekly Report*, January 29, 1977, p. 167.
3. Ibid., March 5, 1977, p. 403.
4. U.S. Congress, Senate Governmental Affairs Committee, "Department of Energy Organization Act," hearings, March 7-April 8, 1977, p. 127.
5. *New York Times*, February 25, 1977, p. D7.
6. Senate hearings, op. cit., pp. 203-13.
7. U.S. Congress, Senate Report 95-164, "Department of Energy Organization Act" (May 14, 1977).

8. A good analysis of perennial energy data collection and analyses problem may be found in U.S. Congress, Senate Governmental Affairs Committee, "Oversight of the Structure and Management of the Department of Energy," Staff Report (December 1980).

9. *Congressional Quarterly Weekly Report*, May 21, 1977, p. 953.

10. U.S. Congress, *Congressional Record*, May 18, 1977, p. S 7948.

11. Ibid., p. S 7958.

12. U.S. Congress, House Report 95-346, "Department of Energy Organization Act" (May 16, 1977), p. 75.

13. U.S. Congress, *Congressional Record*, August 2, 1977, p. H 8262.

14. Senate Hearings, op. cit., March 15, 1977.

15. *National Journal*, January 1, 1977, p. 77.

16. Charles O. Jones, "Speculative Augmentation in Federal Air Pollution Policy-Making," *Journal of Politics* (May 1974): 438-64.

17. These areas are detailed by David Davis, "Establishing the Department of Energy," *Journal of Energy and Development* 4 (1978): 29-40.

18. Daniel Ogden, Jr., "Protecting Energy Turf," *Natural Resources Journal* 18 (October 1978): 845-57; John Nassikas, "A Regulatory Official's Assessment of the New Department of Energy," *Natural Resources Lawyer* 10 (1978): 639-53.

6

Congress Encounters Carter's National Energy Plan

Preoccupied with the energy problem from the beginning to the end of his presidency, Jimmy Carter became inextricably involved in a struggle to enact energy proposals which he earnestly believed to be morally right. Although he originally planned his comprehensive, scientifically based, and interlocking energy plan to exemplify what his particular model of governing[1] could accomplish, his initiative finally led to a Sisyphean effort that exemplified, instead, the failure of his administration.

Although energy was not a major issue of Carter's campaign, it had become crucial by the time he took office because of the acute natural gas shortage. In a February 2, 1977 "fireside chat" with the nation on natural gas, President Carter warned that the United States was facing a "permanent, very serious energy shortage." He ordered energy advisor James Schlesinger to prepare a comprehensive national energy policy within ninety days.

Sharing Carter's technocratic mindset, Schlesinger assembled a group disposed to finding public and governmental solutions to energy policy. Many members of this group had backgrounds in university or public life and favored the conservation orientation embodied in an influential Ford Foundation report.[2] As Schlesinger clearly preferred operating efficiency to time-consuming consensus building, little was done to develop a base of support for the program. Despite a few meetings with industry representatives and government experts, and an opinion survey of 450,000 Americans, which was not much utilized, the Schlesinger cadre isolated itself from special interests in an attempt to insure untainted purity of the final product. With a sense of mission and the satisfaction of making a fresh start on a project of great potential for the future of America, the group labored day and night in virtual secrecy to finish their awesome task by April 20, 1977.

The fruit of this intense effort—the National Energy Plan— was issued by President Carter on April 29. In a national address, Carter announced that he was giving top priority to the formulation and passage of a national energy policy because of the U.S.'s perilous—yet increasing—dependence on im-

97

ported crude oil supplies. He insisted that the waste and misappropriation of domestic oil and natural gas must stop, while domestic production should be increased. Carter proposed to accomplish these ends and reduce projected 1985 oil imports from 12 million to 6 million barrels a day through programs that would (1) produce at least a billion tons of domestic coal to be burned in its place, (2) raise oil prices to encourage conservation and fuel substitution, and (3) subsidize investments in energy technologies. He also proposed strengthening relations between foreign producers and the United States and taking steps to enhance the nation's oil supply security by, among other means, filling a billion-barrel strategic petroleum reserve.

In his first national address on the subject, President Carter put the energy debate in moralistic terms: Energy would "test the character of the American people and the ability of the president and the Congress to govern the nation." To rally the American people, he made his now-famous identification of the energy situation as "the moral equivalent of war."[3] He succeeded in alerting the American people, but he could mobilize them only temporarily.

The tone of the president's speech was consonant with the value perspective that informed the whole National Energy Plan (NEP). While the plan approached the energy problem less dramatically, it treated it as a social and economic issue requiring governmental intervention. Socially, the government was to ensure equitable treatment for all and protect the powerless and disadvantaged. Economically, the government would correct market imbalances and inadequacies, and strengthen market forces that were inoperative or inefficient. The NEP assumed that it was the government's responsibility to deliver the nation from its present state of energy gluttony to a frugal but brighter future. It also assumed that the energy shortage was permanent and would "grow steadily worse," unless "addressed comprehensively by the government." Although the plan sought "fair and realistic pricing" for energy, the government was to decide what the "fair" price should be.[4] Plentiful energy sources such as nuclear power and especially coal should be used instead of scarce or insecure ones such as oil and natural gas, and the government was to direct the transformation. Wherever possible, nonconventional energy sources should be promoted, because many were decentralized or might lead to technological breakthroughs. While nuclear power licensing should be streamlined, the breeder reactor and plutonium reprocessing were unacceptable risks.

Rather than encouraging energy production, the cornerstone of the National Energy Plan was increased conservation and fuel efficiency. Here too, governmental intervention would be required to force the public to make the sacrifices necessary to avoid disastrous shortages and make the transition to energy parsimony.

The Schlesinger team pieced together 113 provisions into one of the most complex legislative packages in U.S. history, and one which would affect almost every aspect of American life. The main thrust of the program depended on regulatory and tax measures that would allow the federal government to discourage or redirect energy use, prescribe efficiency standards for major appliances and industrial products, make fuel choices for utilities and businesses, tax gas-guzzling cars, and levy penalties on businesses burning oil or natural gas and on the public if it used more than a specified amount of gasoline. It proposed subsidizing residential energy conservation, creating mandatory energy-efficient building standards, and extensively reforming utility rates. The latter was to discourage demand by raising the energy rates of large consumers (i.e. industry) and redistributing electricity use to nonpeak periods (i.e. late evening and night). In addition, discrimination by electric utilities against solar and other renewable energies was to be ended, while cogeneration and district heating were encouraged.

The NEP also announced Carter's intention to develop an energy assistance program for low-income people. The two most critical aspects of the program, and by far the most controversial, were the oil and natural gas provisions. Carter planned to tax crude oil production to raise its price to world levels but rebate the tax revenue to the public. Although the ceiling price of newly found gas was to be raised, natural gas price controls were to be extended to intrastate sales.

The plan also proposed moderate adjustments of the energy industry to improve its competitiveness and probity. It condemned energy resource concentration in the hands of a few companies and threatened strong action to promote competition. Carter sought a tripartite National Energy Information System to independently collect and analyze energy data, replacing the audit and verification functions of the American Petroleum Institute and the American Gas Association (industry trade associations) to allow the federal government a clearer picture of domestic energy reserves. The system would include reports on company finances and global operations. An emergency management data system would monitor oil or natural gas shortages.

In line with Carter's proclivity for rational, engineer-like procedures, the NEP promised stable government policies to reassure private investors. (It was claimed that drifting or rapidly changing governmental energy policy had aggravated the energy situation.) The major principles of the NEP were that (1) the government alone could effectively address the energy problem, (2) the government had to convince Americans that there was a serious energy crisis which required personal sacrifices if it was to be overcome, and (3) a great threat was that the United States was highly vulnerable to "potentially devastating (energy) supply interruptions" and that, therefore, imports of oil must be cut. Conservation and energy efficiency were the keys to the entire plan, which had to be "above all . . . fair and equitable to all regions, sectors, and income groups."

Though the purpose of Carter's plan was energy conservation, its immediate effect would be to raise most energy prices, which, unsurprisingly, would make it unpopular. To forestall anticipated opposition, Carter initiated an extensive public relations campaign directed at Congress, industry, and the electorate. Hollywood stars rallied to support the energy program in radio and T.V. commercials. Carter held various town meetings and colloquies with special interest groups; cabinet officers made speeches throughout the nation. A strenuous lobbying effort was launched, involving twenty-four legislative teams, each informed about a different aspect of the complex plan. The president himself led the crusade to develop support for his program.

The first stage in the House of Representatives was auspicious (see Table 6.1). The Interstate and Foreign Commerce Committee handled most of the nontax portions of the National Energy Plan, while the Ways and Means Committee reviewed all the tax measures. To avoid the complications characteristic of Congress's earlier dealings with comprehensive energy legislation, House Speaker Thomas P. O'Neill and his advisors created a single Ad Hoc Committee on Energy to coordinate the consideration of the plan as one package. O'Neill appointed forty members to the committee, of which twenty-seven were Democrats who supported Carter's plan. Viewing the program's success as a test of the Democratic Party and the governing ability of Congress and the administration, O'Neill established strict deadlines, followed the program's progress closely, and personally intervened when difficulties were encountered. He relentlessly appealed to House members for unity and responsibility in their consideration of the bill. As a result, all committee hearings and markups were completed in six weeks and forwarded to the Ad Hoc Committee, which completed its work in three days.

The House committees had a history of supporting energy policies similar to those proposed by President Carter. In 1976, for example, the House Commerce's Subcommittee on Energy and Power compiled a massive record of expert testimony during eight days of hearings on energy issues. The hearings led to a proconsumer bill, sponsored by the subcommittee chairman John D. Dingell, that was very similar to utility rate reform proposals that Carter would later submit. (The NEP team included an aide of Dingell's, who had helped with the 1976 bill.) Another instance of the House committees' basically sympathetic approach to the kind of energy initiatives contained in the NEP was the Ways and Means Committee's approval of an ill-fated energy tax bill in 1975 (see chapter 4).

While there was significant and growing opposition in the House to many of the measures, members moved swiftly and with few modifications, driven by forceful House leadership and shepherded by the Ad Hoc Energy Committee. When dissensions arose, and at times they nearly defeated a key Carter proposal, the House leadership quickly mobilized to squelch it. For example, the House Commerce Committee, which was assigned responsibility for Carter's controversial natural gas measure, was able to defeat decontrol forces on its own Energy and Power Subcommittee that wanted to deregulate natural gas prices. This reversal of the subcommittee's recommendation was sustained by the Ad Hoc Committee, which broadened the definition of "new gas," further weakening opposition to the extension of natural gas price controls. Only legislation concerning the automobile, that indispensable convenience of American life, suffered setbacks. The House Ways and Means committee rejected all suggestions of raising gasoline taxes to cut consumption. It did approve an extra stiff tax on low gas mileage cars, but defeated a rebate system channelling "gas guzzler" taxes to purchasers of high gas mileage cars.

When counterattacks by newly formed lobbying groups opposing the Carter National Energy Plan almost succeeded in breaking the plan's lock-step advance through the House, only the constant intervention of Speaker O'Neill and the Democratic leadership preserved the fragile coalition supporting the NEP. Indicative of the unusual priority given Carter's plan, Speaker O'Neill took the House floor. In one rare and dramatic gesture, he denounced "big oil" lobbyists, and urged Congress to protect "the little man . . . America is watching." He warned that "the future of America is at stake," and demanded that the NEP be approved.[5]

Because of strong Democratic leadership as well as prior organizational innovations, Carter's program was pushed rapidly through the House; it was still virtually unscathed by August 5, 1977. But before the NEP could meet its fate in the Senate, it lost momentum as a result of the August congressional recess and the banking scandal involving budget director Bert Lance. This delay gave NEP opponents the necessary time to organize themselves and devise arguments against the measure.

It was not only this loss of momentum which doomed the NEP in the Senate. While the House committees had reviewed the plan against a background of support for previous energy proposals similar to Carter's—involving deregulation and taxes—corresponding committees in the Senate were generally less sympathetic and accepting of any change and had often opposed Carter-style policies. The newly formed Senate Energy Committee had little experience with key energy legislation issues. This relatively conservative committee lacked a proconsumer majority, and the Finance Committee openly protected industry's interests. Though Senate Majority Leader Robert C. Byrd declared his intention to support the energy plan, he was unable to set and enforce deadlines for committee consideration. His commitment was to

TABLE 6.1
Congressional Action on the National Energy Plan

Carter's Original Proposal	House Decision	Senate Decision	Conference Decision	Final Legislation
1. Grants tax credits for home insulation and energy savings (HR 5263)	Passed 8/5/77	Passed 10/31/77	Maximun $300 credit; conference report filed 10/12/78	Conference report passed by House and Senate on 10/15/78 (PL 95-618)
2. Standby gasoline tax if consumption rises markedly	Rejected 8/4/77	Rejected 10/21/77	—	—
3. "Gas-guzzling" car tax (HR 5263)	Passed 8/5/77	Rejected, but banned their production as part of HR 5037	Passed; conference report filed 10/12/78	Conference report passed by House and Senate on 10/15/78 (PL 95-618)
4. "Gas-guzzler" tax to be rebated to buyers of low-mileage cars	Rejected by Ways and Means Committee 6/9/77	Never considered	—	—
5. Establish mandatory energy efficiency standards for major home appliances, furnaces, etc. (HR 5037)	Passed 8/5/77	Passed 9/13/77	Passed 10/3/77; conference report filed 10/10/78	Conference report passed by Senate report 10/9/78, by House 10/15/78 (PL 95-619)
6. Extend natural gas price controls to all gas sold (i.e. intrastate) but allow higher price ceilings (HR 5289)	Passed 8/15/77	Rejected; approved instead ending federal price controls for new gas 10/4/77	Lift price controls on new gas by 1985, reached 5/24/78, report filed 8/18/78	Conference report passed by Senate 9/27/78, by House 10/15/78 (PL 95-621)

TABLE 6.1 Continued

7. Tax on crude oil (HR 5263) to bring price to world levels, rebate tax to public	Passed 8/5/77	Finance Committee rejected 10/21/77	Eliminated by conference	—
8. Tax on utility and industry to discourage oil and natural gas use (HR 5263)	Weaker form passed 8/5/77	Even weaker version passed 10/31/77	Eliminated by conference	—
9. Government to require utilities to require util- ities to convert to coal from oil and gas (HR 5146)	Passed 8/5/77	Passed but in weaker form than House version 9/8/77	Reached compromise 11/11/77; conference report filed 7/14/78	Conference report passed by Senate 7/18/78, by House 10/15/78 (PL 95-620)
10. Federally directed reform of electric utility rates (HR 4018)	Passed 8/5/77	Finance Committee rejected 9/19/77	Reached compromise 9/1/77; conference report filed 10/6/78	Conference report passed by Senate 10/9/78, by House 10/15/78 (PL 95-617)

the Senate rather than to Carter's plan, so he "let the Senate work its will" on the program.

Moreover, Senate rules precluded the consolidation of power in any one individual or the use of an ad hoc committee to deal with a single bill. Byrd remarked on the impossibility of handling NEP as it had been handled by the House. Therefore, the chairmen of the two committees reviewing the bill, Henry Jackson and Russell Long, were largely responsible for the program's fate, and their views concerning energy policy were often in conflict. To further complicate matters, the NEP was broken up for review into six separate proposals thus giving the opposition six opportunities to revise or defeat the plan.

The administration seemed oblivious to the unsympathetic climate in the Senate and the nature of its deliberations over the NEP. Schlesinger optimistically announced:

> When the original package went to the House, there were all these comments to the effect that the program was being gutted or riddled and so on. Then in August, when the House voted out virtually the entire package, everyone said it was a remarkable triumph. I would not be surprised if we went through the same cycle with regard to the Congress as a whole.[6]

But Carter's plan met its nemesis in the Senate. The six fragments of the bill which were finally adopted bore little resemblance to the NEP Carter had so ambitiously composed (see Table 6.1). For example, while the version passed by the House depended on taxation to insure rapid industrial conservation, the Senate relied on financial inducements. Carter's bill would have distributed a $53 billion tax in cash rebates to needy customers, while the Senate preferred to offer $39 billion as investment credits and tax deductions to industries that converted from oil or natural gas to coal.

Instead of forcing utilities to convert to coal, Senator Jackson offered them $1 billion in loans to assist in the required conversion and authorized spending $1.2 billion to ameliorate coal "boom town" impacts on local communities. Senator Long's Finance Committee departed entirely from Carter and the House on taxes, totally rejecting three of the NEP's crucial tax measures. The controversial Crude Oil Equalization Tax (COET) was acceptable to Long only if the tax would be used for energy and conservation incentives and not simply rebated to the consumer, as Carter proposed. Although he supported the gasoline tax of 4¢ per gallon, Long refused to accept the tax on "gas-guzzling" cars and modified the industrial users' tax on natural gas and oil to an admixture of tax credits for energy production and incentives that was estimated to cost $40 billion through fiscal year 1985, while saving about 2.1 million barrels of oil daily. During the controversies with his committee and his Senate colleagues, Long was able to win crucial battles through successful maneuvering, which reinforced his image as the most powerful of all senators.

The overall strategy used in the Senate differed markedly from that of the House, due to structural differences between the two legislative units as well as the influence of personalities. Wending its way through the Senate, each of the six Senate bills was attached to a minor House-passed bill in order to expedite its passage through Congress:

- S 977, which forced new electric utility and major industrial plants to convert from oil and natural gas (to coal) was combined with S 701, which authorized matching grants for energy conservation in schools and hospitals; these were then added to HR 5146.
- S 2057's energy conservation incentives were combined to become HR 5037.
- S 2104, deregulating natural gas, became HR 5289.
- Electric rate provisions of S 2114 and HR 8444 were attached to HR 4018.
- After a series of deadlocks, ties, substitutions, and filibusters, the Senate passed HR 5289, ending federal price regulation for new natural gas found onshore after two years and gradually deregulating gas produced offshore.
- S 2114 aimed at utility energy conservation and was designed to curb federal authority over electric rates, which were traditionally handled on the state level.
- After six days of debate and the adoption of thirty-four amendments, the Senate passed Long's industrial oil and gas user's tax, which combined tax credits for energy production and conservation. Proposing to save an estimated 2.1 million barrels of oil per day, the bill would cost the government $40 billion through fiscal 1985, a sum which would be halved by an extension of the 4¢ per gallon tax on gasoline through 1985, the only revenue raiser in the Finance Committee bill.

Natural gas was an especially divisive issue, and, although Jackson supported continuing controls, the Senate Energy Committee split evenly 9 to 9 and sent Carter's proposal on extending price regulation, at a higher level, to the floor without recommendation. Although the Energy Committee could not agree on natural gas, the Senate itself had already gone on record supporting decontrol in a 1975 vote. Despite intensive White House lobbying, it seemed likely that the decontrol forces would win again until the timely intervention of James Abourezk (D-S.Dak.) and Howard Metzenbaum (D-Ohio), two mercurial senators who launched a novel filibuster. They managed to block passage of an amendment deregulating natural gas prices for nine days. However, after several attempts, the Senate leadership, with the help of Vice President Walter Mondale, was able to use controversial parliamentary tactics to break the filibuster. The Senate approved a deregulated measure.

Although the last piece of Carter's NEP had been passed, not only were the gasoline tax and several other chunks missing but the House and Senate measures varied widely on crucial questions. A conference committee was thus faced with reconciling opposing and incompatible energy philosophies; it remained stalled for many months, finally writing much of the legislation itself. The group of twenty-five House members and eighteen senators selected to serve on the committee was characterized by diversity. Alignments and loyalties shifted as the members strategically bargained and traded throughout their consideration of the 113 provisions of the House bill and the six separate bills submitted by the Senate. Parts of the bill, although not formally approved, were largely accepted by the conferees in late 1977, including the measure converting utilities to coal and numerous energy-conserving measures. A compromise was also reached on an approach to utility rate reforms. However, further action on the NEP bill's controversial sections was prevented by deep divisions over energy taxes and natural gas. In effect, Russell Long was holding the tax measures hostage for movement on natural gas favorable to his interest, while progress on all the other sections was prevented by the natural gas conferees, who would not act until the natural gas regulation issue was resolved. Thus the entire legislative architectonic hinged on the economically and politically vital question of natural gas policy.

This was the situation when Congress members adjourned for Christmas and when they returned to Washington in January, 1978. The central difficulty lay in the opposition between the Senate and the House. The House supported Carter and favored gas-price controls, although at a higher level, and extended to include gas sold within states (previously, federal regulation affected only prices on gas shipped between states). The Senate, on the other hand, voted for deregulation of all newly discovered gas, a move which would give producers billions of dollars as gas prices rose.

To release the Energy Committee from its deadlock, Jackson proposed a compromise that provided for the removal of price controls on new gas by January 1985, with the stipulation that prices could be frozen any time Congress thought they were rising too quickly. The seventeen Senate conferees resumed their closed-door sessions on February 23, and by March 7 reached a shaky compromise on federal price control of new natural gas that made concessions to deregulation advocates without immediately ending price regulation. The twenty-five House conferees agreed tentatively to analyze the compromise proposal in a "spirit of reconciliation." However, John D. Dingell, an influential opponent of gas deregulation since coming to the House in 1955, while accepting the language of an earlier plan for a "floating cap" to control new gas prices, objected to the compromise on the grounds that it led too directly to deregulation. Dingell's staff had been attempting to reduce the cost and consumer impact of the senators' plan, and Dingell resented the casualness with which it had been given to House conferees without prior discussions and with the obvious approval of the administration.[7]

The March 22 conference was a "standing room only" public session, which one participant called a "mad hatter's tea party." The House conferees voted 13-12 in favor of the Senate compromise, but then substituted for it a detailed amendment built on the same concepts as the compromise, with extensive revisions. This substitution added to the dissension that shook the fragile coalition behind the compromise, and the conference adjourned for the Easter recess in a deadlock. Commenting on the chaos created by holding a public conference, chairman Jackson noted: "You can see why I have urged strongly that we engage in quiet diplomacy. I think these public get-togethers before we get our ducks in a row create nothing but trouble."[8]

At this point Carter intervened. On April 11, he called key conferees for a series of White House meetings in an effort to soothe House Republican anger and resolve House-Senate differences over his natural gas legislation. By April 13, however, Senate conferees had listed eight major areas of disagreement, and the House added four more. They included the definition of new gas that would qualify for higher prices and eventual deregulation, the requirement of incremental pricing devised to force industry— instead of residential users—to absorb most price increases, and how much price ceilings should be allowed to rise each year. When these new points of contention were introduced to an already long list of disputes, the outlook for the bill seemed bleak.

In the meantime, support was mounting among House and Senate conferees for a proposal to split the energy bill into separate sections to vote on individually, as had been done with Carter's package the year before. It was hoped that separation would free the three noncontroversial aspects of the program for passage without having to resolve the sensitive natural gas pricing and major energy tax issues.

On April 20, 1978, one year after he proposed the energy bill, Carter exhorted a joint session of Congress "to fulfill its duty to the American people" and pass his energy legislation "without further delay."[9] Yet, on the same day, Minority Leader John Rhodes, inspired by the donut-shaped cake ironically presented by House Republican leaders on the energy plan's first birthday, described the energy situation as "Congress going in circles around a hole."[10]

On April 21, a major breakthrough occurred in the energy policy debate: a small group of House and Senate conferees agreed to end federal regulation of prices for new natural gas, beginning January 1, 1985. Conference chairman Harley O. Staggers (D-W.Va.) said the compromise, a result of "intensive emotional struggle," was the "best hope we have for resolution of this issue." The compromise contained Energy Secretary Schlesinger's prime objective—the extension of federal price controls to new gas in the previously unregulated intrastate market. The compromise would free the president's energy bill and would deregulate even more gas than the March proposal, which would have gradually removed price controls from newly discovered gas by 1985. However, the outstanding issues of gas pricing and taxes to raise oil prices—especially Carter's wellhead tax on U.S. crude oil—remained points of contention, and the initially optimistic House and Senate conferees began quarrelling. Meanwhile, the opposition had become more visible. James Abourezk, a major Senate force against deregulation, charged that the only beneficiaries of the proposal, which he called a "rip-off" and "rape" of the American consumer, would be "titans of the oil and gas industry," whose "lust for profits has been unmatched in the annals of American business."[11]

The deadlock was finally broken on May 24, when House and Senate conferees accepted a proposal for deregulation; new problems immediately arose, however, with the task of translating the gas agreement into legislative language. Industry partisans, preferring immediate deregulation of new natural gas to complicated, gradual phasing, argued that the compromise's price increase between 1978 and 1985 was too gradual. Objections were also raised against the language giving the president power to allocate gas in intrastate markets.

Nevertheless, a majority of House and Senate conferees signed the conference report (S Rept. 95-1126) on August 18, ending months of bickering and apparently clearing the way for floor action on the agreement. Then, on August 23, in an attempt to send the conference report back to committee, a coalition of Democrats and seven Republicans, proponents and opponents of the gas-pricing deregulation, refused to support the agreement. "This very unusual coalition of senators you see here today," Senator Clifford P. Hansen (R-Wyo.) told a press conference, "has developed because we all have one thing in common—we are all strongly opposed to the natural gas compromise, although for very different reasons."[12] The dissenting group claimed that restrictions on intrastate marketing would reduce producer incentive, forcing consumers to pay higher prices without increasing supplies. This objection gained support among special interest groups and, by the time the bill reached the floor, enthusiasm for it had died. Supporters of deregulation, including many independent gas producers, wanted controls phased out sooner than the plan proposed while labor, consumer, and public interest groups, normally against higher energy prices, complained that the compromise gave away too much. Major industrial consumers of natural gas objected that the plan would force them to pay for a disproportionate share of more expensive gas. Joining industry in opposition was the labor union-backed Citizen-Labor Energy Coalition, headed by William P. Winpisinger, president of the International Association of Machinists.

Critics contended that the administration was now willing to accept almost any kind of an energy bill. Public interest lobbyist James F. Flug claimed that Schlesinger was desperate. "He's willing to do anything and say anything. The operation has lost all credibility."[13]

In a Senate floor speech on September 12, Dale Bumpers (D-Ark.) referred to the "interesting Catch-22 situation," in which senators found themselves in relation to the gas proposal: "It doesn't make any difference how you vote," he observed, "you are going to get it. Gas prices are going to go up if we defeat the bill, and they are going to go up if we pass the bill. You just book that." Depending upon which side one stood, the bill would either increase or decrease gas production, aid or harm the dollar, curb or aggravate inflation, encourage industry's gas use or force a switch to oil, be easier to administer than existing law or spawn "a regulatory nightmare," he said.[14] However, oddly enough, the American Gas Association, representing U.S. gas utility companies, was one of the few interest groups openly working *with* the administration to pass the controversial measure.

The only hope for the bill's survival lay with Carter's lobbyists, who called it the key to meaningful energy legislation for the Ninety-fifth Congress and, like Carter, stressed its importance in maintaining the U.S.'s international economic position and the dollar's soundness in foreign exchange markets. They also claimed that the bill would cut oil imports by an estimated 1.4 million barrels a day.

On September 11, Senate floor debate on the gas bill began—with a flourish. Supporters of the measure narrowly averted a filibuster by agreeing to the opposition's request to wait until September 19 before voting on whether to send the bill back to conference. To expedite its passage, they initiated a recommital which instructed conferees to authorize presidential allocation of gas in an emergency and to eliminate virtually all provisions that related to gas pricing. Majority Leader Robert C. Byrd and Energy Committee chairman Jackson objected that recommital would destroy chances for major energy legislation, not only in the Ninety-fifth Congress but in the future, while Abourezk and Kennedy, on the basis of their objections to the bill, urged recommital. In a 39-59 vote, the move to recommit was rejected.

A day before the final vote on the conference report was scheduled, opponents made what appeared to be a last attempt to send the measure back to conference. Robert Dole (R-Kans.) introduced a motion instructing conferees to approve measures similar to those of the first recommital vote, but it was rejected. One half hour before the September 27 vote, the Senate again debated natural-gas pricing. Senator Metzenbaum, reiterating the defects of the bill, pledged that the gas-pricing issue would not end that day: "It is an issue that will come back time and again to this body." Charles H. Percy (R-Ill.) countered: "It is this compromise or nothing for several years."[15]

A final tally of 57-42 brought the gas issue to a dramatic close. The president rejoiced in the Senate's approval of the conference committee report's approval—"one of the most difficult pieces of legislation that the Congress has ever faced"—claiming: "It proves to our nation and to the rest of the world that we in this government, particularly Congress, can courageously deal with an issue and one that tests our national will and our ability."[16]

Approval of the conference report on energy taxes was expected during the Senate's October 12 meeting. Upon clearance, the tax report and four other bills were placed before the House Rules Committee, which had to approve them before final House floor vote. While the committee was making its decision, Senator Abourezk chose to stall for time and delayed not only the Senate vote on the tax conference report but also action in the House on the five-part package. Meanwhile, in the House Rules Committee, while supporters wanted the gas bill voted on with the other parts in a single vote, opponents tried to convince the committee to reject the package, so that it could be defeated with separate votes.

Until the final roll call, the energy plan was vulnerable to defeat by being sidetracked or picked apart by supporters and opponents jockeying for parliamentary advantage. The Democractic leadership pushed for acceptance of an unusual rule that would combine the five conference reports and allow only one vote on them, hoping thereby to force passage of the controversial measure along with the popular legislation. At the same time, the coalition against the natural gas bill campaigned for a rule that would permit a separate vote on this most controversial part of the package, on the assumption that isolation made it vulnerable to attack. Meanwhile, in the Senate, opponents of the energy tax provisions tried to delay final action on this measure, hoping that House support for the whole package would weaken if the tax language were eliminated from it.

Opponents in the House continued their sharp criticism of the natural gas section, led by John Anderson (R-Ill.), ranking minority member of the Ad Hoc Energy Committee. Anderson charged the bill with being a "merely convenient vehicle for the President to prove his supposed new dynamism, macho, and legislative competence," and said "the House should not begin waging the moral equivalent of war" on the energy problem with "a surrender of our legislative prerogatives."[17]

Nevertheless, the energy tax conference report was passed (60-17), and the House Rules Committee decided to permit only one vote on it. By the narrowest of margins (207-206), the House agreed to consider the five parts as one package, assuring victory for the president with the passage of the natural gas compromise and other nontax measures of the omnibus bill. Had it not been for the eighteen months of vicious arguments, retreats, grueling delays, and drastic alterations of Carter's original plan, the final passage of the energy program might have been considered a major achievement. However, the battered, fragmented version of Carter's original plan placed on his desk on October 15, 1978, was hardly a cause for celebration. The thrust of the president's proposal—to save 4.5 million barrels of oil per day by 1985 through taxation, incentives, and regulatory authority—had been deflected. His standby tax on gas was rejected, and instead of authorizing price controls at higher levels, Congress voted phased deregulation of natural gas. The bill's success could only be measured in terms of its overall significance—ideologically and emotionally—not as a presidential victory or defeat. But certainly the bold intention to dramatically cut imports would not be realized, as indicated in Table 6.2.

TABLE 6.2
Conservation Goals of the National Energy Act, 1978

Provision	Projected Savings of Imported Oil (thousands of barrels per day)		
	Carter's Original Proposals	Enacted Legislation	Critical Estimate
1. Natural gas	700	1–1,400[1]	363–(–1,000)[2]
2. Coal conversion	340–400	300	60–150
3. Utility rate reform	160	0–160	0
4. Conservation subtotal	475	675	NA[4]
a. Building/appliances	280	410	
b. Auto/truck standards	195	265[3]	
5. Tax subtotal	3,480	415	86–216
a. Oil, gas users tax	2,300	0	0
b. Crude oil equalization tax (COET)	230	0	0
c. Gas-guzzler tax	170	80	10
d. Residential tax credits	300	225	76
e. Business energy tax credits	180	110	0–130
Total Optimistic estimates	5,215	2,950	1,404
Pessimistic estimates	5,155	2,390	(–179)

1. Energy Department estimates vary depending upon the amount of oil displaced by increased gas supply (although this gas may replace LNG , propane, and butane as well as oil).
2. Critics found the legislation may actually increase oil imports, as indicated by the minus sign.
3. Assumes that Energy Policy and Conservation Act penalties are increased to the full extent permitted and also that the administration implements truck standards.
4. Because this provision was the least controversial, the critics made no estimate. However, for comparison purposes, the same figure used by the Energy Department was used in the critics' column total.

Sources: U.S. Department of Energy; Critical estimates by Congressional Budget Office; Senator James Abourezk's Office.

Conclusion

The passage of the NEA meant that for the first time in this country's history three major fuels—oil, gas, and coal—would be considered in relationship to one another. The means chosen to accomplish this, however, were those with which Congress was most familiar—regulation and tax subsidies. The price of natural gas would rise gradually toward complete decontrol in the middle or late 1980s. Industrial plants and new utilities would be required to use fuel other than oil or gas, and existing utilities to convert from gas to any other fuel by 1990. Conversion to coal was stressed except in areas where such conversion would be environmentally prohibitive. State regulatory agencies were directed to consider energy conservation procedures, and hundreds of millions of dollars would be spent on home, school, and hospital insulation. Although Carter had intended that two-thirds of the savings in consumption was to come from large taxes on oil, only a mild levy was placed on the sale of gas-guzzling cars. Controls would be used to raise prices and thus increase domestic supplies while reducing demand. However, the changes would be so slow that they would be relatively painless.

Limitations on Government's Ability to Take Bold Action

The Executive Office and Congress appear incapable of creative approaches to new challenges, in part because of the traditional protections given minority groups by the U.S. political system. Paul W. Macavoy of Yale University believes that this built-in means of discouraging rapid, significant energy policy change is further reinforced by the fact that the consequences of the energy crisis have been so complex and disruptive that the polity has had great difficulty in assessing their policy implications.[18]

Indeed, many critics feel that because recent energy legislation was based on previous legislation—notably the Energy Policy and Conservation Act of 1975—it was not very significant. Congress essentially extended existing legislation and added natural gas legislation. There were a few selected incentives for coal and conservation, but almost none for increased production. The legislation's major effect, it seems, was to expand the energy bureaucracy.[19]

Ted Eck, senior economist of Standard Oil Company (Indiana), called the energy package "sort of a non-event. It won't make anybody any money and it won't save anybody any money." He dismissed administration claims that the legislation would limit oil imports: "I don't think anybody in their wildest imagination could claim it would save more than half a million barrels a day."[20] Many critics agreed, and while the administration was more sanguine, as is shown in Table 6.2, it was clear to everyone that the legislative product fell far short of Carter's initial goals.

Originally, the largest energy savings were to result from various oil taxes, but these were dropped from the package, while the natural gas bill, which barely figured in the 1977 estimate, became the centerpiece of the package. The General Accounting Office, the Congressional Budget Office, and the Office of Technology Assessment had, in 1977, concluded that Carter's original plan could not meet its stated objectives even if it were passed intact, and the form of the final bill only increased their pessimism. (See Table 7.1 in the next chapter for details.)

Instead of settling the old Capitol Hill debate between the forces of regulation and deregulation, the new gas-pricing legislation caused new battles in the Federal Energy Regulatory Commission (FERC) and the courts which would continue for years afterwards. The legislation extending price controls to newly found gas in the intrastate market was a main objective of the Carter administration, since most onshore gas had previously been sold in the state where it was discovered and where the seller could charge whatever the market would bear. While combining the intrastate and interstate markets, on the assumption that interstate pipelines should be allowed to bid for new supplies, the legislation provided for eventual deregulation of new gas and created categories by which various kinds of gas must be sold. The new legislation also imposed an incremental pricing system and forced industrialized users to pay more than residential and small commercial users.

Rather surprisingly, especially after so much acrimony and the frequent exchange of insults, many business interests remained neutral toward the new legislation, if not pleased. Articles in numerous trade publications took the attitude that, although far from perfect, the legislation was certainly acceptable and that only time would reveal its full impact. The American Public Power Association declared that it was "nearly impossible to forecast" the act's impact on utilities, and that it represented "only the beginning of a long process of planning and policy making."[21] In a similar vein, the *Real Estate Review* found that, although the NEA was "crucial" to all segments of the real estate market, its impact depended on future action by federal agencies and thus was yet to be determined.[22] Most surprising of all the responses of business, after the bloody and prolonged fighting and wrenching compromises, the natural gas industry was "delighted" by the bill.[23] Traditional coalitions were being rearranged in the pursuit of energy policy.

Consumer groups, although not enthusiastic about the legislation, accepted it. A few public-interest lobbying groups remained adamantly opposed: James Flug, head of Energy Action, asserted that Carter's signing the NEA was the "functional equivalent of surrender in the moral equivalent of war."[24] The press, although predominantly negative, was deeply divided over the legislation's significance. A few journalists were more optimistic. One went so far as to claim that the NEA sealed into law the conviction that, contrary to old and deeply ingrained American values, at least in regard to energy, "more is not necessarily better." The American people, he believed, also saw that "cheaper is not necessarily better, either."[25]

To many believing in a permanent energy challenge and a rational approach, it appeared that Congress had gutted a sensible plan and hobbled the president's powers over energy policy: after Carter had threatened to limit oil imports directly by quotas, the Congress stripped his powers to do so. The House and the Senate refused to allow Carter to ration gas without congressional approval or to restrict consumption directly in other ways. Congress had also rejected legislation preventing citizens from using their cars one day a week; forcing businesses to turn off billboards, neon signs, and interior lights at night; demanding miles-per-gallon standards for new American cars; and restricting petroleum and electricity use by raising prices.

In retrospect, it becomes clear that the bill was drafted too rapidly and tried to cover too much. But its central principle had merit: higher prices rather than moral suasion are necessary to enforce the serious conservation essential to protect the American economy from energy shortages and crises.

Indeed, the impact of the National Energy Plan went beyond actual immediate gain or loss and points toward a reality-oriented energy policy predicated upon the production and control of statistics that are intended to delineate the future in a world of uncertain energy resources. The NEP (and much less so the NEA) epitomized the type of logically preconceived, integrated, and technocratically supported energy policy deemed by many necessary to preserve diminishing energy resources; the NEP also epitomized the belief in energy conservation as the means of avoiding a national catastrophe. Finally, while the resulting act itself was neither theoretically symmetrical nor a piece of intellectual craftsmanship, it indicated the beginning of a major shift in the way the United States perceived the energy problem. Such a change must of necessity be slow and uneven, especially given the great uncertainty surrounding the energy problem today. How permanent or extensive the change in America's perception of its energy problem has actually been is discussed in chapter 11.

Notes

1. See Jack Knott and Aaron Wildavsky, "Jimmy Carter's Theory of Governing," *Wilson Quarterly* (Winter 1977): 49-65.
2. Ford Foundation Energy Policy Project, *A Time to Choose* (Cambridge, Mass.: Ballinger, 1974).
3. U.S. General Services Administration, *Papers of the Presidents of the United States, Jimmy Carter, 1977* (Washington, D.C.: U.S. Government Printing Office, 1977), p. 656.
4. These and following quotes are drawn from U.S. Executive Office of the President, *The National Energy Plan* (April 1977).

5. U.S. Congress, *Congressional Record*, August 3, 1977, p. 2486.
6. Transcript, Department of Energy Press Conference, September 24, 1978.
7. *National Journal*, March 18, 1978, pp. 421-23.
8. *Congressional Quarterly Weekly Report*, March 25, 1978, p. 743.
9. Congressional Quarterly, *Energy Policy* (Washington, D.C.: CQ Press, 1979): 14.
10. *Washington Post*, April 21, 1978, p. A2.
11. Congressional Quarterly, *Energy Policy*, p. 21.
12. *National Journal*, September 9, 1978, p. 1426.
13. Ibid.
14. *Congressional Record*, September 12, 1978, p. 28822.
15. Ibid., September 27, 1978, p. 31821.
16. *Public Papers*: *1978,* p. 1644.
17. *Congressional Record*, October 14, 1978, p. 38352.
18. Paul Macavoy, "Some Thoughts on 'U.S. Energy Policy Options,'" *Materials and Society* 2 (1978): 119-20.
19. Interview with anonymous Congressional Research Service staff member, October 13, 1982.
20. *National Journal*, November 4, 1978, p. 1761.
21. Alan Richardson and Carl Goldfield, "What the National Energy Act Means to Your Utility," *Public Power* 36 (October 1978): 50.
22. Martin Klepper, "The National Energy Act: Its Impact on Real Estate and Real Estate Financing," *Real Estate Review* 9 (Spring 1979): 49.
23. M. Seligsohn, "Almost Too Good to Be True: Natural Gas Bill Delights Industry," *Food Engineering* 50 (October 1978): 24-25.
24. *New York Times*, November 10, 1978, p. D 14.
25. *Washington Post*, November 7, 1978, p. A2.

7
An Anatomy of Failure

To borrow a phrase from the description of the American raid to rescue the hostages in Iran, the National Energy Plan was an "incomplete success." For the third time, U.S. attempts to meet the worsening global energy crisis with strong and comprehensive legislation had stymied, as had the hopes for an integrated energy policy. The one point of agreement among all the participants in the 1977-78 National Energy Act debate was that, even after the NEP's passage, additional legislation was needed, perhaps as early as the following year. Carter himself insisted shortly after signing the National Energy Act, "I have not given up on my original proposal."[1]

Yet before moving on to analyze the next energy battle, it would be useful to assess what mistakes were made by Carter, the qualities inherent in the U.S. political system which caused the particular outcome, and how the various interested parties affected the action on the energy plan.

No Constituency for Self-Sacrifice

Perhaps the most essential factor explaining the plan's failure was the administration's inability to develop a constituency. Gallup polls showed that the administration's efforts to rally the public and underscore the seriousness of the nation's energy problems were ephemeral in their impact. Thus the intended mainstay of Carter's plan—a mobilized, angry, ready-to-sacrifice public—was missing. The president acknowledged his plan's unpopularity and lack of public support in a television address on November 8, 1977:

> I said six months ago that no one would be completely satisfied with this national energy policy. Unfortunately, that prediction has turned out to be right.[2]

Schlesinger had recognized "the basic problem" earlier: "There is no constituency for an energy program. There are many constituencies opposed. But the basic constituency for the major program is the future."[3] Without a constituency, Carter and the congressional supporters of his plan were forced to rely upon ideology in their efforts to secure its passage.

117

Ideology Provides a Guide

Ideological factions in Congress, however, were fragmented by wide-ranging and conflicting interests that often blunted one another's impact or cancelled out each other altogether, paralyzing congressional action. The breadth and diffuseness of ideologies about energy policy exacerbated attempts to take a pragmatic or problem-solving approach, and perceptions of economic interests divided Congress according to state or regional interests, preventing party-based unity. Internal leadership stabilized congressional attitudes and voting patterns toward energy policymaking while Sam Rayburn and Lyndon B. Johnson prevailed (both had represented oil-producing interests in Congress). When in the late 1960s their influence was withdrawn and no dominating ideologies or factions succeeded it, the attitude of many in Congress toward energy issues was often mere indifference.

After the energy crisis of 1973 all the contending interests involved with various aspects of energy policy became more vociferous and visible and their influence on Congress more obvious. The debate's tenor became harsher and more public. When a House Commerce subcommittee at first voted to support decontrol of new natural gas prices and the House Ways and Means Committee voted against President Carter's gasoline tax and rebate plan for buyers of fuel-efficient cars, the president openly blamed oil and auto industry lobbyists for these decisions, claiming that "the people will pay." When the Senate Finance Committee voted out his energy tax proposal, Carter's accusations grew more strident: oil companies were "war profiteering in the impending energy crisis."[4]

The powerful gas and oil company lobby exerted its influence to defeat the tax plans, or at least to secure tax monies for their member firms instead of taxpayers. Lobbyists representing the automobile industry similarly used their influence to prevent the tax on gas-guzzling cars from going into effect. The home-building industry objected to immediate tax credits for homeowners who insulated old houses, on the basis that giving full credits now would raise prices and exacerbate the shortage of insulating material needed for building new houses. Large industrial corporations—including General Motors, Union Carbide, and Anheuser-Busch—formed an Electric Consumers Resource Council to oppose Carter's utility rate reform plan. Fuel oil dealers opposed legislation that might allow utilities to carry out government-sanctioned home inspections, because they might recommend to homeowners to switch from oil to electric heat.

The major utility companies were also well represented on Capitol Hill to oppose proposed utility rate reforms, taxes on their oil use, and forced conversion to coal. Not only industry but also environmentalists, consumer groups, and union lobbyists all contended to influence Carter's energy legislation. Because of the extensive range of the National Energy Plan, it occasioned more lobbying than any legislation in the government history, and the Carter administration was entirely vulnerable to its disintegrating effects.

Division in the House over the National Energy Plan also occurred along traditional party lines. Republican objections to the plan usually concerned its great stress on enforced conservation. One Republican congressman called the plan a "punitive measure" designed to exact burdensome taxes from the American people. However, the Republican's alternative plans were similarly criticized by many House Democrats who said the Republican's tax—OPEC-dictated higher prices for U.S. and world oil—would be collected and retained by the oil companies.

Carter himself has often been blamed for the failure of his program to generate sufficient support for its passage intact. Senate leaders seemed to lack confidence in the man himself, primarily because of his retreats in the face of such tough issues as unpopular nominations, water projects, and tax rebates. Though he changed his political tactics from soliciting public pressure on Congress to applying direct pressure in meetings with congressmen, he continued to offend those on Capitol Hill. Even before he was elected, his relations with the predominantly Democratic Congress began to deteriorate when he attacked the "Washington Establishment" as unresponsive to the vital national issues. The "Establishment" responded with ostracism and ridicule.

As a newly elected president facing myriad problems with little organized support, opposed by a divided and unruly Congress and with few friends on Capitol Hill, Carter was naive in committing himself to the formation of a comprehensive and generally acceptable energy plan within ninety days. To meet the deadline, he adopted a two-part political approach: he functioned as a leadership symbol for the people while the plan was being tailored, but left its formulation entirely in the hands of Schlesinger and a few technical experts. Even attempts by Carter's own staff to inject a broader set of concerns were rejected after they fought a costly battle to even get an audience with the president.[5] Though Carter tried to create an image of openness, partly by dispatching 450,000 letters inviting energy-policy suggestions, his plan was drafted secretly by nonpolitical technicians.

Lack of Participation Hurt Consensus-Building Efforts

This fact alienated not only the experts on Capitol Hill, who had spent years grappling with energy problems, but also special interest groups, private industry, and cabinet members with a relevant expertise who were not consulted. By Carter's own admission, he did not attempt to sell his plan to the Senate until September 1977. Even initiatives from legislators in agreement with the administration's policies were not supported; for example, Senator Edward Kennedy's moves toward horizontal divestiture (e.g. keeping oil companies out of coal and uranium ownership) were not taken up.[6] Civic leaders felt that liberal, urban, and civil rights organizations had also been excluded from Carter's policy development. Even the Department of Treasury complained because it was not consulted on proposed massive energy taxes. (The day the tax plan, drawn up by Schlesinger's staff, was announced, the administration could not describe its likely impact on American households.) Members of the Senate Finance Committee, who had also been neglected, were largely responsible for eliminating the NEP's crucial oil equalization and industrial energy users' taxes. The net result of these exclusions was that factions that had been overlooked felt no obligation to support the energy program in the congressional debates.

Added to accusations that Carter ignored experts when developing a plan that would affect nearly every phase of American life were complaints that insufficient and incorrect information about the plan was given out by White House staff. Even those within the administration did not know who had authority to speak for the program. Carter himself seemed confused about the impact of the plan. He began by calling his legislative efforts "the moral equivalent of war." But, within a week, he said these efforts would not really hurt the American standard of living and would increase employment.[7] Faulty briefings and general lack of coordination were attributed to Carter's personal negligence. There was little communication, for example, between the administration and the two filibustering senators who were working for Carter's original proposal—Howard Metzenbaum and James Abourezk. Abourezk remarked of Carter's staff members, "They don't know what we're doing and we don't know what they're doing . . . they say they're working but we don't know at what."[8] Even congressional staff and lobbyists friendly to the administration complained that there was no timely contact to address the needs and doubts of legislators. Also sharing the blame for the plan's failure was administration's ineffective lobbying effort.

Because the legislative package was written secretly and with great haste, it was riddled with technical errors. For example, some estimates and projections that provided the basis for Carter's proposals conflicted with each other. As the congressional examination uncovered these errors, confidence in the administration was progressively undermined. Major components of the plan were apparently inadequately researched. Congress's own support staffs arrived at several negative conclusions about Carter's plan. The General Accounting Office said, "It is somewhat incongruous to ask Congress to establish a set of national energy goals and then propose a national energy plan that is not expected to achieve them." The Congressional Budget Office accused the administration of being "overoptimistic" in its estimates of what the program would accomplish, and the Congress's Office of Technology Assessment said the Carter program "may not be strong enough to prevent oil imports from reaching levels that could threaten national security and economic stability."[9] A summary of programmatic criticism is displayed in Table 7.1.

TABLE 7.1
Congressional Agency Assessments of National Energy Plan Proposals

NEP Objective	*Criticisms by Congressional Agencies*		
	General Accounting Office	Congressional Budget Office	Office of Technology Assessment
1. Energy growth to less than 2% per year, 1978-1985	Skeptical of sectoral savings	—	Doubts sectoral and aggregate reductions
2. Cut gasoline consumption by 10% from 1977 levels	—	5% reduction might be achieved	NEP prediction too optimistic
3. Cut eventual oil imports to 6 million bbl/day	Imports of 10.3 million bbl/day will still be needed	Possible to reduce by 3.5 million bbl/day. Cut of 8 million bbl/day still needed	Domestic production insufficient to meet needs
4. Double proposed strategic oil reserves to 1 billion bbl	Doubts need, cost, and methods	—	—
5. Expand coal production by two-thirds, to over 1 billion tons/yr	Very unlikely	Unlikely	1.0 billion tons probable level
6. Insulate 90% of all buildings	—	—	70% could be achieved
7. Install solar energy in 2.5 million homes	—	775,000 homes more likely	Inadequate incentives

Source: See note 9.

Poor Congressional Relations

Carter's manner of dealing with Congress has also been faulted. The president's initial approach to working with Congress was to reach members through his influence on the public. Assuming a pedagogical stance, he made televised appeals that were designed to create the necessary public pressure on Congress for the enactment of his program. His mistake was relying on this approach to the exclusion of other possible methods of selling his program, particularly early and direct consultations with congressional leaders.

When Carter's appeals for quick and decisive action on the energy plan were generally ignored and he realized that Congress would not pass his plan in 1977, he invited key congressional figures from the Conference Committee to the White House, in an ineffectual attempt to break the House-Senate impasses on the legislation. Four months later he convened another closed meeting with similar objectives, which also failed to secure the plan's passage and alienated the many conferees who were not invited.

Carter's select and secret conferences were generally criticized, and Congressman Toby Moffett (D-Conn.) found them clearly in violation of House rules. Though Ludlow Ashley (D-Ohio), chairman of the House Ad Hoc Energy Committee, defended Carter's meetings as a necessary means of compromise because the Conference Committee proceedings had broken down, the House voted overwhelmingly to prohibit future closed meetings of select members of the committee. (Individual congressmen, however, continued to meet privately with the president in an attempt to arrive at some consensus that would allow passage of the National Energy Plan.)

Perhaps Carter's greatest mistake was inconsistency; working in bursts, he appeared to become interested in a problem, muster an effort toward its resolution, and then suddenly lose interest. For example he abandoned the energy scene for months between his urgent April appeal and a September 24 speech at Norfolk, Virginia, attacking the nearly victorious deregulation forces in the Senate.

The administration's cause was further weakened because its data analyses conflicted with those using different data bases and assumptions. Confronted with sharply diverging studies and estimates, it was impossible for Congress alone to know which one was correct. Its quandary was illustrated by Congressman Ashley's exasperation:

> Which of the estimates of future oil and gas would we be well-advised to put some stock in? Recently we have had the CIA, the UN, and the Stanford Research Institute give us rather widely different figures, to say nothing of the oil companies and indeed various federal agencies.[10]

The complex nature of the energy problem, combined with such conflicting and insufficient information, exceeded the capacity of rational policy formulation. In the absence of commonly accepted data, ideological considerations become the basis for decision making. Nowhere is this problem cast in sharper relief than in the conflict over natural gas policy during the Carter years.

Natural Gas

Natural gas has been especially problematical since a 1954 Supreme Court decision affirmed the authority of the Federal Power Commission (FPC) to regulate interstate transmission of gas (authority originally granted by Congress in 1938). Under FPC controls, interstate natural gas became an extremely cheap energy source, and consumers—including factories, utilities, and homeowners—availed themselves of great quantities of the clean-burning, readily transportable energy source. Although natural gas producers wanted price controls ended, these manifold consumers of the gas constituted a counter-lobby that pressed for the continuation of price controls. The struggle between these two forces has been continuous since 1954, but at one point, in 1956, attempts to deregulate natural gas prices nearly succeeded. Eisenhower vetoed the legislation because allegations of gas industry bribery and the outrageous behavior of the industry's lobbyists ired Eisenhower and, in his words, "their arrogant defiance . . . of acceptable standards" raised public skepticism about "the integrity of governmental processes."[11] Price regulations remained, and gas consumption boomed.

However, after years of huge increases in demand, shortages began developing in the late 1960s, but only of price-controlled interstate gas. The much more expensive intrastate gas, which was not price controlled, remained readily available, but only in those states that produced the gas.

Diverging Explanations for the Shortage

After more than thirty years of intermittent debate, natural gas shortages seemed finally to be forcing policy change. Yet, despite the consensus about the need to take some action, three diverging schools of thought competed to explain the cause for the gas shortage, and each had its own logic about how to solve the problem.

Some argued that price controls themselves were causing the shortage because they discouraged producers from searching for and marketing more gas; there simply was not enough profit in it. Hence one only need lift the controls and bountiful supplies would appear albeit at a higher price. Others said that producers expected price control to soon be eliminated, and consequently they would be foolish to sell their gas immediately, since much larger profits would be assured if they only waited. Thus rather than decontrols, prices must never be lifted, and this fact must be communicated to producers in certain terms. Knowing that they could not anticipate greater returns in the future, producers would bring their supplies to market and the shortage would be relieved. Finally, some saw the unpredictability of federal policy itself as discouraging production. There had been constant attempts to change natural gas policy in different directions; and, at seemingly any moment, the regulatory bodies or the courts could restructure the entire market. This uncertainty made it difficult for producers to anticipate future market conditions, discouraging them from entering the market or providing gas. The resolution of this problem would be to make a coherent, definitive policy and adhere to it regardless of changing circumstances. With uncertainty removed, supplies would be restored.

Each of these schools of thought had its own vociferous supporters, as well as facts and analyses to bolster it, but each also had its critics and skeptical studies attacking it. Without a clear consensus about what to do, Congress had foundered, and although both President Nixon and President Ford proposed decontrol measures, it was President Carter who finally altered the status quo.

The Carter plan proposed that the price of natural gas be allowed to rise with some control retained, that industrial natural gas use should be taxed to encourage its substitution by coal, and that federal controls be extended to include all natural gas. While this plan did allow higher prices, it also represented an unprecedented expansion of controls, not only over new categories of gas but also over its manifold uses; natural gas would now be regulated all the way from "wellhead to burner tip."

This step was in keeping with Carter's policy of seeking social equity through governmental intervention in the marketplace, but still relying on various market mechanisms to operate within governmentally mandated restraints and incentives. Supporting the third school of thought on gas shortages, the National Energy Plan sought to "guarantee price certainty" to producers, and this predictability was intended to help resolve the supply situation.

Congress Faults Carter's Approach

Despite the fanfare at its launching, the Carter program was greeted with criticism; and in spite of the consensus that something needed to be done, several features made progress on a natural gas policy exceedingly slow. In part, there were problems with Carter's overall presentation of the plan and the strategy he pursued to move it through Congress. In addition to the inconsistencies and technical problems of the overall energy plan, the natural gas portion was uniquely problematical: while most of the plan was designed to force energy consumers to face higher prices, this portion sought to shield consumers and in general keep gas prices low.

The voice of the people is often a guide for congressional action. Although whether or not public opinion can directly influence the course of legislation has been a matter of hot scholarly debate, there is little question that in either case reliance on constituent sentiment for a solution to natural gas issues would be of little use during this period. Public opinion polls showed that while the public wanted action on energy problems, there was no coherent or consistent attitude about what steps ought to be taken. Meanwhile, public concern waned as the months of debate wore on and energy supplies seemed plentiful.

Economic interest groupings were also disarrayed. One key group, the "independent'' small and medium-sized natural gas companies, were outraged by the proposal, which they saw as a sellout of Carter's preelection promise to decontrol gas prices. They organized their own lobbying effort, the Natural Gas Supply Committee, that scored some important victories. However, the larger companies, many of them integrated with oil companies, either did not publicly oppose the Carter plan or in some instances gave it lukewarm support. The reasons for this seemingly surprising support were that many larger companies, would do reasonably well under the Carter proposal and even better by the subsequent compromises devised by Congress, often at the expense of independents who stridently opposed the plan. Large companies felt they could only profit by progress and lose by stalemate.

While unhappy with Carter's original plan, public interest groups generally rejected outright the subsequent compromise. They considered it "regressive" and excessively favorable to the producers. They may have been forced into this position since they were wedded to a civic balance theory which required their opposition to anything seeming to favor "big business." Moreover, many groups—such as labor unions, manufacturers, public utilities, and agricultural organizations—had benefitted from low natural gas prices so they historically had worked to halt any deregulation attempts.

Explanations Change, Alignments Shift

By the 1970s, with spreading natural gas shortages and with natural gas utilities declining to accept new customers, these traditional beneficiaries of low-cost gas began questioning whether the price controls were endangering their vital supplies and generally adding to unemployment and other economic problems. Although the opinion leadership of various interest groups enjoying cheap gas had been gradually shifting their positions, it took most by surprise when the National Association for the Advancement of Colored People (NAACP) suddenly endorsed natural gas price deregulation. This move signalled the breakup of the heretofore monolithic institutional front, which had remained solidly procontrol over the years. As a result, attempts by various legislators to divine public desires and heed the urgings of powerful interest groups became difficult due to the latter's disorganization. Further, without external cues, those in Congress had to rely more on their personal, committee, and party resources for guidance.

This was even more the case because the economic benefits to one's district—a traditional source of policy direction—was, in the case of gas price controls, being reexamined. In part, this was due to the unpredictable impact of various proposed solutions to the natural gas shortages (a subject of increasing controversy), and also due to the spread of doubts among the states as to the most economically profitable (for themselves) course of action. This historical pattern was that regional interests had dictated many legislators' positions on natural gas (as well as numerous other issues) with the South-western gas producers favoring price deregulation and the Northeast consuming states opposing it. However, the natural gas shortages forced many of those opposing decontrol to reconsider their position while uncertainty spread as to what would really be the costs and benefits of continuing price controls and which policy course would actually be in the best interests of a member's district or state. Statistical analysis of the relationship between a state's energy attributes and its congressional representatives' voting on natural gas legislation bears out the fact that, outside of the Southwest, no consistent pattern emerged in the 1977-78 voting on natural gas deregulation. In other words, whether a state consumed much or little price-regulated gas, and whether it was a net energy producer or consumer, had no statistically significant impact on the gas deregulation votes of its representatives.[12] The breakup of the stable coalition of gas-consuming states further deranged both the traditional coalition on natural gas policy and destroyed important signposts used by legislators to guide their voting decision.

Many in Congress sought factual explanations both for the causes of the gas shortage and the potential impact of various proposals. As is so often the case, the experts disagreed even among those who supported nearly identical positions. Further, experts would change their own interpretations and opinions as time passed. A case in point were various studies by the U.S. Geological Survey, the Colorado School of Mines, and MIT, each of which came up with widely varying predictions about the amount of natural gas left to be tapped. Illustrations abound of congressional confusion on the impact of natural gas legislation. Senator Lowell Weicker (D-Conn.) exasperatedly summed up the feelings of many when he said of the Carter proposal: "Nobody knows the consequences . . . including those at the Department of Energy, and certainly including those at the White House."[13] Unable to rely on any external source of guidance, it seems that most members of Congress fell back on ideology to inform their natural gas policy position. Conflicting opinions about how best to serve the public's interest and one's own constituents made compromise exceedingly difficult. The wonder is not that consensus building took so long, but rather that it was ever attained.

Leadership Lacking

Because the congressional system does not require a reconciliation of conflicting goals, coherent energy legislation has been difficult to enact. In fact, as Walter Goldstein asserts, the U.S. "political system was not equipped to implement such an ambitious and sweeping design" as Carter's team had devised. He writes, "The NEP is only the latest casualty of a political system that was intentionally fragmented in its institutions and 'pluralist' in applying veto sanctions."[14]

The Department of Energy, newly created in 1977, reflected this general fragmentation in its inability to implement and coordinate comprehensive energy policy. Secretary Schlesinger admitted that he had not been able to achieve the degree of organizational unity and cooperation within his department that he wanted, primarily because of problems created by several formerly independent agencies being combined into a single new one. Schlesinger's resulting inability to act as a representative voice for the new department eroded his potential for influencing Congress to pass the NEP. Also, failing to consult with other federal agencies and departments which had some authority over Carter's plan, the Department of Energy developed policy that was in some cases contrary to the administration's overall policy. These weaknesses blunted the major tool of using the bureaucracy to influence congressional consideration of the energy program.

It can be questioned whether indeed a democracy is capable of unified action necessary to enact and implement policy as wide-ranging and complex as any interventionist energy program for the United States must be. One of democracy's only means of forcing public recognition of an unpleasant truth is leadership, which had been seriously eroded in many crucial areas when Carter attempted to enact his 1977 energy policy.

Indeed, the difference between the Senate's and House's handling of the NEP is one primarily of leadership. Because of its superior leadership, the House had been able to concentrate on the legislation under consideration instead of on questions of organization as the Senate was forced to do; at the same time, the House's version of the energy plan did not show slavish acceptance of administration policy. If presidential leadership had functioned during 1977 similarly to that in the House, perhaps members of Congress who were sympathetic toward the energy plan would have supported it whether they had been personally consulted during its formation or not. On the other hand, when Carter became president, the office had lost considerable prestige as a result of the Watergate scandal and Richard Nixon's resignation. Congress at the same time was hoping to consolidate the influence over the executive branch it had gained during the Ford administration. Rhetorically at least, it was asserting itself. But even then it spoke not as one voice but as many, and not over issues of national and international significance, but over ones involving parochial interests. Carter worked himself into a no-win position in relation to Congress, which attacked him for showing both too little and too much leadership.

When presidential leadership fails, it is incumbent on Congress itself to demonstrate leadership by substituting appropriate legislation for presidential proposals that are not viable. But Congress can only do this when it has strong leadership and the American people recognize the need for such policy and will demand its creation. If sufficient pressure is placed on Congress and the president, both will respond with leadership and policies adequate for the times. Yet this situation rarely occurs, especially in peacetime. Consequently the president must exercise leadership and use the levers of power at his disposal to build consensus if the nation is to make progress on divisive issues.

Senate majority leader Robert Byrd, Jr., expressed this sentiment. Urging his colleagues to maintain open minds while considering the NEP so that special interests would not prevent unity, he warned however that the 535 members of Congress, "representing all crosscurrents of opinion and pressure," would not be able to provide leadership in the energy battle. "Only one man, under the Constitution, can provide that kind of leadership," he maintained, and that was the president. But Byrd placed responsibility for eliciting this leadership on Americans as a whole: "In the final analysis whether the problem is properly dealt with will basically depend on how the people out in the country perceive it, in Paw Paw, West Virginia, and Plains, Georgia."[15]

Overview

Carter succeeded in enunciating an integrated, comprehensive national energy plan but failed in having it fully implemented. It was the first systematic attempt to create order in the chaotic energy situation. But implicit and apparently false assumptions undergirded it.

Structural Errors

The extraordinary length of the proposed legislation—530 pages—and its breadth which quantitatively covered every aspect of energy production and use, militated against the plan's acceptance. The scope of the legislation was staggering. Its original intent was the government-directed transfer of billions of dollars, part being returned to the consumer and the rest used to pursue politically desirable goals. However, the exact size and mechanics of such transfers were not clarified; they would have required a vast modification of the industrial sector with the redesign or reevaluation of nearly every item sold in the United States.[16]

A large part of the program had been constructed upon data processed through the Federal Energy Administration's Project Independence Evaluation System, which had been devised and utilized by the Ford administration and used in developing the Energy Policy and Conservation Act. However, for reasons of political expedience, the Carter administration altered some of the model's formulae and assumptions, causing charges of manipulated data and weakening the strength and integrity of Carter's propositions.[17]

Another structural weakness of the program was its many internal contradictions between stated objectives and actual content, which though they were exaggerated for political gains, could not be easily dismissed. To illustrate, Carter officials adopted an hypothesis that contradicted economic theory, predicting that although energy prices would be reduced for homeowners, energy demand would also be reduced. The likelihood of such a backward-sloping demand curve occurring was remote.

The result of such structural problems was that Carter's plan vastly over-reached itself in an attempt to include too much, and was ultimately unconvincing. Its lack of clarity and consistency lent credibility to its opponents while alienating its supporters.

Strategic Errors

Strategic errors, such as having the plan constructed in hasty secrecy by technocrats isolated from the broader concerns of special interests, have already been enumerated. In addition the White House misjudged badly the public mood and the malleability of Congress and special interest groups. While there were indications, seized upon eagerly by the White House, that American opinion was shifting toward a less materialistic, more frugal attitude, this change proved ephemeral. Ultimately, the public was dubious of conservation as a substitution for a strategy that would yield plentiful energy supplies.

When the Carter staff sensed the error in its assumptions, it changed its position from warning of the hardships imposed by the program to reassuring the public of its painlessness. This complete reversal increased the skepticism that had greeted Carter's program. In retrospect, it has become obvious that the energy plan would have fared better if it had emphasized production rather than conservation.

The danger of Carter's erroneous perception of the public's attitude toward energy was increased by Americans' deep-seated doubt of the reality of an energy crisis. A main thrust of the administration's public relations effort was toward convincing the public and Congress that the world was indeed running out of energy and would soon face the real crisis, which could only be averted by personal sacrifice. Public doubt about the existence of an energy crisis caused Carter to overstate his case; worse, a highly publicized worldwide oil glut occurred during the same time NEP hearings were being held.

Another of Carter's misjudgments concerned the extent to which he could appeal to the people over the heads of Congress. He assumed that the presidency was invested with great prestige by the American people, whose trust could therefore be exploited to enlist support for his program.

Finally, Carter's planners badly calculated the pivotal role of special interest groups. Expecting to arouse strong antipathy toward them, Carter launched his unprecedented attacks on "war profiteering" and "rip-offs" by special interests, especially oil companies. But this provoked a backlash of sympathy for Carter's targets and worry that the president was unfairly exaggerating their behavior. Every interest group had its representatives in Washington, and singling out one sector for stinging criticism aroused concern as a dangerous precedent and unwarranted intrusion in business-as-usual.[18]

Carter's practice of offending business and industry groups while alienating consumers and environmental groups prevented the formation of a center around which support could be marshalled. No group supported his entire legislation; instead they emphasized their special concerns independently of any coordinated approach. The resulting isolation of congressional leadership and limitation of the White House's power effectively removed the Carterites' control over legislative development. The work of special interest coalitions resulted in the weak policy framework known as the National Energy Act.

Presidential Qualities

The ultimate source of many of these problems can be traced back to President Carter himself. He combined the rational, analytic, concrete predisposition of an engineer with the transcendental faith, moral certitude, and philosophical arrogance of a southern preacher. Embodying both positions, he often seemed to suffer from the weakness inherent in them rather than benefit from their strengths. It is with head-shaking incredulity that one hears the president's response to an interviewer who asked: "Do you have any doubts? About yourself? About God? About life?" Carter's answer: "I can't think of any."[19]

This "born again" self-righteous attitude helps explain the failure of his energy program. The energy problem represented for Carter a fundamental challenge to the American people's moral worth, as evidenced in his July 15, 1979 address, where he told of the "invisible threat" striking at "the very heart and soul and spirit of our national will," which was a crisis of confidence evidenced by the lack of tough, morally inspired public action on energy. With only slight hyperbole, it can be asserted that for Carter the American people represented a giant soul that needed saving, and he was just the man to do it.

Behind this transcendental message of inspiration was the mind of an accountant. A prodigious worker, Carter adhered to a mechanistic world of inputs and outputs and of cost/benefit tradeoffs. He believed strongly in the possibility of social engineering and morally imbued pragmatism, at times espousing Bentham-like utilitarianism, always holding the "people's" best interests (the greatest good) in mind.

The government was to be the instrument of this morally inspired redirection of activities. Carter would replace the nineteenth-century concepts of "free markets" with a government-directed program (perhaps inspired by seventeenth-century social philosophy). Unrestricted freedom of choice would have to make room for a higher authority's moral guidance. The functions of setting prices, regulating performance, distributing wealth, assuring equity, preserving the environment, and protecting future generations would all be moved from the hands of producers and consumers (to the extent it resided there) and invested in those of ambitious "mandarins" who control public institutions.[20] Moral instruction and value-oriented pragmatism were to be the order of the day for the government, leaving industry to scramble as best it could to toe the new line.

Yet, in terms of designing policy and building programs, there was an important gap between Carter the preacher and Carter the engineer. He had the tools and the technocrats and he had the firmly held moral convictions, but no way to link the two, and no way to make a decision between two equally worthy goals. Competing claims and conflicting choices caused Carter to send to his supporters and opponents many mixed signals, and he continued to break his promises and change course in midstream. Perhaps Carter was only the product of an American value system which emphasizes moral rectitude, a special mission, and practical know-how. He had learned to be a manager and operate mechanical systems. But as a leader he failed, for he did not know how to lead, guide, persuade, and (often overlooked) chastise others. Carter relied on his experts (who were to create the perfect plan); on his pollsters (who were to monitor and report on the flow of national moods, needs, and responses); and on his media experts (who were to provide the right touch to achieve the right effect). However, the manager's beautiful machine became merely a petard upon which was hoisted Carter and the NEP. The failure of leadership meant that Carter's successor, Ronald Reagan, would have less resistance to devolving the national energy policy structure.

Notes

1. *New York Times*, November 14, 1978, p. D1.
2. U.S. General Services Administration, *Public Papers of the Presidents of the United States: Jimmy Carter, 1977* (Washington, D.C.: U.S. Government Printing Office, 1978), pp. 1985-86.
3. U.S. Congress, House Ad Hoc Committee on Energy, "National Energy Act," hearings, May 5, 1977, pp. 118-82.
4. *Public Papers: 1977*, p. 1783.
5. James L. Cochrane, "Carter Energy Policy and the Ninety-fifth Congress," in Craufurd D. Goodwin, ed., *Energy Policy in Perspective* (Washington, D.C.: Brookings, 1981), p. 589.
6. There had been repeated attempts at both horizontal and vertical divestiture of the oil companies. Although the issue received significant attention in 1975 and especially 1976, Carter was loath to address the issue until he had his energy package safely through Congress. Consequently, the issue has remained buried after the defeat of divestiture forces in 1976. See *Oil and Gas Journal* (July 4, 1977): 30.

7. *Washington Post*, December 14, 1977, p. A-4.
8. Congressional Quarterly, *Energy Policy* (Washington, D.C.: CQ Press, 1979), p. A-3.
9. U.S. General Accounting Office, "An Evaluation of the National Energy Plan," EMD-77-48, July 25, 1977; U.S. Congress, Congressional Budget Office, "President Carter's Energy Proposals: A Perspective," 2nd ed., staff working paper, June, 1977; U.S. Congress, Office of Technology Assessment, "Analysis of the Proposed National Energy Plan," August 1977. See also U.S. Congress, Ad Hoc Committee on Energy, "Briefing on the National Energy Act," committee print no. 5, June 7, 1977.
10. Ad Hoc Energy Committee, p. 152. See also *National Journal* (July 9, 1977): 1068.
11. *Public Papers of the Presidents of the United States: Dwight D. Eisenhower, 1956* (Washington, D.C.: U.S. Government Printing Office, 1958), p. 256.
12. Pietro Nivola, "Energy Policy and the Congress: The Politics of the Natural Gas Policy Act of 1978," *Public Policy* 28 (Fall 1980): 512.
13. Ibid., p. 533.
14. Walter Goldstein, "Politics of U.S Energy Policy," *Energy Policy* 2 (September 1978): 187. See also Milton Russell, "U.S. Energy Policy Options," *Materials and Society* (1978), pp. 113-17.
15. *New York Times*, April 21, 1977, p. B8.
16. John Hill, "An Assessment of the Carter Administration's Proposed Energy Program," *Natural Resources Lawyer* 10 (1978): 615-23.
17. Barry Commoner, *The Politics of Energy* (New York: Knopf, 1979), ch. 6.
18. Kevin Phillips, "The Energy Battle: Why the White House Misfired," *Public Opinion* 1 (May/June 1978): 13.
19. Interview with President Jimmy Carter, televised on Public Broadcasting System, October 31, 1980.
20. Irving Louis Horowitz, "Social Science Mandarins: Policymaking as a Political Formula," *Policy Sciences* 1 (Fall 1970): 180.

8
Congress and Carter's Second National Energy Plan

Carter's second National Energy Plan (NEP II), launched in 1979 despite the setbacks suffered by his earlier plan, contained three major initiatives: an Energy Mobilization Board for setting energy development projects on a "fast track" that would cut bureaucratic delays and red tape, the Synthetic Fuels Corporation—a multibillion dollar effort to foster development of alternative sources of oil largely by tapping coal and shale oil—and a massive windfall profits tax on decontrolled oil, to pay for the Synthetic Fuels Corporation. This tax was the largest single-item tax measure ever passed by Congress and was designed to recapture part of the difference between the controlled price of oil, which would be lifted in 1981, and the much higher world price. Overall, NEP II was more successful than the earlier NEP.

Background

After the gruelling battles over energy policy in the first two years of the Carter administration, the second half of the first term was expected to be a period of relative calm when the Ninety-fifth Congress's achievements in energy policy could be consolidated, diminished though they were. The Energy Department was especially in need of respite in order to organize structurally. However, the Carter administration's plan to carefully and thoughtfully construct a second stage of national energy policy was swallowed by external events far beyond U.S. control.

There had been little in Carter's third State of the Union Address, economic report, or budget message to indicate that energy would be a major priority for the administration in 1979. Price decontrol was not mentioned, though the documents encouraged solar energy development and warned against foreign oil dependence. The seriousness of the growing world oil shortage caused by the revolution in Iran was not immediately recognized, because the United States received merely 5 percent of its imported oil from Iran. However, when the Iranian-induced shortfalls cascaded dramatically and caused the second major world oil shock, gas lines appeared throughout the nation and gasoline prices shot skyward.

When increasing dissatisfaction in Congress over the energy situation forced the administration to take action, Carter made his second national address on energy, prepared in great part by the interagency task force under the direction of the White House Domestic Policy Staff. Despite its almost overwhelming number of proposals and actions, this April 5, 1979 speech presented Carter's former position unchanged: U.S. oil prices must be raised to world levels to discourage consumption, but oil companies must be prevented from unfairly reaping profits. Acting under the authority of the 1975 Energy Policy and Conservation Act, Carter would begin decontrol on June 1, 1979, and all controls would expire on October 1, 1981. In the same speech, but without directly linking his request to the decontrol measure, Carter urged Congress to pass a windfall (excise) tax on oil to recapture "huge and undeserved" profits.[1] (The fate of this proposal is discussed in a later section of the chapter.)

The accident at Three Mile Island nuclear plant, the lines of motorists awaiting gasoline, the tense world oil market, and international economic summit meetings combined to keep energy a primary administration concern. Demonstrating his expressed interest in solar and renewable energy, Carter sent the first presidential solar energy message to Congress on June 20, 1979, and with considerable publicity dedicated a new solar water-heating system for the White House. He proposed that 20 percent of the nation's energy needs be provided through solar sources by the year 2000, and called for an ambitious series of solar aid programs to achieve this objective. Despite the encouragement that these proposals represented, the modest funding increases they were given by the administration showed that solar energy at best was a moderate priority.

In fact, oil was the Carter administration's major energy interest. But more fundamentally, Carter was becoming increasingly convinced that energy represented a crucial turning point for the United States, and that only drastic action might save the nation from permanent decline. Chief domestic policy adviser Stuart Eisenstat recommended that Carter use the energy crisis to galvanize Americans to action and divert the blame for energy problems from himself to OPEC.[2]

Carter mysteriously postponed an energy speech planned for July 5 and, after holding a domestic summit meeting with opinion leaders at Camp David, spoke dramatically to the nation on July 15, calling for a "restoration of American values" and common purpose, and a counteraction to the deepening national despair. He presented energy problem-solving as a key test of national unity and a "standard around which we can rally." Responding to what he termed a "loss of confidence in the future," Carter sought to allay the public's anxiety by outlining a massive energy program.[3] His plan included immediately levying import quotas; requiring utilities to burn coal instead of oil over the next decade; a solar bank; an Energy Mobilization Board to cut through the red tape which delayed domestic energy projects; a government Energy Security Corporation to bankroll synthetic fuels (synfuels) production; new tax and conservation incentives; and presidential authority to ration gasoline.

To many, however, these initiatives were mere palliatives disguising more fundamental problems that could be overcome only by strong national leadership. Yet while Carter was attempting to lead a fractured, demoralized administration into an all-out, wide-ranging battle over energy policy, the general response to his July 15 speech indicated that he would not succeed in turning the energy issue as a whole to his political advantage. The *New Republic*'s acerbic attack was typical of the criticism being directed at NEP II:

> Carter has taken every half-baked scheme he could find and lumped them all together in an incoherent mass, hoping at once to satisfy every powerful interest group with a stake in energy, to give the electorate the impression that he has taken bold and decisive action, and to avoid causing consumers the slightest pain.[4]

The Energy Mobilization Board

One of the most controversial elements of Carter's plan was his proposed Energy Mobilization Board (EMB). Critics considered its rationale, which was to expedite the process of launching vital domestic energy projects by slashing through bureaucratic obstacles, "clever sophistry" to conceal a "power grab."[5] Their concern was based on EMB's power to impose time limits for regulatory decisions on projects classified "critical energy facilities," take over the state and local agencies' decision-making powers if timetables were not met, and waive environmental regulations. Once construction was under way, the EMB could also override other legal delays, unless public health or safety were "unduly endangered." Any judicial review of the EMB's decisions would be bound by a strict timetable.

Environmentalists particularly feared the threat posed by the board to air and water quality laws. The EMB could also waive procedural requirements of federal, state, and local laws that guarantee citizen access to information on and participation in planning.

Although the president affirmed his desire to protect the environment, his proposals concerning the EMB had alienated many of his supporters. Congressman Toby Moffett (D-Conn.), who had been present at the Camp David summit meeting in July, remarked, "Clearly Carter has changed. There's been a backing away from conservation and social equity." Leaders of eleven major national public citizen organizations called a press conference to attack the EMB concept as threatening "not only environmental laws" but also laws that affect the public's rights in "every segment of society: business, labor, consumers, farmers, ranchers, native Americans," as well as the railroad, trucking, and local and state government sectors.[6] David Bower, president of Friends of the Earth, called the proposals "simplistic and dangerous. They threaten to unravel the basic principles of our government; government by law; equal justice . . . checks and balances, and the delegation of authority between the states and the federal government."[7]

There was general concern in Congress that Carter's proposal transferred too much power to the president. As a result, both the House and Senate requested a voice in specific board decisions, although some feared this would only replace procedural and legal red tape with the legislative variety. The House Subcommittee on Energy and Power asked that both houses be given a veto over EMB actions, while the Senate suggested congressional approval of major EMB decisions. Although Carter assured Congress that there would be checks on the board's authority to waive environmental procedures, to complete a "critical energy facility" the board could override a variety of rules, even those dealing with air pollution (subject to presidential veto and limited judicial review). Meanwhile, there had been an effort in Congress to establish a board similar to the EMB before Carter's announcement, and some members wanted to go beyond the White House position with a tougher EMB.

Congress Takes the Initiative

Consensus building on the issue was slow; congressional and energy industry representatives had difficulty identifying their spokesmen within the White House, because responsibility for ongoing policy information on the EMB was diffused. When the president began his lobbying attempt to swing an independent Congress to his side, the Energy Department was being reorganized by its new chief, Charles W. Duncan, Jr., and political voices and views were multiplying. As a result, Carter not only forfeited what his advisers had billed as "another chance to show [himself] as a man on top of his job and in charge of his staff,"[8] but lost control of the EMB issue. Congress once again seized the initiative and did not return it.

During mark-up in the Senate Energy Committee on September 19, the EMB was empowered to override substantive state and federal law, except when such an override would "unduly endanger public health or safety." This reflected the president's desire that the agency's override power not be totally unrestricted.

The Energy Mobilization Board legislation was the first part of the president's energy program to reach the Senate floor, and was initially approved largely intact. Rejecting amendments which would have added to or diminished the EMB's power, the Senate approved the Energy Mobilization Board (68-25) on October 4. The passage of the EMB bill without major changes was facilitated by the White House-endorsed efforts of private lobbyists from corporate and organized labor to enlist senators' support for the original bill. In the Senate version the EMB, consisting of a chairman and three members appointed by the president, would place certain energy projects with high priority status on a "fast track" by establishing and enforcing strict timetables for them. President Carter described the bill's Senate passage as "a major step forward in the joint effort to achieve energy security for our nation."[9] However, a coalition of fifteen Republicans, mostly conservatives, and ten Democrats, who were virtually all liberals, opposed the legislation. The Republicans were concerned about state and local governmental authority becoming subordinate to a federal instrument, the Democrats about the EMB's extensive power to override environmental laws.[10]

While the Senate's approval did not guarantee passage of Carter's whole program, it indicated that Congress viewed the energy situation as critical and conceded that governmental obstacles to certain kinds of industrial construction had become so insurmountable that specific mechanisms were necessary to overcome them. Further, despite the deep divisions that had characterized the Senate Energy Committee in the past, it was unified in support of its EMB bill, and this solidarity consistently discouraged attempts to defeat the EMB.

While the EMB's legislative journey in the Senate had been relatively simple, the House reported two widely varying bills. The first, from the House Interior Committee, made the EMB so weak as to be practically meaningless. In the second, from the House Commerce Committee, the board could recommend to the president the waiver of practically any law, and the president could accept the recommendation provided neither house of Congress objected. Carter reacted by protesting that he had not intended the EMB to have such broad authority, while his chief domestic policy advisor, Stuart Eisenstat, supported the Commerce Committee's version, demonstrating the confusion over the EMB proposal in the White House. Eisenstat then stated that the administration wanted the bill which was originally submitted to Congress, empowering the board to override substantive laws only with regard to plants already under construction. Carter added that he did not intend the board to have the power to preempt substantive laws, particularly those on environmental standards. Congressman John D. Dingell (D-Mich.), sponsor of the Commerce Committtee bill, observed: "After the last couple of days, I find it difficult to ascertain the administration's position on anything. The administration has the capacity to surprise its friends and please its enemies."[11]

The White House Deserts Its Supporters in the House

For a time, it appeared that a consensus in the House supported Carter's position of wanting a stronger EMB than was provided for by the House Interior Committee, but the Commerce Committee's measure was a problem.

The key issue was whether Congress would permit the waiving of substantive federal and state laws in order to hasten the development of energy projects. A compromise bill, offered by Congressman Morris Udall (D-Ariz.), chairman of the House Interior and Insular Affairs Committee, and supported by a bipartisan group of House conservationists, would have made the EMB more powerful than the House Interior Committee's version, but would have eliminated the controversial override clause included in the House Commerce Committee's version. While Udall hoped to win broad approval by basing his proposal on White House specifications, he found the administration had changed its position. Although claiming neutrality, the administration noted that it favored Dingell's amendment over Udall's, since it allowed fewer opportunities for delays through judicial challenges.

Udall's move was defeated 191-215, as was a proposal by Congressman Robert C. Eckhart (D-Tex.) to eliminate substantive override authority from the Dingell bill. Although Carter had indicated his strong support of Eckhart's amendment, it was clear that administration lobbyists had deserted Udall. Udall's embarassment was compounded because his position was much closer to Carter's "official" position than was Dingell's, which Carter tacitly supported. Carter aides explained that they supported Dingell in order to obtain a stronger bargaining position in the conference committee which could inevitably settle conflicts between the House and Senate versions of the EMB. However, the administration assured environmental and western groups which opposed a strong EMB that it would return to its original position in conference.[12]

Environmental, public interest, and state groups lobbied unsuccessfully to curtail the board's override and waiver. They were particularly concerned that the board's power—to recommend to the president waiving federal law in order to expedite construction of an energy project—could allow override of federal clean air or water standards or permit construction in national parks. League of Women Voters' president Ruth Hinerfield said that, although her organization supported an EMB, it was "dangerous to allow a potentially narrowly focused group to run roughshod over our environmental laws and laws guaranteeing citizen participation in government." John Dingell countered these objections by asserting that without some limited override provision, the EMB could not succeed as a "fast track" agency in clearing the way for construction of synfuel plants and other energy projects. Congressman Jim Wright (D-Tex.) concurred that elimination of the override capability would "make shambles of any opportunity Congress might have to expedite energy projects."[13]

On November 1, 1979, the House approved creation of the Energy Mobilization Board by a vote of 299-107. The House's version differed from the Senate's in empowering the board to override substantive federal laws such as environmental guarantees with the consent of the president. Although this extension of power was not in the administration's original proposal, White House officials expressed general satisfaction with the legislation.

The conference to resolve House-Senate differences was impeded by the tenacity of both extreme positions. After a stalemate of several months, there seemed to be no other course than to capitulate to the adamant Dingell, who insisted on some sort of substantive waiver position. The continuing deadlock was broken when Carter lobbyists made it clear that they would accept a bill in nearly any form. So enough votes were changed to give victory to the Dingell position. As a result, some members, including Udall and Eckhart, felt betrayed by the Carter administration, not only on the House floor but also in committee, when Carter failed to keep his promise not to support a substantive waiver. They therefore refused to sign the conference report, so that only the barest majority was secured. They also generated opposition in the House by suggesting that western and environmental interests had not been considered in the conference.

Udall and his associates had their revenge on Carter when the House expressed its dissatisfaction with the conference report and sent it back to committee, effectively killing the EMB measure. A pivotal role in this action was played by the Republicans, who, although initially providing support for the conference report, withdrew it when presidential candidate Ronald Reagan's opposition was seen as an opportunity to embarrass Carter in an election year by scuttling an important section of his energy package. Ironically, Carter in effect destroyed his own handiwork. Had he supported the Udall bill, or even remained neutral, it would in all likelihood have been passed by the House. Then the chances of stalemate in conference would have been minimized because the Senate bill, like Udall's House measure, had no substantive waiver so there would have been no controversy.[14]

Unresolved Questions

Many important questions concerning the EMB remain unanswered and could become crucial if other legislation should be devised in the wake of an energy emergency. Among these is the advisability of creating a new bureaucracy such as the EMB to cure the ills of an old bureaucracy. While this approach countered conventional wisdom and aroused public and congressional fear of intrusive and juggernaut-like government, it was consonant with Carter's emphasis on having governmental institutions balancing interests and guiding energy policy. Essentially, the EMB would have substituted the judgment of four presidential appointees (three part-time and not subject to the regular conflict-of-interest legislation) for that of independent federal, state, and local regulatory bodies, and could have prevented the application of federal and state laws. Nevertheless, despite Congress's reluctance to concede more power to the executive, especially the president, the Carter proposal passed both houses of Congress before it was stopped by the combined opposition of members concerned about states' rights, various state and county officials, and environmentally oriented groups.

Also, as the lobbying efforts of those favoring expanded energy projects became more intense, concern over health and environmental factors lessened, indicating that developmental concerns can eclipse environmental interests, and that for expediency fundamental protection laws can be set aside. It is also noteworthy that conservatives paid little attention to a bill that would concentrate power in the hands of a few Washington appointees until Ronald Reagan expressed his opposition.

Synfuels Controversy

Although the technology required for a synfuels industry had existed for decades, and synthetic fuel was one of the earliest fossil fuels used in quantity during the ninteenth century, its relatively high cost had interrupted its commercialization.[15] In 1975 and 1976, after the energy crisis and spiraling oil prices made the development of a large-scale synfuels industry seem viable with modest federal stimulation, President Ford proposed it. Although Ford's proposal was then rejected by Congress, the issue was reconsidered after the turmoil of 1979; the House approved legislation HR 3930, which was aimed at assuring synfuels producers a governmental market. In essence, HR 3930 extended federal aid to companies producing synfuels and mandated that the Defense Department purchase 500,000 barrels per day of synfuels by 1984.

Congressmen John Dingell and Richard L. Ottinger (D-N.Y.), however, opposed the synfuels bill, warning that it removed Congress's control over the financial aspects of the program. And congressional analysts predicted that with heavy government investment in plants and the wide discrepancy in price between synfuels and conventional oil and gas, the cost of the program would far exceed the original estimate. Nevertheless, the House rejected two amendments offered by Dingell to curtail authority in defense-related energy production and to remove the president's authority to command petroleum businesses to provide the government with synfuels. It also rejected amendments offered by Ottinger requiring congressional approval of large loan guarantees and contracts. Ottinger noted that the energy issue attracted some of the "largest and most voracious sharks . . . who would like to get their teeth into the federal treasury." Without congressional control, he commented, we are going to "roll out the barrel and damn the cost."[16]

Amendments proposed by Robert H. Michel (R-Ill.) and Morris Udall were also rejected. Michel's amendment, which involved funding the synfuels program from the windfall profits tax on crude oil, was opposed by House members who thought the linkage would prevent funding if the tax were not passed. Udall's proposal would have prohibited government purchasing of synfuels from the eight largest oil companies in order to discourage development of energy sources controlled by a few oil industry leaders.

The House Gets Synfuels Fever

However, enough synfuels program skeptics were finally won over by House enthusiasm and voted overwhelmingly in favor of HR 3930 on June 26, 1979, demonstrating Congress's vulnerability to an attractive idea of unknown merits and liabilities if it is accompanied by public agitation and a demand for action. Majority Leader Jim Wright remarked, "The public wants bold action. . . . The time has come for us to do everything within our power to break the stranglehold upon this country that foreign nations are asserting. . . . We are going to declare our energy independence."[17] Finally, without pause for a recorded vote, the House approved a proposal to quadruple the legislation's goal for synfuels production.

The bill, an amendment to the Defense Production Act of 1950, would require the government to encourage production of the equivalent of 500,000 barrels a day of synfuels by 1985 and 2 million barrels a day by 1990. The House further authorized $3 billion worth of synfuels price supports over the $2 billion recommended by the Banking Committee. The House version of the bill, however, ignored the means by which the program would be implemented.

To build a synfuels industry was only a secondary aim of the bill; its major purpose was to demonstrate national independence from oil imports so that OPEC could no longer raise prices with impunity. However, the coal and oil industries remained cool to the proposal, fearing government disruption of their operation.

Synfuels Enthusiasm Becomes Widespread

Despite estimates from the Congressional Budget Office that the measure would cost taxpayers $18-$22 billion, synfuels fever had hit Capitol Hill. In the Senate, Jackson pushed a synfuels bill (endorsed by fourteen of the nineteen members of his energy committee) for the construction of fifteen synfuels demonstration plants to the tune of $5 billion. The fever spread to the White House. In a breakfast meeting on June 1, 1979, Carter was convinced by congressional leaders to support the principle behind the House bill,[18] even though his second NEP, sent to Congress on May 7, 1979, foresaw only a modest synfuels industry and a minor government role in its development. After a period of soul-searching at Camp David, Carter decided to develop a synfuels program that would outreach the House measure. In his July 15 message, he proposed a massive commitment to develop the synfuels industry, offering as an impetus an $88 billion federal investment.

According to the president's plan, liquids and gases from coal, biomass and peat, oil shale, and "unconventional" natural gas were to provide a major alternative to imported oil, producing the equivalent of 2.5 million barrels of oil by 1990, when an estimated 30-40 plants would be operating. An Energy Security Corporation (ESC) would coordinate synfuels production. While previously Carter had found the estimated costs of synfuels production prohibitive ($27-45 a barrel compared with the OPEC oil at $22 per barrel), he now decided that most of the $88 billion investment, in the form of a trust fund, could be derived from the windfall profits tax on crude oil; an additional $75 billion private investment would be stimulated through tax credits.

Carter's proposed corporation would be an independent, government-sponsored entity, managed by a seven-member board of directors. The ESC would invest trust fund monies and could even establish government-owned and-operated synfuels plants, although the administration suggested that the ESC attempt instead to "maximize its leverage within the private sector." The corporation could offer price guarantees, contracts, direct loans, and loan guarantees. In his enthusiasm, Carter asserted, "Just as a similar synthetic rubber corporation helped us win World War II, so will we mobilize American determination and ability to win the energy war."[19]

Senator Jackson's support of a synfuels program notwithstanding, the Senate had not yet had the opportunity to consider either of the proposed synfuels measures. As a result, they referred the House-amended S 932, which contained the synfuels authorization, to the two committees having clearest jurisdiction over the synfuels program—Energy and Banking. These committees jointly reported two very different bills to handle synfuels.

The Senate Energy Committee proposed a massive program depending heavily on government intervention and including a synthetic fuels corporation which could own or operate plants. However, instead of the $88 billion requested by Carter, $20 billion would be provided in a first stage of the program and after three years, if Congress did not object, the other $68 billion would be authorized.

The Senate Banking Committee's more modest program did not include founding a corporation or government operation of synfuels plants. Subsidies would be limited to $3.9 billion in formal loan guarantees and price supports rather than direct outlays. Neither the Energy nor the Banking Committee's bills made use of a windfall profits tax.

The Senate, rejecting the Banking Committee's bill, adopted the Energy Committee's proposal on November 8, 1979. Before passing the program, however, the Senate changed certain aspects of it, creating a more general bill that encouraged conservation, gasohol, and solar energy by authorizing $13 billion toward these ends. These added provisions necessitated original work by the House conferees, but finally the Energy Security Act (PL 96-294), closely resembling the Senate version, was passed by the House by 317-93 on June 26, 1980. The measure was promptly signed by Carter.

Both Industry and Environmentalists Skeptical of the Program

Although the congressional victory for the synfuels program might suggest widespread support for the proposal in the energy industry, the industry, in fact, had attempted to halt the program, but was restrained by fear of public condemnation for advocating governmental noninterference.[20]

Before the Senate passed the synfuels bills there were attempts to mollify opponents, especially those in industry. In response to the concern of the oil companies (which dominated the synfuels industry) that government would be unfair competition for privately owned plants, senators suggested that the companies be given subsidies and tax advantages to induce them to develop substitute fuels. Furthermore, Carter agreed to withdraw the proposal that the Energy Security Corporation be given authority to build and operate plants with governmental funds.

Nevertheless, industry experts criticized the synfuels program as technologically premature and claimed that even with the creation of the Energy Mobilization Board—which would expedite construction of the plants—the existing laws restricting pollution would prevent companies from acquiring sites. In Senate testimony most experts endorsed a slower program, organized in stages, to prevent locking industry into tested but still ineffective technologies. A Senate Budget Committee consultant asserted that meeting the president's production goal of 1.75 million barrels a day would require "wartime effort and significant diversion from the rest of the economy." The Congressional Budget Office also endorsed a go-slow program to "provide information about costs . . . that would reduce the risks to both the private sector and the government in initiating a full-scale program."[21]

Environmentalists expressed concern about a hasty, massive commitment to developing a synfuels industry before its environmental and health effects were determined, especially since environmental impact statements and other provisions of the National Environmental Policy Act could be bypassed. They also claimed that the proposed Energy Security Corporation would place excessive emphasis on producing fossil-based synfuels. Due to the large investment of tax dollars and guaranteed private sector construction, they said, other innovative programs for developing renewable biomass synfuels sources would be neglected.

Although an Energy Department study released in July 1979 concluded that the production of up to 2 million barrels a day of synthetic fuel "appears feasible in terms of current environmental restraints," it also said that this level of production could create the following: violation of clean air laws due to pollution from the synfuels plants; heavy demand for water which could cause shortages in the West; production of tons of solid wastes including toxic materials; land disruption and water pollution from large-scale coal and shale mining; and production of carcinogens from coal liquification, endangering workers using or transporting the fuel.[22]

Windfall Profits

After two years of struggle by the Carter administration to bring U.S. oil prices up to world levels, the gap was wider than before, and the attempt to contain inflation impeded plans for removing price controls. Besides seeking an acceptable program to raise U.S. oil prices and cut imports, the administration had been attempting to reduce communication and coordination problems it had been having with its allies on Capitol Hill. After weeks of preparation, Carter announced his decision on April 5, 1979, to attack the economic problem of supplies by raising prices, and the political problem of windfall oil company profits by taxing them. He would exercise his presidential power to decontrol oil prices, admittedly a "painful step," and requested that Congress pass a tax that would take half of the oil companies' so-called windfall profits as U.S. oil prices rose to world levels. Appealing to the people rather than Congress, he called for a public outcry: "Unless you speak out" on behalf of the tax measure, warned Carter, the oil industry "will have more influence on the Congress than you do."[23] In line with his predisposition to equity, Carter wanted the tax to be used to aid low-income families, sponsor mass transit, and finance alternate-energy development, particularly of synfuels. However, Congress ultimately put the money in general revenues in order to directly control it, and, although Carter wanted a fixed rate of 50 percent on the oil profits, established a variable rate with numerous exceptions.

Public Reaction

Carter's proposal was immediately attacked by consumer groups and pro-control forces as leading to higher prices and massive profits for oil companies. Because it would reduce production and incentives, it was also condemned by the oil industry and its supporters, and others who wanted energy to be handled in a "free market."

The oil industry denounced the windfall tax as a perpetual excise tax levied on oil production, not on profits.[24] The industry maintained that all profits from decontrol were needed to finance the search for crude oil and that the $6 billion generated by Carter's plan would be "minimal" compared with the industry's own outlay to boost oil and gas production.[25]

While the oil producers were united in their opposition to the windfall profits tax, they did not present a monolithic front. Anxious to express their particular version of entrepreneurship and independence, smaller companies and "wild catters" joined the battle with their own lobbying effort. Jack Allen, president of the 5,000-member Independent Petroleum Association of America, expressed the attitude of the small oil companies: "We don't want to be tarred with the same brush as the oil majors."[26]

Despite the industry's protests, it was clear that decontrol would bring a bonanza of additional revenues to the oil companies. A Congressional Budget Office study estimated that they would receive an additional $82.9 billion by 1985, if real oil prices were to remain constant, and more if prices rose.[27]

External events reinforced and appeared to justify Carter's position. Much higher quarterly oil company profit reports coincided with White House oil policy pronouncements and congressional votes and also served to increase public support for punitive measures against the companies. In the days following the president's April 1979 speech, quarterly earnings reports profits were up between 40 and 80 percent. Summer profit announcements—showing even larger rises—increased pressure on the House to act favorably on Carter's proposal. Even the usually intransigent Senate Finance Committee was finally spurred to action by embarrassingly high third-quarter company profits.

Decontrol: The End of an Era

Carter's move to decontrol oil prices was unexpected and raised a sharp but brief storm of controversy. Although he attempted to shift the responsibility to Congress by claiming he was merely acting under existing law (the Energy Policy and Conservation Act, discussed in chapter 4, gave the president power to alter controls after a mandatory period lasting until June 1979), his decision to decontrol left the liberal Democrats in Congress, his purported allies, with no overarching leadership. Carter's failure to link the removal of price controls to the windfall tax measure was questioned. Apparently, though he considered doing so, he decided against it because it could cause congressional opponents of the tax measure to join forces with opponents of decontrol to defeat him.

The opposition in the House to Carter's decontrol measure proved largely symbolic. House Speaker Tip O'Neill, while supporting an extension of controls, admitted that he could not conceive of an extension being legislated. Procontrol members in the House Commerce Committee received no support from the Energy Subcommittee chairman Dingell, who finally conceded that there was insufficient support for controls in either the House or Senate. Toby Moffett and others in the Commerce Committee who fought for retaining price controls were consistently defeated, although the Democratic Caucus, in a nonbinding vote taken May 24, 1979, voted for retaining controls by a 2 to 1 margin. Finally, the House Democratic leadership averred to the president and, to avoid an enervating fight, kept proposals for continuing controls off the House floor until October, when support for such measures had died down.

In the Senate, supporters of continuing oil price controls fared even worse. Senator Edward Kennedy embodied the liberal proconsumer, prointervention position. He denounced price decontrol as "bad economic policy . . . bad energy policy, and . . . bad for the country." Reiterating Carter's contention that the tax proposal represented "a classic confrontation" between big industry and the people's interests, Kennedy went further:

> The overbearing power of the oil lobby has exerted its influence in two new and unacceptable ways. First, it has intimidated the Administration into throwing in the towel without even entering the ring on the issue of oil price decontrol. And, second, it has also intimidated the Administration into submitting a token windfall tax that is no more than a transparent fig leaf over the vast new profits the industry will reap.[28]

Yet, despite vociferous but scattered protests over Carter's decontrol move, the issue was not voted on in 1979 or 1980 in the Senate, where procontrol sentiment was even weaker than in the House. Energy Committee chairman Jackson admitted that even in his own committee most members favored price decontrol and that he did not have the votes to support his own procontrol sentiments.

The Windfall Profits Tax

Despite oil industry opposition, the House began work on Carter's tax proposal shortly after it was announced. The tax-writing Ways and Means Committee was the arena for the crucial fight over the plan. Liberal Democrats wanted to raise the percentage of the windfall tax, while Republicans wanted either no tax or a plowback provision requiring oil companies to invest their profits in energy exploration or production. Tax rates were raised but Republicans received no support for their plowback measure.[29]

When the Ways and Means proposal was on the House floor, it was ambushed by two committee members from petrobelt states. Jim Jones (D-Okla.) and Henson Moore (R-La.) proposed a substitute measure, which would reduce the tax and provide for its eventual termination in 1990. The substitute measure prevailed on June 18. However, to reduce maneuvering and conflict, Ways and Means chairman Ullman allowed the tax itself to be voted on without any stipulation about how the funds would be used, thus frustrating special interest groups who might fight for a share of the revenue and congressional committees that would contest jurisdictions over control of the spending plans. (This maneuver greatly speeded the legislative process but precluded holding hearings on how the money should be spent, and the question was never put to a vote.)

The Carter administration, unhappy about the laxness of the House measure, urged the Senate to be more exigent, hinting that price controls could be reimposed. However, Russell Long (D-La.), chairman of the Finance Committee and well known as a friend of oil and gas interests, had jurisdiction over the bill. (His effectiveness in eviscerating Carter's earlier proposals was discussed in the preceding chapters.) Long was resigned to having some tax because he feared without it Carter would withdraw his decontrol plan. He compared the inevitability of the tax to old age: "When you think about the alternatives, you don't feel so bad about it."[30] Even so, after months of delay, when his committee finally reported the bill on November 1, 1979, it was weaker than either Carter's proposal or the House measure. The revenues to be generated under the Long bill would be half those under the House measure and numerous exemptions had been included, although, as the president had requested, portions of the expected revenue were to be earmarked for various programs.

When the bill was reported in November, five Democratic and six Republican members of the Finance Committee filed a statement protesting its diluted form. While the bipartisan group declared most of the bill "fair," it claimed that "several special exemptions are allowed which are unjustified because they do not enhance production and because they significantly reduce badly needed revenue."[31]

This direct challenge to Long, unprecedented in his fourteen-year chairmanship, cannot be attributed to any decrease in his effectiveness as an individual senator. In fact, Long had protected his prerogatives of committee chairman far better than most. He not only conducted a majority of Finance Committee meetings himself, but saw to it that the subcommittee chairman, so powerful in the House, would have little formal authority, especially in drafting legislation. He was also more successful than most chairmen in having the committee's Democratic staff members work for him directly, in function if not in title. The committee staff regulated information flow so that it directly benefited Long, at times to the disadvantage of others. In accordance with his style, the committee's seating plan when bills were drafted placed members so that their aides and personal staff could not be immediately adjacent, thus reducing their ability to provide technical support and clarification of details. Also, by manipulating committee rules, Long could call meetings, structure debates, schedule bills, and control the order of amendments.

Considering Long's power and obvious talents, the mini-revolt of the eleven Finance Committee members demonstrates a basic change in the Senate itself. A Senate staffer suggests an aspect of this change: "The new committee members are smarter politically as well as analytically. They are trying to move the committee by force of argument, not by plea to the conscience, as often was the case in the past."[32] The causes and consequence of this change in Congress as a whole will be considered in later chapters.

Responding to the Finance Committee complaint and the unhappiness of the Carter administration over the watered-down windfall profits bill, Majority Leader Robert Byrd put tremendous pressure on other senators to stiffen it. Byrd and Finance Committee member Abraham Ribicoff (D-Conn.) offered an amendment that would also tax oil newly discovered or produced by expensive, technologically complex tertiary methods (e.g. injecting chemicals into wells). After failing to table the motion, Long and his supporters began a filibuster against it. After several attempts at cloture, a compromise was reached which softened Byrd's amendment but retained its basic form, including the tax on newly discovered oil. The Senate's amended bill was passed on December 17, 1979, by a margin of more than 3 to 1.

There was considerable speculation in both Houses over the amount of revenue that could be raised under the various proposals. Skirmishes broke out over the accuracy of predictions, which varied widely. That the question was more than academic was proven when Daniel P. Moynihan (D-N.Y.) had an amendment adopted by the Senate that would postpone a phaseout of the tax until 90 percent of an arbitrarily estimated yield of $210 billion had been collected. Thus, an arbitrary estimate of revenues would determine the duration and level of taxation.

Conference and Signing

A conference held to iron out differences between the House and Senate versions of the legislation made the usual compromises, often exactly at midpoint between the two competing measures. Controversy over three issues—taxation of newly discovered oil, exemptions for independent producers, and a termination point for the tax—delayed final agreement on the bill until March 1980.

On April 2, 1980, Carter signed PL 96-223, the Crude Oil Windfall Profits Tax Act, which differed from his original proposal in three important respects. Whereas Carter had requested a permanent tax, Congress chose a phaseout procedure that would end the tax in the early 1990s, depending on how quickly the $227.3 billion was raised. Second, while Carter wanted the funds placed in a special Energy Security Trust Fund and then apportioned to poor families, mass transportation, and alternative energy projects, Congress preferred to retain control over all windfall tax revenue by placing it in a general revenue fund. Finally, special, regional, and local influences managed to have Carter's proposed 50 percent rate changed to a highly variable rate with numerous exceptions.

Overview

Although Energy Department officials agreed with oil industry representatives that some production would be lost as a result of the tax, they also claimed that production would ultimately go up if price controls were removed. They also pointed out, in line with the general thrust of Carter's administration, that if decontrol was to be fair, it must be balanced by a windfall tax. Thus, one of Carter's last major energy initiatives at least expressed his concern for equity. However, another major aspect of his energy policy position—reliance on massive government activities to direct, encourage, or supplement energy-related activity, such as the Energy Security Trust Fund—was not included in the final legislation.

While Carter clung to these convictions throughout his tenure, he did reverse his position on price control. During his 1976 campaign, Carter doggedly insisted that price controls be retained on oil and gas, but after the election his administration proposed the Crude Oil Equalization Tax (COET, see chapter 6) and set October 1981 as the deadline for lifting controls, placing Carter squarely in the decontrol camp. Further, despite his constant vilification of the oil industry, Carter at least partly adopted its view that terminating price controls would provide companies with the necessary incentives to locate and produce oil.

This position change is partly attributable to the declining influence of Carter's circle of liberal advisors and the rising influence of technocratic advisors such as Energy Secretary Schlesinger, who became increasingly outspoken on the necessity of freeing energy companies from government control. An even more significant cause of the position change was a growing decontrol sentiment in Congress, where, although some held out for controls, the notion of price rollbacks had all but disappeared. In dialectical fashion, the liberals and free marketers arrived at the windfall compromise.

A final reason for Carter's position change was an apparent lack of feasible alternatives. It was generally believed that controls were necessary so that windfall profits would not be gathered by oil companies because of temporary increases in world oil prices. However, when oil rose to $7, $15, and finally $35 per barrel, and there seemed to be no hope of a quick technological solution, some action seemed mandatory. When no viable alternatives to price control offered themselves, short of a complete restructuring of the U.S. economic system, conventional wisdom began to caution that continuing controls merely aggravated shortages and energy policy problems in general.

Despite several congressional attempts to sabotage the windfall profits measure, its modest success ultimately proved to be the greatest legislative and domestic policy victory of Carter's administration.

Historical Reversal: Domestic Producers Subsidize Consumers

The two major thrusts of U.S. energy policy in the aftermath of the embargo merely increased oil importation from foreign sources, which Carter had identified as among the greatest threats to American security. First, price controls were a disincentive to domestic production and encouraged consumption by signalling "artificially" low prices to the consumer. Second, special programs passed by Congress to protect independent refiners required domestic producers to subsidize the refiners' importation of foreign crude. Meanwhile, the windfall profits were shipped abroad to foreign producers, aggravating balance of payment deficits. The essential consequences of these policies was that consumers and refiners of petroleum benefited at the expense of oil producers—a reversal of the pattern that held since the oil depletion allowance of 1928. It has been calculated that the costs of controls, including the administrative costs of regulations, were about $4 billion a year.[33]

In the contest over the distribution of wealth resulting from energy policy, two sectors of the oil industry were in competition with each other: crude oil producers and oil refiners. The Emergency Petroleum Allocation Act of 1973 and the Crude Oil Windfall Profits Tax Act of 1980 reduced profits oil producers would have received. The consequence of these and related acts was a U.S. petroleum policy that between 1973 and 1980 consciously favored all crude oil users (both consumers and refiners) over producers, through price controls and entitlements, which blocked the transfer of billions of dollars from users to producers.

According to statistical analyses,[34] congressional positions on energy pricing policy are determined by a combination of ideology and constituent's economic interests. To a large extent, the regulation of the petroleum industry was explicitly designed by Congress to redistribute wealth at the cost of economic efficiency and was therefore not the result of a conspiracy but rather of the coincidence of the interests of certain influential groups. Petroleum refiners, consumers, and liberals competed in policy contests with oil producers, conservatives and libertarians. The attack on the energy problem was indeed the moral equivalent of war, but it was a civil war.

But why did the coalition of liberal-consumer-refiner interests, which had predominated in the policy contest for five years, lose to the producer-conservative coalition? In part, the loss was another manifestation of the larger ideological shift toward the right which culminated in Ronald Reagan's conservative victory in 1980. Another reason was the success of the argument that the inefficiency of price controls and regulations caused widespread economic damage and dislocation, and that pursuing distributional goals through energy policy reduced the total amount of benefits to all. The structural reason is explored in chapter 10.

Notes

1. U.S. General Services Administration, *Public Papers of the Presidents of the United States: Jimmy Carter, 1979* (Washington, D.C.: U.S. Government Printing Office, 1980), p. 610.
2. Elizabeth Drew, "Phase: In Search of Definition," *New Yorker* (August 27, 1979): 45-73. See also *New York Times*, October 14, 1979, p. D7.

3. For details of the program, see *Public Papers*, pp. 1235-41. For a discussion of the public relations campaign, see "Carter at the Crossroads," *Time* (July 23, 1979): 20-23. Shortly after this speech, Carter fired cabinet officials, including Energy Secretary James Schlesinger.
4. "A Cowardly Failure," *The New Republic* (August 4, 1979): 6.
5. *Washington Post*, October 14, 1979, p. D7.
6. "Perspective: Jimmy Carter: Anti-environmentalists," *Audubon* (September 1979): 9.
7. *New York Times*, September 2, 1979, p. 4.
8. Drew, *Phase*, op. cit.
9. *New York Times*, October 5, 1979, p. D1.
10. M. A. Conant, "Hopes for Long Awaited EMB," *Petroleum Economist* 46 (December 1979): 500; "Senate Decides on Its Version of EMB," *Public Utilities* 104 (October 25, 1979): 39-40.
11. *New York Times*, September 13, 1979, p. D5.
12. "House Returns EMB Bill to Conferees: Survival Doubted," *Oil and Gas Journal* 78 (July 7, 1980): 50-51; *National Journal* (July 5, 1980): 1105.
13. *New York Times*, November 1, 1979, p. D5. See also July 17, 1980, p. 18.
14. See *National Journal* (July 5, 1980): 1105; *Energy User's Report* (July 3, 1980): 3; *New York Times,* June 30, 1980, p. 4.
15. See Richard H. K. Vietor, "Synthetic Liquid Fuels Program: Energy Politics in the Truman Era," *Business History Review* 54 (Spring 1980): 1-34.
16. *Congressional Record*, June 26, 1979, p. H5119.
17. Ibid, pp. H5146-47.
18. *Science* 205 (July 13, 1979): 167.
19. *Public Papers*, p. 1138.
20. *New York Times*, September 21, 1980, p. C1; *Science* 205 (September 7, 1979): 978-9. See also R. C. Moe, "Government Corporatons and the Erosion of Accountability: The Case of the Proposed Energy Security Corporation," *Public Administration Review* 39 (November 1979): 566-71.
21. U.S. Congress, Senate Budget Committee, "Costs and Consequences of Synthetic Fuels Proposals," hearings, September 5, 1979, pp. 7-36.
22. U.S. Department of Energy, *Waste Disposal, Cooling and Related Environmental Impacts Associated with Synthetic Fuel Plant Siting and Design Criteria*, prepared by Water Purification Associates (Springfield, Va.: NTIS, 1979) (ET-78-C-01-3182).
23. *Public Papers*, p. 612.
24. "Swearingen Blasts Carter Windfall Comments," *Oil and Gas Journal* 77 (April 30, 1979): 132; "Excise Tax Called Economic Ingnorance," *Oil and Gas Journal* 77 (June 11, 1979): 43.
25. "Profits are Crucial to Ending Energy Shortage," *Oil and Gas Journal* 78 (May 28, 1980): 78; J. G. Wingertabs, "Search for Oil Depends on Profits." *Euromoney* (July 1979): 53 ff.
26. "IPAA Arms to Fight Carter Excise Tax," *Oil and Gas Journal* 77 (June 11, 1979): 84-5. See also U.S. Congress, Senate Finance Committee, "Crude Oil Tax, part 2," hearings, July 12, 1979.
27. Congressional Budget Office, *The Decontrol of Domestic Oil Prices: An Overview* (Washington, D.C.: U.S. Government Printing Office, 1979); "Those Windfall Profits," *Fortune* (June 18, 1979): 65-66. Office of the White House Press Secretary, "Fact Sheet on the President's Program" (April 5, 1979). Cf. U.S. Congress, House Interstate and Foreign Commerce Committee, "Updated

Analysis of the President's April 5, 1979 Crude Oil Pricing Plan," committee print, April 1979.
28. "Behind the Big Furor of the Windfall Tax," *U.S. News and World Report* (May 14, 1979): 23-24.
29. Treasury Secretary Michael Blumenthal warned that the plowback provision would distort the market, by artificially increasing incentives to invest in oil, and erect further barriers against new companies entering the business. Industry lobbyists countered that the provision, while it did give established companies a tax advantage over newcomers, would encourage investment in oil projects which would otherwise be uneconomic. See U.S. Congress, House Ways and Means Committee, "Windfall Profits Tax and Energy Trust Fund," hearings, May 9-11, 16-18, 1979, and W. Michael Blumenthal, U.S. Congress, House Interstate and Foreign Commerce Committee, "Domestic Crude Oil Decontrol, 1979" hearings, May 16, 1979, pp. 339-411, for oil industry perspectives.
30. "Fight to Tax Oil," *Time* (April 23, 1979): 27.
31. U.S. Congress, Senate Finance Committee, "Crude Oil Windfall Profit Tax Act of 1979," report, November 1, 1979, pp. 132-85.
32. *National Journal* (April 12, 1980): 602.
33. Joseph Kalt and Peter Navarro, "The Energy Crisis," *Regulation* (January/February 1980): 41-43. See also Walter J. Mead, "Performance of Government in Energy Regulations," *American Economic Review, Papers and Proceedings* 69 (May 1979): 352-56.
34. Edward J. Mitchell, "The Basis of Congressional Energy Policy," *Texas Law Review* 57 (March 1979): 591-613.

9

The Reagan Administration and the Retreat from Governmental Planning

The 1980 Republican victory, which swept Ronald Reagan into the White House and a Republican majority into the Senate, dramatically accelerated a reversal already under way in U.S. energy policy. President Reagan's persuasive manner, in tandem with increasing congressional skepticism about the efficacy of governmental manipulation of energy supply and demand, made it easier to push for a deregulated energy market. Since the 1980 election also eliminated from Congress many senior liberal Democrats who had been highly active in energy policy, such as Al Ullman, it was much harder for Congress members favoring a strong government role to resist the Reagan administration initiatives to cut energy programs.

Conservative Republicans in Congress and President Reagan have been markedly successful in returning the United States to an era when the energy industry and the government cooperated amiably with each other. The equity concerns that were an integral part of congressional energy policy since 1973 have diminished. Instead, forces advocating a minimum of governmental involvement in energy planning have become predominant. Specifically, the Reagan administration has been largely successful in fostering an energy policy consisting of untrammeling the oil-producing companies; reducing governmental energy organization and its attendant regulatory accoutrements; strongly supporting nuclear energy while cutting all other energy technology development; and eliminating past administration commitments to environmental quality and energy planning, conservation, consumer protection, and emergency preparation.

The emphasis on government-based solutions to energy problems, including conservation, energy market regulation, and emergency planning, had reached their highwater mark under the Carter administration. The energy policy pendulum has swung back, and Reagan has pressed hard for a quick return to the preenergy crisis system of organization. Congress has resumed many of its more passive characteristics and has greatly reduced its involvement in new energy legislation, yet has often tried to defend the existing energy policy system.

Administration Plans

Reagan's keystone policy is reliance on free markets rather than on federal programs to govern energy policy. This direction was manifested by the energy policy task force report, which Reagan commissioned during his election campaign.[1] The report, issued on November 5, 1980, urged Reagan to end federal government support for synfuels development, eliminate regulations directing utilities to convert to coal, accelerate nuclear power development, establish emergency supply procedures that "rely as much as possible on the private sector," fill the Strategic Petroleum Reserve rapidly, eliminate federal conservation programs, and rely instead on market forces as "the most effective way to bring about energy conservation throughout our economic system." It also called for decontrolling oil and gas, opening up public lands for exploration, and reducing burdensome environmental standards. Reagan's often repeated insistence that the Department of Energy (DOE) be disbanded was not stressed in the report, although the government was urged to move away from the "fads of government bureaucrats" and to pare bureaucracies. The Reagan administration policies largely conform to the report's recommendations.

The Reagan free market approach has been clearly demonstrated in the third National Energy Plan,[2] which the administration has taken pains to call a "policy plan," that is, a plan for a policy rather than a policy itself. It was issued in mid-July 1981 in fulfillment of the DOE act's requirement for a biennial report to Congress. Those members of Congress who favor an aggressive governmental role or who are concerned about environmental preservation, conservation, or solar energy are critical of it. Congressman Richard Ottinger (D-N.Y.) says it has "little substance or intelligence," while Senator Gary Hart (D-Colo.) observed that it jeopardizes national security by failing to provide a program to reduce oil imports, and contravenes the serious initiatives in energy policy taken in recent years. He calls it in sum "an irresponsible policy."[3] True to form, the "policy plan" emphasizes Reagan priorities, encouraging governmental support of nuclear power, including nuclear waste disposal and fast breeder development, while relegating renewable energy, synfuels, and environmental protection to the private sector, to be handled automatically by rising prices. The most radical departure occurs in conservation and renewable energy. Carter and the Ninety-fifth and Ninety-sixth Congresses had encouraged these through an array of financial incentives, regulations, and demonstration projects. The task force plan targets them for elimination.

Social concerns are shifted to the states which, the biennial report argues, are best able to deal with poor people suffering from high energy prices. The report asserts that, "as a practical matter, holding energy prices down is ineffective as a means of helping people on low or fixed incomes." Consumer protection, either as a program or a priority, is dismissed.

The plan does not indicate that the government will play an active role in handling energy shortages or emergencies. While the report admits that "free markets will not work perfectly during a severe disruption," they do "work more smoothly, with greater certainty and ultimately more fairly than complex systems of price and allocation controls managed by the government."[4]

Lack of Contingency Planning Worries Congress

The administration's unwillingness to develop an intervention strategy to handle an energy emergency, or even to admit responsibility for such a role, has worried some in Congress and has frequently led to congressional attempts to thwart the Reagan stance. But, echoing the theme of its "policy plan," the Reagan administration told Congress that no replacement was needed for the government's expiring authority to allocate oil in a crisis.

The depth of congressional unease with this position was indicated by several attempts to preserve the expiring presidential energy emergency authority. One attempt, spearheaded by the new chairman of the Senate Energy and Natural Resources Committee, James McClure (R-Idaho), was deflected by the administration, and authority expired on October 1, 1981. A few months later, a weaker bill giving the president emergency authority to set prices and allocate fuel in a crisis easily passed the Republican-dominated Senate, 86-7; the House also passed the measure 246-144. Reagan then vetoed the measure, explaining that emergency controls "can only shift losses from one set of Americans to others, with vast dislocation and loss of efficiency."[5] The Senate failed to override the veto. Subsequently, a new proposal was introduced that would allow oil prices to rise so as to balance energy supply and demand, and the resulting price increase would be taxed away; a great part of the revenues would be returned to the states as energy aid to the poor. While this and similar measures have not yet been enacted, they do underscore Congress's desire to have an energy policy that promises more equity and reliability than the uncertainty inherent in the Reagan administration approach.

For their part, Reagan administration officials maintain that the mere establishment of emergency control and planning authority in advance of a disruption sends an inappropriate signal to the private sector that it can count on federal intervention to protect its access to crude oil or products during a shortage. They claim further that an energy shortage will provide the ultimate proof of the free market's ability to deal with allocation problems. Some experts have challenged administration contentions that a combination of free market forces and the Strategic Petroleum Reserve would prevent undue hardship to the poor and to regions which rely heavily on imported oil. They doubt it would effectively guarantee supplies to farmers, police, firemen, hospitals, and defense installations.[6]

Reagan's Drive for Decontrol

Campaign promises made it clear that decontrol was a major priority for Reagan and many newly elected members of Congress. As a candidate, Reagan claimed that "there is more oil in Alaska than there is in Saudi Arabia," and "with decontrol, we could be producing enough oil to be self-sufficient in five years."[7] No energy experts have been found who agree with these assessments. Shortly after taking office, Reagan used his authority to decontrol oil prices immediately rather than letting them expire automatically in late 1981.[8]

Oil: An Easy Victory

The weak procontrol forces deteriorated even further after Reagan took office. Attempts to block Reagan's decontrol of crude oil were undertaken in both the House and the Senate, but they did not hinder, let alone halt, the deregulation of oil prices. Toby Moffett (D-Conn.) and Robert Roe (D-N.J.) offered resolutions in the House opposing Reagan's policy and, although such resolutions do not have the force of law, they were still defeated. Moffett's claim that decontrol would contribute to inflation and "deal a body blow to energy users, both residential and industrial"[9] proved unconvincing to his fellow representatives. Howard Metzenbaum (D-Ohio) led a quixotic attack in the Senate seeking to attach a rider to vital legislation in order to force members to take a public position on decontrol but, as in the House, this attempt was in vain.[10]

According to a Congressional Budget Office report, a consequence of Reagan's immediate decontrol decision will be an extra $8 billion in tax receipts, set off against an extra $1.9 billion in expenditures for oil destined for the Strategic Petroleum Reserve. It has also been estimated that oil companies would be receiving $3.6 billion of the additional money charged consumers.[11]

Natural Gas: A Major Battle Looms

A consistent free market approach would argue for removing controls from gas prices. The highly complex 1978 Natural Gas Policy Act generally allowed gas prices to rise gradually until 1985, when most categories of gas would become decontrolled.[12] However, in July 1981 Reagan's Cabinet Council on Energy and Natural Resources recommended that decontrol of wellhead prices of newly discovered gas be speeded up, joined by decontrol of prices of presently flowing gas, over a three-year period.

Besides fitting in with administration economic philosophy, a speedup might provide substantial revenue if it included a windfall profits tax, a great temptation in the face of alarmingly high projected budget deficits. While there is debate within the administration over the size of this potential revenue, the annual tax yield might well rise to $10 billion, a very attractive total. However, in July 1981 Reagan dispatched a handwritten letter to Congressman Glenn English (D-Ohio), promising to veto any such bill. Senate Majority Leader Howard Baker (R-Tenn.) told Reagan in early November 1981 that Congress would not agree to speed up the gas decontrol timetable unless it could also impose a windfall profits tax on natural gas similar to the tax on oil. Senator McClure, Energy Committee chairman, agreed with Baker's stipulation.

In light of this adamant congressional stance, natural gas producers are beginning to admit they may have to accept the tax; some feel they may need to announce a concession publicly in order to get a decontrol proposal moving. On the other hand, consumer groups are strongly opposed to any such acceleration of the decontrol schedule, charging that homeowner's gas bills would rise sharply, with a consequent increase in inflation. Despite attempts to decontrol some gas prices by regulatory manipulations,[13] the Reagan administration seems unlikely to secure the legislation needed to lift gas price controls. Even so, the administration began the Ninety-eighth Congress by proposing a decontrol plan, but no measure was ever passed by either house.

Removing Impediments to Fossil Fuel Production

Opening Public Lands for Exploration

The opening of federally controlled lands and offshore tracts for oil and mineral explorations complement oil decontrol policy. The year 1981 was a record in the twenty-eight-year history of federal offshore oil and gas leasing, with the number of tracts and the amount of acreage leased almost doubling those of 1980. A new five-year lease plan proposes opening for exploration and drilling 875 million acres of undersea property.[14]

In addition to this undersea activity, Interior Secretary James Watt sought to open up 1 million more dry land acres, including wilderness and wildlife areas, for exploration in the next five years. Watt temporarily extended a moratorium on oil and gas leasing in wilderness areas until after the Ninety-seventh Congress went out of session, but then began trying to lease 5 million acres while Congress was impotent to stop him.

While some in Congress, such as Morris Udall and House Speaker O'Neill, have expressed deep concern over the interior secretary's program and have confronted him sharply, it seems unlikely that there will be any substantial congressional intervention on this land-leasing issue even though the House passed legislation blocking Watt. If anything, the plan will be slowed because of lack of resources or interest by the oil exploration companies. When told of the Watt plan's size, one oilman reacted: "I don't see how it would be possible."[15] In February 1982, Congressman Manuel Lujan, Jr. (R-N.Mex.), acting on behalf of the Reagan administration, introduced legislation that would bar drilling and mining in federal wilderness areas for the rest of the century, but also made it easier to withdraw federal lands from the "wilderness" classification.

Although Democratic congressmen and environmental groups initially reacted to the proposal with surprised gratification, after closer examination they realized that the proposal's enactment could devastate the wilderness system. Congressman John F. Seiberling (D-Ohio), chairman of the Interior Committee's Public Land Subcommittee, claimed that the bill would mean "the wilderness would continue only at the discretion of the President."[16]

Watt's successor, Clark, is likely to pursue similar policies but in a low-key manner.

Tax Relief for Oil

Reagan also used tax relief incentives to expedite his tax cutting proposal in 1981. When he first outlined his across-the-board tax reduction plan in February 1981, no mention was made of special tax relief for oil. By June, negotiations over the terms of a tax cut between the White House and the chairman of the Ways and Means Committee had broken down, and the administration decided to submit its own tax reduction bill. The only oil provisions included in Reagan's proposal was a $2,500 exclusion for royalty owners from the windfall profits tax on crude oil. The windfall profits tax had become law during the Carter administration and was considered at the time the political price the oil industry had to pay to achieve decontrol of domestic crude oil.

Since then, oil interests have been working at reducing the tax, and although Robert Dole (R-Kans.) was sympathetic, as chairman of the Senate Finance Committee he was chiefly concerned with getting a major tax-cut bill passed by the August 1, 1981 deadline set by the president. An amendment reducing the tax on new oil was worked out in the Senate committee. The House Ways and Means Committee, hoping to pass its own bill, included tax breaks for royalty owners and independent producers. It was outmatched by a Republican-sponsored House bill (Conable-Hance), giving even larger tax breaks to many varied actors in the oil industry. The president found a revised version of Conable-Hance acceptable. A bill passed the House containing more tax breaks than a Senate bill—$16 billion versus $6 billion. To placate a group of Democrats who had been firmly opposed to any changes in depletion allowances and to keep the tax bill on schedule, the conferees agreed to a compromise of a $12 billion oil tax cut with no depletion language. Both houses accepted the conference report and the president signed it. Except for some early stiff resistance from the Treasury Department, the administration slid from a position of no specific oil tax relief to a tax break of $12 billion, willingly aiding oil resource owners and investors to obtain the desired income tax reduction.

"Getting Government Off the Backs of the People"

Ending Oil Company Prosecution. When oil price and allocation controls were lifted by President Reagan early in 1981, Energy Secretary Edwards assured Congress that there would be "no amnesty" for violators of the previous controls. Funds were appropriated to keep the Economic Regulatory Administration in operation until the overcharge cases were settled or handed over to the Justice Department for litigation. By spring, Democratic Congressmen expressed skepticism that the oil companies would ever be prosecuted. Congressman Albert Gore (D-Tenn.) introduced at an oversight hearing an exhibit from the DOE's controller's office showing that only 40 out of a possible 125 notices of violation could be issued and only 45 cases brought to trial under existing staffing. Six months later, Rayburn D. Hanzlik was brought in as chief of the Economic Regulatory Administration. He announced a reorganization that eventually cut his staff from 1,800 to 344 and his field offices from 47 to 8. He described his goal as putting his agency "out of business" and the law he was appointed to enforce as "a monster the courts would no doubt throw out."[17]

Scrapping the Allocation/Entitlement System. Before the end of oil price controls and allocation in January 1981, independent refiners were able to obtain guaranteed supplies of oil at controlled prices under Energy Department programs. Citing free market arguments, administration spokesmen stated after deregulation that no special treatment for the refining industry was needed and that if the industry shrank as it adapted to decontrol, the government should not meddle.

The independent refiners replied that they would be happy to compete in a free market but that none existed. They pointed out that OPEC sets world oil prices and that those U.S. firms with access to the cheapest OPEC oil have an unfair advantage. From the independents' point of view, a fair solution would have been a contingency plan in case of another oil shortage or price spiral that would assure them of supplies at equitable prices.[18]

Encouraging Nuclear Power

To provide needed energy, the Reagan administration foresees an important role for high technology and especially nuclear energy.

There are both economic and political reasons why Reagan has made an exception to his free market philosophy in the case of nuclear energy. Undoubtedly each step of the administration's pronuclear argument is open to counterarguments, but it is especially noteworthy that its entire position is counter to the administration's own general rhetoric of governmental nonintervention and free market economics.

The Reagan economic position favoring nuclear energy may be summarized as follows: A free market for nuclear energy does not exist now. While all forms of energy are subsidized in different ways, sudden withdrawal of government assistance to nuclear power would require such large immediate adjustments that chaos might result. In addition, Reagan is the prisoner of past policies that have committed the country to a nuclear industry that is now an important component of the country's electrical generating capacity. But the industry is weak and requires a governmental presence. It is faced with difficult technological problems requiring sustained investment, which firms will undertake only with massive government assistance. Much basic research needs to be done, but the rewards appear too far off in the future for industry to underwrite them unassisted. The safety factor is an enormous cloud hanging over the industry's head, and companies involved are unwilling to assume responsibilities for all the risks. Environmental and procedural blocks have hobbled the industry; their removal could revivify it. The nuclear waste disposal problem in this country has yet to be solved satisfactorily either economically or politically. For all these reasons, therefore, the government must nurture and protect nuclear power.

There are also political reasons why nuclear energy is supported by the administration and "soft" energy not: Reagan's political supporters include nuclear interests and pronuclear adherents. Further, a former member of Reagan's Council of Economic Advisors and two high Treasury Department officials have told me that the Reagan administration support for nuclear power is based in part on antipathy toward environmentalists and conservationists, who oppose Reagan's philosophies.

Nuclear Power Plant Licensing Incentives

Describing the present Nuclear Regulatory Commission (NRC) licensing system as a "morass of regulations that do not enhance safety but that do cause extensive licensing delays and economic uncertainty," Reagan announced that the secretary of energy will "give immediate priority attention to recommending improvements in the nuclear regulatory and licensing process." Plants should not take 10-14 years to license, he said in his October 8, 1981, statement; the 6-8 years "typical in some other countries" should be the objective.[19]

Although no specifics on what is expected from the NRC were included in Reagan's statement, the NRC has prepared legislation for introduction to speed up nuclear plant licensing. A draft of the legislation includes proposals for: "preapproving" power plant sites in advance of any specific requests for permission to construct a particular plant; standardizing nuclear plant designs which would then have blanket approval; and a one-step licensing procedure that would consider plant construction and operation permits concomitantly rather than separately.

Congress may greet these proposed alterations skeptically, as it did similar Carter administration initiatives. Yet there is also strong pronuclear sentiment on Capitol Hill, which has already attempted to close out citizen participation and intervenors from nuclear licensing procedures.[20]

The Clinch River Fast Breeder Reactor

Making an exception to its insistence that free markets and private enterprise guide policy developments, the Reagan administration has assumed responsibility for disposing of nuclear wastes generated by atomic power plants across the country, as well as for developing the controversial and expensive Clinch River Fast Breeder Reactor (CRBR). The CRBR has been under continual attack, especially in the House, and during his incumbency President Carter tried to kill it. Nevertheless, it has survived and the administration has given strong backing and funding to the CRBR, resorting to unusual stratagems to promote it.[21]

CRBR's funding became a major energy issue during the Ninety-seventh and Ninety-eighth Congresses. The project, located in Tennessee, had become the strongly favored project of the senior senator from that state, Majority Leader Howard Baker. Partly because of Baker's pressure, the project had been able to stave off repeated attempts to scuttle it, squeaking by with as little as one vote. Because it is so politically risky for a senator to grievously offend the majority leader, CRBR continued to survive despite its worsening cost/benefit ratio. But Baker, apparently tiring, reduced pressure on his colleagues and the project was killed by the Senate in 1983.

International Proliferation and Reprocessing

Although the Reagan administration does not favor nuclear weapons proliferation, neither is it preoccupied by it. During his election campaign, candidate Reagan said that he did not think it was "any of our business" whether other nations acquired nuclear weapons.[22] The administration's current approach appears embodied in a December 1980 memo written for the presidential transition team by James L. Malone, at the time a foreign agent for overseas nuclear clients, including Taiwan's power corporation. The Malone memo recommended gutting the Nuclear Nonproliferation Act of 1978, which acted to curb U.S. nuclear exports that had potential use in nuclear weapons.[23]

In accordance with his pronuclear position, the president, in his first major statement on nuclear proliferation, July 1981, said: "The Administration will not inhibit or set back civil reprocessing and breeder reactor development abroad in nations with advanced nuclear power programs where it does not constitute a proliferation risk."[24] This is a clear departure from the Carter administration.

The reaction to the president's nuclear position has been sharp. Jeremy J. Stone, director of the Federation of American Scientists, labeled the position a "rhetorical cover for the desire to sell reactors abroad."[25]

Yet the administration argues that by making plutonium more widely available in domestic and international commerce, and by becoming "a reliable and very competitive" merchant in international nuclear commerce, the United States will have the greatest leverage over client states. The United States can then use this leverage to dissuade nonnuclear states from acquiring their own nuclear weapons. This policy has been applauded as a "refreshing change" by Dixon Hoyle of Westinghouse, and "a new realism" by Myron Kratzer of International Energy Associates, Ltd.[26]

Nonetheless, it seems likely that other countries will see in the administration's position an implicit endorsement of the effectiveness of current safeguards and other controls, of plutonium as a commercial nuclear fuel, and of reprocessing as an unassailable national right. Such a perception could make it more difficult for the United States to try to prevent other countries from following this lead.

Congress has been decidedly unhappy about the administration position. The Senate reacted to the president's July nuclear proliferation statement by passing, 89-0, the very next day a resolution which called for tightened restrictions on "dangerous nuclear trade," a temporary world moratorium on transfers of uranium enrichment and reprocessing equipment, and a strengthening of International Atomic Energy Agency safeguards. The House joined the Senate with a similar resolution the same day. The Senate and House have held a variety of hearings bringing out the proliferation implications of administration nuclear sales policy and have sought new curbs on the export of nuclear technology and related material.[27]

Cutting the Budget: Selective Dismantling of the Bureaucracy

The Eclipse of Solar and Conservation Programs

In contrast to nuclear power's favored status, solar energy budgets have been severely slashed under Reagan. Demonstrating that the "soft path" of renewable energy and passive solar designs are clearly out of favor, the Reagan administration has sought to practically eliminate all funding for solar research and demonstration programs. It has also formally renounced the Carter goal of meeting 20 percent of the nation's energy needs from solar sources by the year 2000, arguing that the free market, not the government, should determine the nation's energy mix.

TABLE 9.1

U.S. Department of Energy Budget for Research and Development by
Energy Supply Source, Fiscal Years 1978-1983

Energy Source	Expenditure by Fiscal Year (in millions of dollars)					
	FY1978	FY1979	FY1980	FY1981	FY1982	FY1983
Conservation[1]	538	631	779	644	143 (384)[2]	22
Fossil Energy	784	760	858	994	417 (566)[2]	107
Solar and Renewables	532	671	751	714	314	82
Magnetic Fusion	332	355	350	394	454	444
Nuclear Fission[3]	1,202	1,092	1,198	1,031	1,087	830
Total	3,388	3,509	3,936	3,777	2,415	1,485
Percent of total devoted to nuclear	45	41	39	37	64	86

1. Includes state conservation grant programs.
2. Figure in parenthesis includes 1981 deferrals.
3. Does not include basic research.

Source: Subcommittee on Energy, Nuclear Proliferation and Government Process, Senate Committee on Governmental Affairs.

Note: For consistency in comparisons, figures were taken from the president's annual budget request. Variations may occur due to changes in accounting over the years. In addition, due to differences in accounting practices, the figures may vary somewhat from appropriation levels cited by congressional appropriations committees.

By contrast, solar industry lobbyists point out that "high technology" solar projects, such as complex solar tracking equipment and sophisticated photovoltaics, continue to receive funding. They assert that these not only are part of the "hard path" and benefit the largest aerospace, electric, and oil companies but also dry up funds that would otherwise go to lower-risk, small-business projects that have greater promise of immediate payoff. They say that with high interest rates and heavy military spending, there will be little venture capital available for the small entrepreneurial firms.[28]

Because of Carter's emphasis on solar energy, some accused him of "solar socialism"; Reagan budgets have been labeled by solar advocates "nuclear totalitarianism." Nuclear research will rise from 37 percent of the DOE's FY 1981 research and development budget to 85 percent in FY 1983 (see Table 9.1).

While funds for every Energy Department research and development program have been cut, except nuclear fission and fusion, conservation has been the hardest hit, falling from $799 in FY 1980 to about $22 million in FY 1983. Dropping governmental incentives for conservation has been one of the most controversial energy policy changes. To the Reaganites, emphasis on conservation implies personal sacrifice, limits on future economic growth, and a dismal future for America and capitalism. Within a month of his inauguration, Reagan, by executive order, lifted controls on building temperatures and withdrew federal standards that were to have been imposed on home appliances. This, of course, was in keeping with the free market argument that rising prices, especially if they result from decontrol, will encourage the most appropriate forms of conservation and that government interference with private decisions will only hinder effective conservation and economic efficiency.

On the other hand, Thomas Stelson, Carter administration conservation and energy program director, attacked the Reagan approach before a congressional subcommittee, characterizing it as based "upon ignorance with respect to both the free enterprise system and the energy conditions of the United States." Congressman Ottinger, a champion of solar energy and conservation, called the new policy "misguided" and maintained that the administration position is "not corroborated by any studies."[29]

The Senate has also been a stronghold of proconservation sentiment. A Governmental Affairs Subcommittee on Energy held hearings during which several of its members expressed dismay at the Reagan plans, and attempted to restore conservation programs. Senator John Glenn called the costs "about as pound foolish a move as I've seen on Capitol Hill." Energy expert S. David Freeman (who was also director of the TVA) testified that "market forces are heavily tilted in favor of energy production and against conservation. [Energy] production organizations have access to capital on terms that would be the envy of the average energy consumer."

Ultimately, the argument hinges on the effects of high energy prices. The Reagan people foresee massive investments in energy supply production; assuming a free market exists, conservation advocates hold that with a truly free market, massive investment will go into increased energy efficiency. While it is unlikely that Congress will restore solar energy and conservation programs to their former importance, it has acted as a brake, slowing the determined drives by Reagan to eliminate them.

Congress Reluctant to End Department of Energy

To complement the reduction in programs and regulations, Reagan forces have sharply diminished and hope to abolish the DOE, which to some is a symbol of Carter's "big-government" approach to energy policy.[30] Reagan appointed former South Carolina governor and dentist James B. Edwards as energy secretary. Edwards, who is pronuclear and prosupply in his orientation, drastically reduced staff and streamlined reporting procedures. Edwards has repeatedly stated that his mission was to preside over the agency's dissolution. In a 1982 speech, Edwards said, "I want to be the first Cabinet member . . . to close down a department. I want to close down the DOE, bury it once and for all, and salt the earth over it so it won't spring up again."[31] The DOE has shrunk from 19,927 employees in January 1981, when Reagan took office to 16,717 in July 1982. Although he never succeeded in this goal, and has been replaced by Donald Hodel, a former Interior Department official, the administration remains committed to DOE dismantlement. But Congress is unenthusiastic about proposals to terminate DOE and is unlikely to act on them soon.

Backing Off from Synfuels Support

Paralleling the decline in the size and activities of DOE is the diminishing Reagan support for the synfuels effort. The Synthetic Fuels Corporation (SFC), established under the Carter administration, was an early target for the Reaganites and received prominent attention in Stockman's "black book" of budget cuts. In this document, OMB authors warned that the project had powerful supporters including an "array of business and labor interests that would benefit from government-subsidized construction programs." They forecast strong "negative public and media reaction" and bipartisan resistance from congressional delegations anticipating synfuels plants in their states, namely West Virginia, Kentucky, Ohio, Alabama, and Illinois.

Stockman's prediction was correct, and sharp congressional protests about anticipated cuts were not long in coming. Representatives from the oil companies that would benefit from the program, especially Gulf Oil and Union Oil, lobbied at the White House and Congress to assure continued synfuels funding.[32]

Reagan synfuels policy is slightly ambivalent, favoring reduction of governmental projects subsidizing certain forms of energy production, yet the administration would like an alternate energy source in case there is another disruption of imported oil. If the alternative were relatively cheap, it would be appealing, but synfuels now seem very uneconomical. Clearly the synfuels fever that gripped first Capitol Hill and then the Carter administration has subsided. The original 1992 goal—to stimulate production amounting to about 2 million barrels of oil a day—has been substantially reduced. The target is now only one-fourth of the original goal and even this is unlikely to be met.

The enthusiasm for synfuels in Congress has faded in large part because its cost has risen while oil prices have fallen. Although long-time energy specialists in Congress such as John Dingell (D.-Mich.) have continued to push for synfuels, they have met with only modest success since Reagan's election. (Yet it is congressional interest in synfuels that has kept the program from being pared back even further.) In addition, there continues to be skepticism about the ability and willingness of the private sector to undertake a meaningful synfuels program, especially since several major private projects have been cancelled. Senator Jackson has said: "We have waited since the 1940s for the private sector to develop synthetic fuels. And we will wait until well into the next century if we abandon the . . . Energy Act."[33] His prediction now appears to be correct.[34]

Government Hastens Coal Production, Undermines Consumption

The Reagan administration's confidence that market conditions favor coal dictates a governmental policy of simply getting out of the way. This confidence is resulting in proposals to promote production while removing subsidies that promote consumption. The administration is aggressively encouraging coal exploration and production on federal lands, suggesting changes in the clean air laws that would permit wider coal burning,[34] and reducing federal surface mining land reclamation regulations.

The Reagan administration has not pushed for enactment of eminent domain legislation for the construction of coal slurry pipelines. These pipelines would be the major alternative to expensive railroad coal transportation. But the administration holds that the enactment of federal eminent domain legislation would intrude on matters that should be left to the individual states to decide. This position greatly adds to coal costs since it is extremely difficult to create a low-cost transport alternative. Congress has not passed legislation to help let the slurry pipelines be built, siding instead with the politically potent railroads.

An important Carter administration policy was to increase coal use by prohibiting utilities and industries from using natural gas and oil (effectively turning them to coal use), and by strongly supporting coal technology research. The Reagan administration's approach has been entirely different. Instead of mandating coal use, it is minimizing government intervention in private decisions and allowing energy-consuming facilities to determine which fuel they will use.

Conclusion

Reagan's energy policy displays a reliance on measures that contributed to some of the problems of the 1970s. Tax write-offs for oil producers, dependence on more and more production of fossil fuels, and an absence of planning, goal setting, or support for conservation were the main features of the United States position when it faced the first energy crisis. Reagan's energy program illustrates a return to these attitudes, with the addition of some new wrinkles that stem from his ideological posture and the political exigencies he faces. Yet his policy is also to try to circumvent some of the other problems that helped create the shortages of the 1970s. Natural gas regulation, environmental and air quality restrictions, fuel allocations, and highly cautious nuclear power licensing have all been identified as factors leading to those shortages, and their elimination are Reagan priorities.

Reagan and his administration are unwilling to engage in overall energy planning or even to draw up designs for emergencies. Because of their free market philosophy, they advocate fostering more production through decontrol of oil and natural gas. Decontrolling oil came easily, but natural gas presents still-unsolved political problems. The administration does not share others' concerns about conservation and protection of the environment, willingly exchanging such considerations for the possibility of increased production from greatly expanded offshore leasing and unprecedented exploration in federal wilderness and wildlife areas.

Despite the program of immediate price decontrol and the opening of vast acreage for oil exploration, Reagan's prediction of self-sufficiency by 1986 is chimerical. Nearly all predictions of U.S. crude oil production show continued decline, although the rate of decline will be less sharp than if controls had been continued. Decontrol cannot reverse the United States' long production slide, only slow its rate of descent.

Reagan officials willingly face political embarrassment by cutting back on measures that would reimburse the public for past overcharges, ending programs for small independent refiners, and drastically reducing programs such as weatherization and fuel assistance for those with low incomes. But their free market philosophy does not preclude a fascination with and strong support for nuclear technology, including reprocessing and the breeder reactor, despite opposition from responsible advisers within the government, and despite the risks which no market participant is willing to underwrite. The cost reduction argument is applied stringently to all energy programs save nuclear research and development.

Resurgence of the Free Market Philosophy

The resurgence of the free market forces in Congress has not taken place in a vacuum. Not only were new members swept into office on Reagan's coattails, but even those who had supported government intervention were becoming impatient and dissatisfied with federal energy programs. Late in the Carter administration, the Energy Department produced a study that indicated only 5 percent of the increase in energy efficiency (per unit of gross national product) since 1972 was attributable to government programs; most savings in projected energy growth since 1972 resulted from slower economic growth and higher energy prices.[35] This report signalled a turning away by both the executive and the legislature from massive federal intervention to construct a comprehensive energy-pricing policy.

Those favoring free market forces argue against the two central tenets of the

Carter era. First, contrary to Carter's assertions, they claim the world is not running out of oil faster than market participants think. Therefore, there is no need for government intervention to change consumer and industry behavior, and alternative fuels need not be made available any earlier than is economically optimal. The world market is not fragile, so any disruptions can be handled through a world oil market that has sufficient flexibility to distribute oil during an emergency. A loss of oil anywhere in the world raises prices (thus reducing demand) everywhere. Further, in the long run there can be no artificially increased oil prices, and oil prices can only rise to the backstop price of alternative fuels.

Second, free market advocates do not believe that the public welfare is served by government intervention. They point to the inequities of past energy policies, such as those which subsidized the flow of capital into petroleum production, and conclude that government policies respond to the dominant organized group, rather than principles of economic efficiency. Intervention presupposes that the government has the wisdom and political will to devise proper policies and can make the correct decision about who will have energy supplies and who will go without them. Further, when the government assumes an interventionist stance, it is accompanied by great economic and social costs both direct and indirect. For example, a large bureaucracy is required to devise regulations, and their work will be followed by expenses resulting from protracted legal battles. Price policing, auditing, reporting, etc. are all required to insure compliance with decisions once they are reached and litigation is completed. The costs of these are borne by the general taxpayer as well as the companies involved in energy production and distribution, which increases the total cost to the consumer. Society's labor is deflected from more productive purposes. Free-market advocates point to the patent inequities of recent federal interventions, especially the windfall profits provisions. (The windfall gain principle was inequitably applied. Oil, coal, and uranium prices have all gone up markedly since 1967, but only oil was singled out for the windfall penalty.) Federal attempts to increase equity and redistribute income by means of energy policy have not been encouraging either. For example, poor people who do not have natural gas hookups do not benefit from artificially low gas prices, but owners of large houses and heated swimming pools often do.

On the basis of these arguments, free market advocates conclude that a comprehensive national energy policy is not desirable. At most they will allow a government role in residual areas, such as long-range energy options (e.g. fusion and breeder reactors), while insisting that private enterprise totally dominate decisions about exploring for and producing, distributing, marketing, and pricing an evolving blend of fuels.

A drawback to this approach is that the world rarely operates according to classical economic theory, and even when it does the failure to intervene can hurt a nation severely. For instance, during the 1973-74 embargo some oil companies withheld their supplies, anticipating greater profits from higher prices. (There are many social critiques of classical economics, but these cannot be recapitulated here. Other problems of a national energy policy which relies singularly on corporate actors are discussed in the next chapter.)

It is clear that in its implementation, the Reagan energy program harbors many inconsistencies and is heavily weighted against administration opponents (liberal Democrats, environmentalists, and conservationists) and in favor of its supporters (western and Sun Belt energy producers and their representatives in Congress, and the nuclear industry). It is a policy based on the assumptions that the United States contains much undiscovered oil and gas, that nuclear energy is safe and economically competitive, that the environment can withstand additional degradation, that oil-exploring nations will neither restrict—voluntarily or involuntarily—production nor sharply raise prices, and that if there *is* a shortage, the free market will resolve the problem. If such optimism is justified, the Reagan policy may be a wise one. If on the other hand any of these hopeful assumptions proves false, the United States may be in for a repeat of the energy shortages of 1973-74 and 1979.

Notes

1. "President-elect Reagan's Task Force on Energy Transition," Halbouty report, November 5, 1980 (Washington, D.C.: mimeo, 1980).
2. *Securing America's Energy Future: National Energy Policy Plan* (Washington, D.C.: U.S. Department of Energy, July 1981).
3. *Congressional Quarterly Weekly Report*, August 1, 1981, p. 1424.
4. *National Energy Policy Plan*, p. 2.
5. "Message from the President of the United States," veto—S. 1503, March 22, 1982 (Washington, D.C.: U.S. Government Printing Office, 1982).
6. See U.S. Congress: House Committee on Energy and Commerce, "Standby Petroleum Emergency Authority Act of 1981," report no. 97-363 (Washington, D.C.: U.S. Government Printing Office, 1981). The full defense of the Reagan administration position was presented in an Energy Department study, "Preliminary Analysis of Federal Energy Emergency Preparedness Strategies," reprinted in *Congressional Record*, March 24, 1982, S2737-S2742.
7. *Wall Street Journal*, August 5, 1980, p. 26.
8. This step only preceded by seven months the October 1, 1981, expiration date set by President Carter under the 1973 Emergency Petroleum Allocation Act as amended and extended.
9. *Energy User's Report*, February 5, 1981, p. 213. Congress's mood about oil prices and free markets had changed dramatically since 1974, when it voted to roll oil prices back to lower levels (see chapter 2).
10. Independent oil and gasoline dealers and independent oil refiners did lobby against the decontrol move, arguing that they would be forced out of business by unfair practices of the major oil companies. However, a Department of Energy report found no evidence that the major refiners were subsidizing their own gasoline stations to drive independent gas stations out of business, and this lessened

the impact of their claims. The independent refiners also have sought special legislative remedies that would give them preferential treatment, but these efforts have not been successful. See "The State of Competition in Gasoline Marketing," U.S. Department of Energy, Office of Competition, January 1981.

11. U.S. Congress, Congressional Budget Office, "Effects of Immediate Decontrol," January 29, 1981 (mimeo).

12. The 1978 Natural Gas Policy Act was the result of eighteen months of political savagery and compromise that ended the forty-year control regime of the 1938 Natural Gas Act. A comprehensive analysis of the 1978 measure may be found in the U.S. Congress, Environmental Study Conference, *Fact Sheet* (February 4, 1981). The Act's implication are discussed in "U.S. Gas Price Decontrol Debate Centers on Cloudy Market Views," *Oil and Gas Journal* (July 13, 1981): 33-37.

13. See *Washington Post*, April 8, 1982, p. A15.

14. This figure is about twice the acreage proposed in the original Carter plan proposed in June 1980. Despite the record-setting drilling activity in 1981, which also included the most gas produced from leased fields and the largest federal revenues from drilling rights and royalty earnings, only 283 million barrels of oil were produced from offshore tracts, the second lowest total in ten years. Further, drilling activity was down about 30 percent in 1982 compared to the previous year. The industry has remained depressed since 1982.

15. *Washington Post*, February 14, 1982, p. A3. See also *New York Times*, August 4, 1981, p. D15. The 1964 Wilderness Act gave Watt until 1984 to issue wilderness oil leases before 80 million acres come under permanent protection, and he exploited this opportunity. As might be expected, this plan was opposed not only by environmental groups, but also by individual oil companies who complained that the plan was too large, moved too quickly, and was too different from previous operations. The history and current situation of this issue is discussed in the *Congressional Record*, August 9, 1982, H5459-H5474.

15. *New York Times*, February 25, 1982, p. A23.

16. *Washington Post*, January 12, 1981. Personnel figures were provided by Mr. Hanzlik's office.

17. Independent producers argue on their own behalf that: (1) consumers have benefited from the competition independents have provided and would be at the mercy of the major oil companies if the independents are forced out of business; (2) a sound domestic refining capability strengthens national security; (3) farm states and rural areas depend on small, independent refineries; those areas have been increasingly abandoned by major oil companies; (4) a contingency plan for the next crisis would avoid bidding wars and lessen the need for rationing.

18. The administration with its often stated antiregulatory position has not exempted NRC from 12-percent 1982 budget cuts dealt out in the fall of 1981. No relief from the cuts are given despite the addition of many new responsibilities: contract work to accelerate licensing of light water plants, funds for research and licensing at the Clinch River Breeder Reactor (CRBR), and money to support safety issues in the wake of the Three Mile Island nuclear power plant accident. The cutback, combined with the new duties, reduced funds for the 1982 activities by about $45 million, according to *Science* 214 (November 13, 1981), p. 761. NRC officials estimate about 75 percent of the required reductions must come from research support. This flies in the face of a report of the President's Nuclear Safety Oversight Committee (now disbanded), which concluded in September 1981 that the NRC should engage in new research. The committee listed eight new urgent re-

search problems on which no significant work is currently being done and eleven other areas in which work needed improvement. The report urged a redrafting of the NRC's long-range research plan with a concentration on more up-to-date concerns and less support for previous undertakings.

19. Congress is ideologically diverse and resists facile generalization. But clearly, just as there is deep antinuclear sentiment on Capitol Hill, there is also very strong support for nuclear energy. A major expression of this sentiment has been concerted drives among some factions to expedite reactor licensing and construction. For example, in 1982, the House Appropriation Subcommittee on Energy and Power attached three riders to the Nuclear Regulatory Commissions appropriation bill. These riders would speed up nuclear power plant licensing methods, including siting and impact assessments, and would freeze the public and critics out of licensing procedures. While nuclear intervenors were upset, the Appropriation Subcommittee's measures were neutralized by other committee action; yet it did signal the existence of a strong pronuclear sentiment in certain parts of Congress. See *Washington Post*, April 30, 1982, p. A15.

20. "DOE internal memo reveals manipulation of NRC and Congress in attempt to obtain licensing exemption for Clinch River Breeder Reactor," Natural Resources Defense Council, Press Release, December 8, 1981 (Washington, D.C., mimeo).

21. This statement was reported in the *Washington Post*, February 1, 1980, p. A 3.

22. Malone subsequently became assistant secretary of state for oceans and international environmental and scientific affairs, a position which has a major role in U.S. proliferation policy. Coauthor of the memo W. Kenneth Davis, then of Bechtel Corporation and now deputy energy secretary. See *Washington Post*, March 8, 1982, for a review of Malone's controversial performance.

23. White House Press Release, July 16, 1981 (Washington, D.C.: White House, mimeo).

24. *Science*, 213 (July 31, 1981): 523.

25. William J. Lanouette, "Reagan Loosens Controls on Plutonium and Unleashes a Flood of Worries," *National Journal* (August 7, 1982): 1376.

26. For example, see U.S. Congress, Senate Committee on Governmental Affairs, "Nuclear nonproliferation policy," hearings, June 24, 1981. Two laws have been passed recently strengthening U.S. nonproliferation efforts: Public Laws 97-113 and 97-90.

27. "Photovoltaic Industry Position Paper on Federal Photovoltaic Programs" (Mountain View, Calif.: Strategies Unlimited, Co.); P. K. Munjal and S. L. Leonard, "Third Party Financing of Photovoltaic Power Plants for Electric Utility Service" (El Segundo, Calif.: January 1982). Aerospace Corp., prepared for the U.S. Department of Energy.

28. *Science*, 212 (April 24, 1982): 1424.

29. Rogert Sant et al., *The Least Cost Energy Strategy* (Washington, D.C.: Mellon Institute, 1981); Marc Ross and Robert Williams, *Our Energy: Regaining Control* (New York: McGraw-Hill, 1981); National Audubon Society, *Audubon Energy Plan* (New York, 1981); Nat Bruce Hannon, "Energy, Labor and the Conserver Society," *Technology Review* (March/April 1977): 47-53.

30. In his January 1982 State of the Union message, the president repeated his call for dismantling DOE. In the summer of 1982, the administration found congressmen, albeit reluctant ones, willing to introduce legislation merging DOE into the Commerce Department, where the commerce secretary would oversee both commercial and energy policy. In keeping with its pronuclear emphasis, three of the four

proposed energy assistant secretary positions would have responsibility for nuclear issues. Only one assistant secretary would be assigned to cover fossil fuels,
conservation, solar, planning, and emergency programs. This plan was killed by
Congress.

31. *Science* 211 (February 6, 1981): 903.
32. *Congressional Quarterly Weekly Report*, July 25, 1981, p. 1341.
33. Synfuels are caught in a dilemma. If oil prices rise, demand is reduced and new
reserves are brought into production, so synfuels remain relatively too expensive
compared to conventional oil. If oil prices fall, synfuels become even more expensive in relative terms. Thus, without major technological progress, synfuels will
remain more costly than conventional oil, regardless of world oil prices.
34. The Clean Air Act of 1970 and the resulting regulations, especially those of the
Environmental Protection Agency, have limited coal use in electricity and heat
generation. The limits on emissions of sulfur dioxide, nitrogen oxides, and partic-
ulates have been highly controversial in the United States, and coal's role in creating "acid rain" has become a focal point of domestic and international contention. There is widespread agreement that the Clean Air Act is highly imperfect
and in need of modification; however, there is little agreement about what should
replace the present arrangement. Despite the Reagan administration drive to
change (some would say weaken) clean air laws to permit greater coal use, if the
laws are changed at all, it will likely be in the direction of tougher standards.
35. U.S. Department of Energy, "Briefing Materials on *Trends in Energy Use and
Conservation*" (Washington, D.C.: DOE, Office of Policy, Planning and Analysis, April 14, 1982).

PART TWO
THE IMPLICATIONS

10
The Politics of U.S. Energy Policy

Three Perspectives

Attitudes toward energy use are usually rationalized by an assessment of the amount of usable energy readily recoverable in the near future. Such assessments, however, vary widely. The supply perspective[1] urges the use of what it envisions as abundant resources; the energetics perspective maintains that energy resources are scarce and in need of careful husbandry; and the conservation perspective takes a position between these extremes. The conflict over energy use, which has resulted from this divergence of opinion concerning availability, is deep, acrimonious, and strongly influenced by economic interests and ideologies. Yet if the United States is to arrive at a coherent energy policy, some basis of agreement about energy use must be found.

Supply Perspective

Historically, the supply perspective has predominated. Within it three approaches have molded national policy in accordance with a particular facet of the general theory of abundance. The most influential of these has been the approach encouraging domestic oil companies to control and produce more petroleum. It has resulted in government policies such as granting oil depletion allowances and special tax credits and imposing an oil import quota. There have also been numerous sub rosa agreements that assist U.S.-based international oil companies by giving them secret tax write-offs or using them to distribute foreign aid while manipulating them as instruments of foreign policy.[2] Another approach encourages policy that gives a larger role to the government in the regulation of oil companies and in the overall preservation of the free enterprise system. This policy has generated numerous probes and investigations of the oil industry by congressional committees, the Federal Trade Commission (FTC), and the Department of Justice. Although their ultimate purpose is to protect the free market, the industry views these regulations as hostile to its commercial interests, for those who most often benefit from them are small, independent companies that complain of "unfair" competition from larger companies. Also, such practices have raised arguments over where government encouragement of efficiency-producing competition ends, where protectionism and favoritism begin, and what constitutes a truly free market.

A third approach seeks to protect energy users by discouraging producers from unfairly taking advantage of consumers or accruing excessive profits. Thus the government must supervise markets and prices and make judgments about what is just and equitable. The decision to control interstate natural gas, crude oil, and gasoline prices was influenced by this approach, which asserts that low-cost energy should be available to increase production and employment and raise living standards. Energy producers, it argues, should themselves help subsidize the consumer by limiting their own profits.

Although these approaches disagree over methods, they basically concur in their premises and goals. Therefore, except where noted, the term *supply perspective* will henceforth refer to the first and dominant approach—governmental encouragement of energy production.

It should be kept in mind that U.S. energy policy has never been the result of any rational plan but rather of a struggle between various interests. Prior to 1973, insignificant attempts at balanced strategic planning had been made at the presidential staff level and occasionally by the Interior Department, but these were either ignored or denigrated by operational agencies, which themselves were often captives or open supporters of the oil industry. When conservation has been advocated, it has been by presidential or congressional planning staffs whose influence has been very limited.[3]

The supply perspective has predominated except during the energy crises of the 1970s. At that time the two other perspectives—conservation and energetics—made temporary inroads. While the supply perspective has survived the challenge, at least for the time being, and has returned to official favor with the Reagan administration, each of the three competing perspectives still claims to offer the only means of escape from the societal chaos which could ensue from an energy shortage.

Salvation, according to supply perspective supporters, lies in gaining access to abundant fossil fuels, including strip-mined coal, and moving forward with transitional sources, such as the light water and especially the breeder reactor, to the ultimate energy source—fusion. This view's defenders, many of whom are economists and oil company executives,[4] claim that the earth's petroleum supplies are enormous. Even an unrelenting critic of oil companies and nuclear power, consumer advocate Ralph Nader, maintains that the world is "drowning in oil." Staunch supply perspective supporters also insist that energy and economic growth are interdependent, that any large reduction in a society's available energy will result in catastrophic social and economic dislocation. They consider conservation merely a form of deprivation that camouflages a reduction of living standards and a retreat from important social and ecological goals; they claim that active government intervention on the supply side of the energy equation interferes with individual rights and erodes the free enterprise system. President Reagan accurately expressed this perspective when he asserted that conservation is "being hot in the summer and cold in the winter."[5]

The traditional supply perspective gives a central position in policymaking to corporations and a significant but subsidiary role to government officials, while university experts are expected to supplement the contributions of both these groups. The small, stable, closed elite group that then controls energy policy largely excludes the public, partially because citizens are supposedly unprepared to understand the complex and subtle issues involved and lack the means of becoming so prepared. Policy makers thus protect each other's economic interests and status designations.

Although the ultimate goal for the supporters of the supply perspective is abundant energy at a low price, they argue that higher prices will make more energy available by encouraging the search for new sources of petroleum and natural gas and may even create new, ultimately cheaper, conventional and unconventional energy sources. Because the proponents of the supply perspective believe the alternative is the destruction of advanced industrial society, they are willing to risk environmental damage and threaten public health and safety for the achievement of their goals.

Conservation Perspective

Supporters of the conservation perspective, on the other hand, view petroleum and natural gas supplies as constrained and rapidly disappearing; they contrast other nations' higher energy efficiency with that of the United States, where, they claim, 50 percent of all energy is wasted. They maintain that the federal policy of consistently stressing energy production over conservation interferes with overall economic efficiency.[6]

When the conservation perspective was delineated in a controversial 1974 Ford Foundation energy project report,[7] it was immediately adopted by a segment of academic and policy analysts and soon became highly influential in Washington, especially in Carter's 1977 National Energy Policy. The NEP assumed that economic growth was not dependent on increased energy consumption. If institutional and market barriers were removed, society would gradually become more energy-efficient while any decline in living standards which might result would be merely temporary.[8]

The conservation perspective gives the key role in energy decisions to the federal government as arbiter of intergroup conflict and regulator of the equity consequences of energy system changes. The NEP defines this role: "The energy problem can be effectively addressed only by a government . . . dealing with it comprehensively." This includes creating incentives for conserving energy, preventing energy companies from reaping windfall profits, compensating for wealth transfers among regions, and undertaking energy development projects that are too risky or expensive for the private sector.

The government would also set conservation standards, forcing industry to build energy efficiency into its activities.

The supply and the conservation perspectives differ radically, particularly on equity concerns. Whereas the former sees inequality as driving market mechanisms (and indeed every human endeavor), the latter aims at as much equity as possible, necessitating governmental intervention throughout the energy system.

The conservation perspective's objective is to regulate a transit through the immediate future of scarcity into a more energy abundant future. If energy waste were drastically reduced and energy-efficient technical innovations promoted, oil and gas demand and imports could be drastically cut. With federal government regulation and new technology limiting environmental damage, abundant U.S. coal reserves could easily permit temporizing until a plentiful energy source is discovered. The conservation perspective emphasizes advanced technologies to increase use of coal (e.g. coal gasification) and renewable sources of energy (e.g. biomass conversion, solar photovoltaics), with direct solar radiation and other low-technology sources as important supplements. Dangers to be avoided, according to conservationists, are supply disruptions, exhausting oil reserves, balance of payments deficits, and foreign policy problems caused by foreign oil reliance or energy wars.

The conservation perspective assumes that modifications in values are needed to solve the energy problem; public education and energy extension services could reduce energy consumption. Moral suasion could reduce the need for economic sanctions.

Energetics Perspective

The energetics perspective derives partly from radical social criticism and offshoots of traditional economics. It contends that the amount and form of available energy dictates the social, economic, and political structure of a society. From this perspective, the energy crisis is an endemic and systemic problem that can be permanently resolved only by radical changes in society's structure and values. The world's resources are part of a closed ecosystem, which is affected in its entirety by every subsystem's intake or output.[9] Society should be reminded of the just law of the thermodynamics, i.e. that energy can never be created. In both social and natural systems, energy efficiency is the key to survival, growth, and maintenance. Accelerating energy-linked economic development will merely increase entropy and create social disorder. Energetics perspective's proponents welcome the cheap energy era's demise. To them it means that values will change; environmental pollution and destruction are slowed while centralizing, antidemocratic, large-scale energy technologies are replaced by locally controlled, humane, participatory, and simple energy technologies. A safer, more resource-abundant future will be inherited by our children.

Unlike the supply and conservation perspectives, which emphasize industry and government actors respectively, the energetics perspective stresses the citizens' role in arbitrating and implementing soft-energy paths. Societies will become more democratic and therefore, following the Jeffersonian ideal, non-aggressive. They will experience a rebirth of community values, while their citizens will become more compassionate and self-actualizing. As a challenge to mainstream conventional wisdom, this world view has excited strong criticism and skepticism.[10]

In sum, the supply perspective argues that once freed from excessive governmental interference, the energy market would establish an equilibrium. The conservation perspective argues that to protect long-term social interests and safeguard society from disastrous supply disruptions, government should assume responsibility for setting prices, allocating supplies, overseeing and supporting research, correcting market inadequacies, and substituting itself where markets are nonexistent or inefficient. The energetics perspective believes that policy should encourage public participation and provide the requisite information, thereby limiting dangerous and destructive energy exploitation and substituting a low-technology, soft-energy path, responsive to the citizenry's true needs and to the finite nature of energy resources.

Shifts among Perspectives

Before the 1970s, when the supply perspective predominated, the government provided a stable, industry-led set of actors with depletion allowances, import quotas, and similar kinds of aid.[11] Previous to the Nixon administration, most energy policy conflicts were between various approaches within the supply perspective, and these caused a gradual shift of national concern from producers to consumers of energy. At the same time, an environmental and natural resources protection movement began to reemerge after a quiescent period following the Progressive Era. In the late 1960s this movement won victories that directly and indirectly began to erode the dominance of the supply perspective. As the energy situation deteriorated in the early 1970s the remedies that were proposed by the Nixon administration were designed to reinforce the classic supply perspective. Under the grandiose notions of Project Independence lay merely a proposal for transferring energy production costs from producers to the general public (by granting research and development subsidies, eliminating consumer subsidies, and externalizing social and environmental costs). This alone could supposedly solve all the energy problems which state planning and state-owned oil corporations (solutions offered by the conservation perspective) were deemed incapable of resolving. The still nascent energetics perspective was not considered an option.

In the early 1970s, energy shortages brought forth a cacophony of charges and countercharges which eventually resulted in the emergence of the conservation perspective, haltingly at first under President Ford. The rhetoric of Nixon was replaced by a stalemate under Ford, caused by conflict among a variety of approaches to energy problems. Ford initially advocated a program to encourage domestic production, but congressional forces favoring consumers, price controls, and governmental intervention strongly opposed him. Although Carter had been won over by the conservation perspective, the supply side still had strong proponents both in Congress and the executive branch. The compromise that was achieved, while seeming to favor the conservation side, actually protected the supply-side prerogatives, except in relation to a few key issues such as windfall profits and the continuation, until 1985, of some natural gas price controls; but even these were only delays rather than defeats.

As the conservation perspective began to dominate energy policy initiatives, the energetics perspective emerged. Without attracting as much attention as the conservationists, the energeticists were nevertheless able to disseminate their ideas. Carter went so far as to meet with soft energy's chief advocate, Amory Lovins, and the energetics perspective was presented in a favorable light at congressional hearings.[12] However, after the initial flurry of interest, this high-level attention has receded. The conservation perspective reached its apex in 1979-80 with the enactment of the National Energy Act, the synfuels corporation, and the windfall profits measures which allowed the federal government to foster new technology through subsidies, directly manipulate markets, and redistribute some of the benefits accruing from possession of petroleum resources.

Ronald Reagan's election in 1980 was a supply-side victory. It resulted in the expansion of nuclear energy research and development, the opening of federal lands for oil and gas exploration, and an easing of regulatory hurdles facing energy projects. Under the Reagan administration, the supply perspective is again in favor, primarily at the White House, although Congress, too, is sometimes willing to allow market forces free reign.

The reasons behind the continuing predominance of the supply perspective must be fundamental and compelling, especially considering the sizeable evidence against its validity and that it has not yet led to a steady supply of energy at a stable price—its goal—upon which the future of advanced industrial society supposedly depends. The limited information supporting the supply perspective and arguments raised to justify its apparent failure are inadequate to explain how it has been able to win sufficient political and public support and to have influenced energy policy history so strongly. But it can be explained by the ideological relations among the three perspectives, and by the U.S. political system's nature. The following examination of these factors has both practical and theoretical significance.

Ideology and Stability

A fundamental factor contributing to the supply perspective's success and longevity, besides the inertia built into any widespread social system, is the symbiotic relationship that exists between government and industry in the United States. The supply perspective's implementation, espoused by the elites of these two sectors, has cost consumers billions of dollars over the past fifty years, through import quotas and oil depletion allowances, among other subsidies. Yet with rare exception, these elites have retained public approval, largely because real energy prices declined under their influence. (Despite rapid price increases, in constant dollars, gasoline today is about as expensive as it was during the early 1950s.) The united front presented by these elites protects their class interests and discourages any challenge to the supply perspective. Even when challengers arise, their pressure cannot be sustained because their institutional base is weak compared to their opponents, and they are usually caught up in the same technocratic values that dominate the supply perspective. Further, the ideology that supports industrialization and economic growth for its own sake continues to be attractive. The American cultural values of increasing prosperity, freedom, independence, and opportunity allow conventional economic wisdom to rationalize and legitimize the energy industry's activities.

The supply-perspective domination of U.S. energy policy demonstrates the truth of Galbraith's theory that power accrues to those who control scarce resources. Because large corporations, with their greater organization and discipline, control energy resources, they are able to influence specific policy decisions and even limit the boundaries of policy discussions.[13] An outstanding example of their influence occurred shortly after the oil embargo, when some consideration was given to divesting oil companies of their marketing functions or restricting their domination of the nonpetroleum elements of the energy industry (pipelines, coal mines, etc.). Although these initiatives were supported by some in Congress, by consumer and public interest groups, and by labor unions, the oil companies were able not only to suppress them (through meetings with policy makers and large-scale public relations campaigns), but also to expand their scope of activities into nonenergy areas.

In addition, the supply perspective offers status and wealth to many participants in the corporate-political system which it sustains. It has been especially rewarding for those in the highest positions of the hierarchy of elites who have been able to translate their economic success into social influence and prestige. (Included in this category are, for example, the Mellons and Rockefellers and, indirectly, Presidents Johnson and Nixon and Senators Long and Kerr.)[14]

Given these reasons, it seems surprising that the conservation and energetics perspectives have managed to have so much influence. Because the putative benefits from conservation accrue largely to future generations, any rationale advanced in its favor must rely essentially on moral suasion rather than economic interest, as traditionally defined. Although religious movements have always attracted followers by promising future bliss and redemption in exchange for sacrifice, most successful political movements promise immediate but morally justified material gain. Excluding the occurrence of another Middle East war, revolution, embargo, or continuing price escalation, there are no immediate material incentives for accepting the conservation or energetics approaches. Although prudence, uncertainty, and pessimism would urge their adoption, these attitudes imply ideological assumptions that directly threaten current power arrangements. Therefore, no elite coalition or mass movement has appeared, or is likely to develop, in support of a prolonged energy conservation program or a shift to less convenient technologies. Moreover, there is no elite leadership at this point to enforce the discipline required by the unpopular perspectives. Without some external change in the energy situation, the elites have little to gain and much to lose by failing to support the supply perspective.

Most important, unless a case for the conservation or energetics perspectives could sway the public, the changes they entail would, by challenging the legitimacy of the currently dominating elites, endanger the political system itself. It is precisely this kind of threat that causes resistance to the conservation and energetics perspectives in nearly all sectors of society; merely considering them raises questions about the values and myths that provide this country's political and social legitimacy. Materialism, market orientations, and the producing systems would be directly challenged in the United States if these perspectives were to win wide support. Production would be guided by principles of social utility rather than by individual tastes, large corporations, powerful mass media, or vested interests. A political force with its own elite would be needed to deal explicitly with large corporations, a multitude of organized interests and institutions, and practically autonomous governmental entities. There is no existing group powerful or wise enough for this role.

Energetics and conservation perspective supporters know that slight adjustments of values will never lead to their perspectives' eventual dominance, that they face a prolonged battle with the supply perspective for control of society, and that they have only narrow political and economic bases to draw upon. They can offer no rationalizing ideology that is likely to be widely adopted by either the elites or the mass public. While the pessimistic predictions of energy resources appeal readily to some, especially to those academically oriented, there is no shortage of empirical evidence on any side of the argument. The energy debate is not so much over what the facts are as which facts are significant.[15]

The Stability of the Energy Policy System

The supply perspective continues to dominate the energy debate not only for the ideological reasons already cited, but also because of factors inherent in the U.S. energy policy system itself. Recent large-scale changes in the energy supply picture have brought about only incremental and minor changes in U.S. energy policy. If one assumes that existing but untapped fuel supplies are sufficient and that economic incentives are all that is needed to assure their recovery, this lethargy can perhaps be justified. On the other hand, if one admits that because fossil fuels and uranium supplies are limited and in great demand (and their acquisition and extensive use environmentally ruinous), a change in consumption patterns is called for. It can then be argued that the unresponsiveness of U.S. political leadership constitutes a dereliction of public responsibility. The reasons why there has been so little policy adaptation by the political system deserve consideration.

Traditionally, two principal theories have been used to explain the structure of the American government.[16] One of these, the pluralist theory, posits that a multitude of interest groups compete for control over policy, and that the content of the political process is largely the result of this competition and of bargaining and compromise between the leaders of the groups and the political authorities who represent their interests. Because of the multiplicity of interests—often manifested by advocacy and veto groups trying to constrain one another—the political process becomes largely the unintended consequence of the ebb and flow of competition. As each group increases its demands, the government must expand the area of its responsibilities and, as more is expected of it, appears to accomplish less. Policymaking is incremental and riven with fundamental conflicts over values.

The elitist theory posits that the political agenda is determined and controlled by elites who, although they may head different institutions of American society, agree concerning the nature and direction of that society. Their institutional interests, however, do not always coincide, especially when policy boundaries are expanding and interfering with one another.

An analysis of the evolution of U.S. energy policy seems to confirm the elitist interpretation over the pluralist. Although complex, chaotic, and often acerbic competition has been an important element in energy policy decisions, this does not adequately account for much of the policy outcomes described in earlier chapters. For while the energy policy contains contradictory elements, it was nevertheless determined by a relatively closed and small group of organizational elites. There was no monolithic elite consistently controlling every move made by the state, but rather a stable group of institutional leaders who often cooperated to share in the mobilization of resources and arrange interorganizational coalitions to dominate and formulate the political agenda.

An overarching U.S. energy policy did not exist in the postwar period. With rare exceptions, action taken in the area of energy was simply the automatic result of decisions made in other areas and based on extraneous considerations such as national defense or economic growth. Post-World War II energy policy goals were to expand supplies to meet anticipated demand, to transfer those risks to the larger society that the private sector was unwilling to take, and to meet increased energy demand by importing foreign oil. As a result, citizens paid a higher price for energy than could be justified by its cost, much to the advantage of particular producers.[17]

Reciprocity Enhances Stability

Energy producers developed a reciprocal relationship with certain elements of the policy system, especially with government officials in the executive and legislative branches. The energy industry enjoyed privileged access to policy makers through a variety of coordination and cooperation mechanisms. Industry's pattern of producing larger amounts of increasingly cheaper energy was necessary for policy makers to meet social objectives in other areas. The two sectors shared a common conception of the role that the energy industry should play in American society. This relationship remained largely intact throughout the shortages and price increases of the 1970s. Considering the latter's magnitude, the stability in the energy policy system is remarkable.

Further, although specific actors in the energy arena have circulated (in Pareto's definition), the same cohorts of elites and technical experts continue to play key roles in the government, in industry, and in the private "nonprofit" sector. As was pointed out earlier, agencies within the government are not fundamentally altered by reorganization but rather come to represent greater and greater agglomerations of the original interests and participants in new combinations and with an occasional new interest added. Throughout these changes the energy industry's interests continue to be reflected in federal energy policy organizations, and the industry's relative bargaining power remains largely unchanged.[18]

While major energy decisions continue to be made by a limited set of actors, a narrow technocracy exercises a disproportionate control over the framing and implementation of these decisions because of the highly technical nature of many energy problems. This is particularly true of energy research policy. The strong supply orientation found among technocrats is generally shared by energy decision makers and is related to the so-called engineering mentality, which tends to emphasize complex, exotic, and sophisticated technologies and ignore or downplay their external and social costs.[19]

New Groups Dilate Policy Boundaries

Energy policy's boundaries have expanded to include new areas, as newly mobilized groups demand to be included in the decision process. Those that represent narrowly defined interests and are easily organized are likely to form effective pressure groups. When they have attained sufficient influence, they may be included in consultations and their opinions solicited. They then demand participation in the policy process, and if they are strong enough, a special agency will be created through which their interests can be formally represented in the decision-making hierarchy. Consumer and environmental protection groups and solar agencies have been formed for such purposes. However, while these newly included groups unbalance the traditional power arrangement and often put producers on the defensive, they have not been fully integrated into the policy framework. Complex decisions are still made sequentially and narrowly by simplistically addressing seemingly unrelated issues as they occur. Because of this the nation's energy future remains unprotected; and the vitality of the supply perspective continues unabated.

In sum, a long period of falling energy prices brought political leaders and energy industry officials into a close symbiotic relationship, although more recent changes in the energy situation severely strained these closed energy subgovernments or "triangles." Because the number of policy participants and audiences was increased, the neat triangles became sloppy hexagons, which aggravated the problems of policy management. Further, the interdependence that exists throughout the energy picture caused foreign governments to become indirect participants in the energy policy process. The continual expansion of the policy system to include these new interests and organizations, formed in reaction to the energy crisis, has brought about a condition approximating stalemate.

However, these new clusters of citizens, whose interest in energy policy had been latent (those having macroeconomic, employment, environmental, health, or safety interests, as well as foreign policy and national security interests), have been mobilized.[20] The pressures created by these groups have been dealt with in part by creating a variety of ad hoc groups, commissions, study panels, and committees. In addition, they have raised energy policy in the public consciousness, and the Democratic and Republican parties consistently address energy in their platforms, with their presidential candidates including energy issues in their campaign rhetoric. A new party—the Citizen's Party—has even been formed around what began, at least partially, as an energy issue.

Although the impact of the Citizen's Party has been slight, the success of

Europe's environmental parties indicates the potential power of such political movements organized around energy/environmental issues. Other avenues have been used by these groups to exercise influence over energy policy. For example, recourse to court, administrative, and legal action now offers considerable leverage when used as a dilatory tactic by those opposed to certain energy policies. However, these tactics have provoked numerous calls in Congress and the executive for limiting lengthy administrative and court procedures, and this pressure has resulted in tangible policy changes. The attempts to create an Energy Mobilization Board to override opposition to energy projects might also be viewed in this context, as well as the more recent procedural modifications under the Reagan administration to speed nuclear reactor construction.

The present energy policy situation is dominated by the supply perspective, despite the prolonged battles over energy which are punctuated by occasional victories for the conservation perspective, such as the windfall profits tax. But even these gains are usually compromised, as they were when the windfall profits tax was emasculated, auto mileage and clean air standards relaxed, and concessions on oil and natural gas pricing won. The cumulative energy policy record preserves the prerogatives of the energy industry.

Although a proliferation of actors and increased competition at the pluralistic level have made the policy control of energy elites less obvious, the course of the energy policy system has been deflected only slightly, which is remarkable in view of the public attention given the energy issue and the political interests involved. The storm of battles and momentary dividing of spoils merely distracts attention from the essential wars and their winner—an elitist system that sets the basic parameters of decisions about energy, if not always the discourse around these decisions.

Dilemmas of Energy Policy

The continuing conflict over energy policy is partly due to the nature of the energy problem itself. The energy policy's goals are inherently contradictory, and thus as one goal is approximated and its reasonably appeased supporters disappear, the supporters of other goals become more militant. Thus continual clashes result. Conflicting goals have made political competition over energy issues sustained and intense, encompassing every political arena. This competition continues because energy politics is primarily oriented toward rearranging the government's action agenda and affecting the way public authorities handle energy issues, and only secondarily toward enlisting public support. Finally, deeply entrenched values are often in competition with each other in energy politics, and while single-focus energy interest groups are stable, coalitions are not. They can only hope for an uncomfortable *modus vivendi*, which is constantly threatened by disintegration as conditions change.

Although the events of the early 1970s—the oil shortages and especially the embargo—brought public demands that the national energy situation be at least minimally supervised by government, this recognition was not accompanied by a widespread appreciation of the complexity and subtlety of the situation. There still are serious structural problems that elude resolution but which do not enjoy a very high level of public awareness:

1. Because segments of the United States are large energy exporters that profit enormously from escalation of energy prices, the energy situation is largely a zero-sum game (any gain in one quarter is subtracted from another quarter). Those who control energy resources gain financial and political leverage only at the expense of others.
2. The complexity of energy problems inevitably results in disagreement about the definition of the problems and their solution. Policy battles revolve around the control, use, and interpretation of data, and experts are deployed as the tactical situation dictates.
3. Because energy problems are practically inseparable from economic problems, solutions must be viable in both areas.
4. The momentum already achieved through the large, complex, technological infrastructure, which now supplies the nation with energy in various ways, would make change difficult and costly in terms of capital equipment, human training, and lifestyle, and would also require modifications in the nation's social structure. Consequently, there is a strong tendency to maintain a status quo, which inhibits the development of new energy sources and styles of energy utilization.
5. Energy policy not only dictates the distribution of wealth and status but also influences ideologies, values, institutions, and behavior, even as these factors influence the formation of policy. Purely economic or technological approaches to energy policy often founder because of sociological and political forces.
6. The great variety of energy sources and uses and the connections between them make any neat formulation for conceptualizing energy problems practically useless.
7. The various goals of energy policy are often mutually exclusive. Reducing imports to preserve national security and balance of payments depletes domestic energy reserves and causes environmental degradation. Holding down inflation through "artificially" controlling or restraining energy prices stimulates consumption. Allowing prices to rise, on the other hand, usually results in the added cost being paid primarily by those least able to afford it: the elderly and the poor. When the government intervenes to subsidize alternative technologies, such as synfuels, the cost can be exorbitant relative to conventional fuels. When the government "force feeds" a technology—whether through direct transfer of money, as with the

Clinch River Breeder Reactor, or indirectly, through tax write-offs, loan guarantees, or special depreciations—there is danger of the nation prematurely committing itself to an inadequate or short-lived technology. However, if market forces are relied upon entirely, the nation may be deprived of effective energy technologies by the inherent limitations and short-sightedness of the free market.

8. The creation of effective energy policy strains traditional values. National or even local "social engineering" entails planning for society and thus restricts individual freedom in some way. But without it, energy decisions often result in a maldistribution of costs and benefits during the production process. Those who are strip-mined, polluted, and poisoned are usually least able to participate in the benefits of energy expansion or to control their own destinies, and future generations are seldom considered in decisions that will determine the habitability of their environment.

Notes

1. David W. Orr, "U.S. Energy Policy and the Political Economy of Participation," *Journal of Politics* 41 (November 1979): 1027-56.
2. U.S. Federal Trade Commission, *The International Petroleum Cartel* (Washington, D.C.: U.S. Government Printing Office, 1952); U.S. Congress, Senate Foreign Relations Committee, "Multinational Corporations and U.S. Foreign Policy," report, January 2, 1975; Carl Solberg, *Oil Power* (New York: New American Library, 1976).
3. Crauford Goodwin, ed., *Energy Policy in Perspective* (Washington, D.C.: Brookings Institution, 1981), esp. chs. 1 and 5.
4. Richard Mancke, *The Failure of U.S. Energy Policy* (New York: Columbia University Press, 1974), p. 11; Maurice A. Adelman, "World Oil Cartel: Scarcity, Economics and Politics," *Quarterly Review of Economics and Business* 16 (Summer 1976): 7-18. Representative examples of oil corporation perspectives are to be found in Gulf Oil Corporation, *Annual Report* (Pittsburgh, 1979): 4-5; Exxon Corporation, *EXXON, USA* (Houston, 1976): 27-31; Mobil Oil Corporation, "Observations," *Parade Magazine* (advertisement), October 18, 1981, p. 9.
5. See also Gulf Oil Corporation, "Conservation," *The Orange Disc* (Spring 1981): 25, 30; *Wall Street Journal*, August 5, 1980, p. 26; *New York Times*, February 6, 1981; and Mobil Oil's attack on strong conservation, equating it with "economic stagnation," *New York Times*, October 18, 1974, p. 41.
6. *Energy User's Report*, January 8, 1981, p. 25. The conservation perspective is embodied in the U.S. Executive Office of the President, *The National Energy Plan* (April, 1977). See also Robert Stobaugh and Daniel Yergin, eds., *Energy Future* (New York: Random House, 1979).
7. Ford Foundation Energy Policy Project, *A Time to Choose* (Cambridge, Mass.: Ballinger, 1974).
8. Roger Sant et al., *The Least-Cost Energy Strategy* (Washington, D.C.: Mellon Institute, 1981); Marc Ross and Robert Williams, *Our Energy: Regaining Control* (New York: McGraw-Hill, 1981); National Audubon Society, *Audubon Energy Plan* (New York, 1981); Bruce Hannon, "Energy, Labor and the Conserver Soci-

ety,'' *Technology Review* (March-April 1977): 47-53.

9. Kenneth Boulding, "The Social System and the Energy Crisis," *Science* 184 (April 19, 1974): 255-57; Barry Commoner, *The Poverty of Power* (New York: Knopf, 1976); Harold Barnett and Chandler Morse, *Scarcity and Growth* (Baltimore: Johns Hopkins University Press, 1963); Amory Lovins, *Soft Energy Paths* (New York: Harper and Row, 1979); William Cottrell, *Energy and Society: The Relation between Energy, Social Change and Economic Development* (New York: McGraw-Hill, 1955). Many of these authors see an important link between the thermodynamic principle of entropy and economic activity. See Nicholas Georgescu-Rogen, *Energy and Economic Myths* (New York: Pergamon, 1976).

10. See Hugh Nash, ed., *The Energy Controversy* (San Francisco: Friends of the Earth, 1979); David Rossin, "The Soft Energy Path: Where Does It Really Lead?" *The Futurist*, June 1980, pp. 57-63.

11. For a detailed analysis of the implications of various incentive programs, see Joseph Kalt and Robert Stillman, "The Role of Governmental Incentives in Energy Production: An Historical Overview," in *Annual Review of Energy, Volume Five* (Palo Alto, Calif.: Annual Review, 1980), and David H. Davis, *Energy Politics*, 2nd ed. (New York: St. Martin's, 1978).

12. *Wall Street Journal*, March 16, 1981, pp. 1-19; U.S. Congress, House Interstate and Foreign Commerce Committee, "Middle- and Long-Term Energy Policies and Alternatives," hearings, March 25-26, 1976.

13. John K. Galbraith, *The New Industrial State* (New York: New American Library, 1968), 3rd rev. ed., p.67. For a theoretical discussion of this point, see Charles O. Jones, *An Introduction to the Study of Public Policy* (Belmont, Calif.: Wadsworth, 1970), especially chs. 2 and 3; and Peter Bachrach and Morton Baratz, "Decisions and nondecisions: An analytical framework," *American Political Science Review* 57 (September 1963): 632-42. Examples of this process in action include Davis, *Energy Politics*; Goodwin, *Energy Policy*; Robert Engler, *The Politics of Oil* (Chicago: University of Chicago Press, 1961) and *America's Energy* (New York: Pantheon, 1980); and Norman Ornstein and Shirley Elder, *Interest Groups, Lobbying and Policymaking* (Washington, D.C.: CQ Press, 1978).

14. Examples of this process may be found in Richard O'Connor, *The Oil Barons* (Boston: Little Brown, 1964); Allan Nevins, *A Study in Power: John D. Rockefeller* (New York: Scribner's, 1953); Robert Engler, *The Brotherhood of Oil* (Chicago: University of Chicago Press, 1977); Burton Hersh, *The Mellon Family* (New York: Morrow, 1978); Robert A. Caro, "The Years of Lyndon Johnson," *Atlantic Monthly* (October, November 1982); Anne Morgan, *Robert S. Kerr: The Senate Years* (Norman, Okla.: University of Oklahoma Press, 1977).

15. Although there is an immense literature discussing the size and availability of energy resources, useful illustrations of the questioning of the problematical nature of the energy supply can be found in Richard Kerr, "How Much Oil? It Depends on Whom You Ask," *Science* 212 (April 24, 1981): 427-29; Elliot Marshall, "Energy Forecasts: Sinking to New Lows," *Science* 208 (June 20, 1980): 1353-56; U.S. Congress, Senate Energy and Natural Resources Committee, "Energy, An Uncertain Future: An Analysis of U.S. and World Energy Projections through 1990," committee print, December 1978; John Bridger, "Backing into the Future: On the Methodological and Institutional Biases Embedded in Energy Supply and Demand Forecasting," *Technological Forecasting and Social Change* 21 (June 1982): 229-40.

16. Much ink has been spilled on this topic. Among the major exponents of the pluralist theory are Truman and Dahl, while Mills, Prewitt, and Stone have espoused the elitist position. David B. Truman, *The Governmental Process*, 2nd ed., (New York: Knopf, 1971); Robert A. Dahl, *Who Governs?* (New Haven: Yale University Press, 1961); C. Wright Mills, *The Power Elite* (New York: Oxford University Press, 1956): Kenneth Prewitt and Alan Stone, *The Ruling Elites* (New York: Harper and Row, 1973).

17. All energy sources, including fossil, nuclear, and solar, are heavily subsidized. A Princeton University study estimated that in 1977 routine federal subsidies exceeded $6.5 billion, not including research and development costs. This figure included $1.5 billion in oil and gas depletion allowances, $1 billion for utility tax breaks, and $300 million in federal services to the nuclear industry. The total did not include the subsidy provided by the Price-Anderson Act, which removes from utilities the liability of a serious nuclear accident. The Union of Concerned Scientists calculated this subsidy to be worth at least $1.8 billion annually. *Nucleus: A Report to Union of Concerned Scientists Sponsors* 3 (Fall 1981): 2. Another recent study found that investor-owned utilities received federal assistance at a level of $3.0 billion in 1979. Donald E. Smith, *Comparing Capital Costs: Federal Assistance to Electric Utilities* (Washington, D.C.: National Rural Electric Cooperative Association, 1981). For a theoretical discussion of these points see Leon Lindberg, "Energy Policy and the Politics of Development," *Comparative Political Studies* 10 (October 1977): 355-82.

18. Charles O. Jones, "American Politics and the Organization of Energy Decision Making," in *Annual Review of Energy, Volume Four* (Palo Alto, Calif.: Annual Review, 1979). The continuing pattern was most recently confirmed in a study described by David Rogers, "Oil Emerges as Leading Hill Patron," *Washington Post*, September 15, 1981, p. A2; and in a historical analysis by J.R. Bond, "Oiling the Tax Committees in Congress, 1900-1974," *American Journal of Political Science* 23 (November 1979): 651-64.

19. For example, see Theodore Roszak, *Where the Wasteland Ends* (New York: Doubleday, 1972); Barry Commoner, *Science and Survival* (New York: Viking Press, 1966).

20. Olson's theoretical discussion and McFarland's empirical examination address this point. See Mancur Olson, Jr., *The Logic of Collective Action* (Cambridge: Harvard University Press, 1976); Andrew McFarland, *Public Interest Lobbies: Decision Making on Energy* (Washington, D.C.: American Enterprise Institute, 1976).

11
Prognosis for Congress's Role in Energy Policy

In its use of energy resources, the United States has traditionally been able to follow the same pattern of continual expansion that has characterized its economic and physical development. Free access to abundant natural resources has determined to a considerable extent our national character and the structure of our political system and has allowed many national problems, particularly those relating to equity, to be rapidly resolved through sharing a growing resource base and by decreasing the real cost of energy.[1] The demands of newly organized interest groups could be satisfied without taking anything away from the dominant groups. But because of traditional reliance on this solution, a sudden change to an epoch of shrinking resources and scarce energy (an "era of limits" or the "zero-sum society") may alter the political orientation of America more radically than that of any other nation in the world.[2]

The Challenge before Congress

The machinery of politics in a modern environment of limited resources must be geared to handle increasingly complex, technical, and interrelated problems, rather than traditional issues of distribution or ideological orientation that concerned previous generations. Yet the only apparent solutions to proliferating national problems involve the strategy—unprecedented in peacetime—of requiring sacrifice from the people, prompted by moral incentives. The failure of this method could necessitate the use of direct sanctions to enforce lower living standards, a last resort employed in America during wartime only.

The energy crisis introduced major questions concerning resource constraints. Even in normal times neither Congress nor the executive branch is well prepared to formulate energy policy as a comprehensive, coordinated set of interrelated national goals. The government's role has been restricted primarily to the management of public resources, limited regulation of certain utilities, and an occasional intervention, as when it instituted the natural gas price controls, the oil depletion allowance, and the mandatory oil import quota program, each to the benefit of a certain interest group. Even when a national program has been built around a specific issue, as with the Rural Electrification Administration, the Tennessee Valley Authority, and the Atomic Energy Commission, the traditional pattern was repeated; special benefits accrued to special interests which "captured" the regulators or agency and seemingly dictated policy. Although the energy policy developed within specific areas might be coherent, as was civilian nuclear power policy, it was isolated from the broader contexts of total energy resources and uses.[3]

Since 1973, those in favor of a strong central administration, including presidents Nixon, Ford, and Carter, saw in the energy crisis and its aftermath an opportunity to expand the White House's role, not only in managing short-term energy problems, but also in setting and controlling the larger agenda of energy policy. This hope was frustrated by a hostile and assertive Congress that wanted the energy problem solved but was unwilling or unable to take definitive action, or to surrender some of its prerogatives so that the president might do so. (Rationing and emergency planning are pertinent examples of this.)

Many private interests, especially those involved in the creation or transformation of energy resources, had been forced by the environmental movement of the 1960s to absorb some of the costs of their activities—such as strip mining, air pollution, and general environmental destruction—which had been previously absorbed by society. The energy crisis allowed them to transfer some costs of their operation back to the general public (i.e. the consumer) and the environment (through environmental degradation).

Congressional Assertiveness

Systematic changes in governmental processes have made the presidency the dominant and aggressive center of American government. While events following Watergate have caused many to challenge this pattern's validity, the White House has been the initiator and coordinator of much recent energy policy.[4] Because of slack resources and declining real energy prices, there had been little public awareness of energy's key role in society or the desirability of exercising close governmental control over it. But energy is now a seamless web of interlocking concerns linking industrialization, foreign affairs, cities, transportation, agriculture, taxes, and many other policy areas, and any change in one area causes change throughout the whole system. In the past, energy problems were addressed piecemeal; frequent energy surpluses permitted a gradual solution to emerge. Congress has recently contributed to this piecemeal approach through its tendency to create more and more programs, leaving little time for meaningful oversight and improvement of already existing programs. The rationale for this great expenditure of congressional time and effort has been the notion that new programs will effectively solve the nation's problems. But as quickly as one problem is solved, another appears.

Internal Factors

Congress's increased activism is due to many changes, both internal and external. One of the most significant internal changes in Congress has been the diffusion of power, which is partially a result of the numerous reform procedures of the past decade.[5] As was noted earlier, most congressional committees are at least indirectly involved in energy policy and there is significant overlap of jurisdictional responsibility among them. This dispersion of power and authority contributes to the fragmented nature of Congress's attempts to devise a policy, and to the proliferation of activities based on members' parochial and personal interests. The smooth exercise of power through the committee system is now threatened from within, as for example by committee members who seek their own interests apart from the commonly shared (although hierarchically defined) committee goals, and by the multiplication of subcommittees. Externally, it is threatened when the committees constantly challenge each other's turfs in the struggle for publicity, power, and control of emerging issues.

Congressional activism in energy policy has been encouraged by the increasing sophistication and size of staffs, which allow Congress to assert its position independently from the executive branch, thus providing an incentive for activity in a field previously of limited interest to many in Congress and permitting involvement in policy at the earliest stages (sometimes in advance of the executive). At the same time, increased staff resources have resulted in an even greater dispersion of power within Congress. The fact that practically every member has an energy specialist on staff and experts readily available through both committee and the ancillary staffs (such as the Congressional Research Service), increases the power resources of House and Senate members and provides them with an incentive to establish their own fiefdoms of prestige and to rely on their independently derived analyses and positions. (This area is discussed at length in chapters 12 and 13.)

A final important change, brought about by social and organizational pressure, has been the House's increased participation in energy affairs. In the past, most imaginative approaches to energy policy were generally found in the Senate. The increasing assertiveness of the House can be explained by more than mere resentment at being overshadowed in this popular area. Tax revenue measures, the bailiwick of the House, are often integrally related to contemporary energy legislation (e.g. crude oil equalization and windfall profits taxes). Finally, because House members are up for election every two years, they are more directly pressured by the public to take action on energy matters and are forced to serve as an ongoing plebiscite on energy policy, a role no other institution, including the Senate, can match.

External Factors

Added to the internal changes that have impelled Congress to play a more active role in energy policy are external factors such as public opinion and lobbying by special interest groups and the executive agencies. (Other important external environmental changes are discussed in chapter 1.) Political leaders have never paid so much attention to public opinion polls as they do today, although public sentiment has always been an important part of the foundation upon which Congress legitimizes its activities. Beyond creating concern for maintaining elective office, public opinion also dominates three long-standing philosophical perspectives that can justify congressional assertiveness in energy policy. First, some members view their role as that of interpreter of the public mood. They claim to have a special mission in a democracy to translate their perceptions of public will into energy policy. Another, and probably much smaller, school of thought holds that it is incumbent upon Congress to educate its constituents about energy problems. It holds that Congress is uniquely situated to help guide the country toward a better future; a seat in Congress provides a "bully pulpit." A third philosophy, closely related to the first, posits that it is Congress's job to chastise the executive branch where it has failed and to confront it with the public sentiment in areas where further action is needed.

It is clear that the American people by no means present a unified voice on energy policy. Popular attitudes are characterized by an ignorance of the energy problem's realities and by confusion, bewilderment, and contradiction concerning the means to its solution. This lack of consensus has made it practically impossible to devise a generally satisfactory policy on energy, calling instead for trade-offs between opposing but highly valued goals. The public has failed to recognize the contradictions between its goals and complains about the failure to attain one goal while it ignores progress made toward another.

Although lobbying is deeply entrenched in the American system of government, it has never been so highly organized or well funded as it is today, especially in the energy policy arena, where a few powerful lobbying groups of a relatively narrow orientation have grown into an extremely involved circuit of lobbyists. With the proliferation of energy interests among the 385 standing committees and subcommittees, the hundreds of registered energy lobbyists, the criss-crossing of influence affecting energy legislation, and the coterie of congressional liaison offices attached to all executive agencies, it requires an extraordinary amount of inside knowledge to follow the power struggles behind each major piece of legislation, let alone to participate in them.[6]

The increased complexity in energy affairs allows Congress members to play one group against another or use one group's information to neutralize that of an opposing group. Lobbying then becomes a key instrument in legislative and policy battles, and this truism becomes most obvious when counterlobbying tactics are *not* used. Carter's failure to consider such machinations and to effectively deploy his own lobbying efforts contributed to the evisceration of his initial energy program.

Another factor that has encouraged congressional assertiveness is the consistent failure of U.S. presidents to present unified energy plans in a convincing manner, for even if plans are at least superficially cohesive, the deep divisions in Congress destroy the plan's coherence. Congress then feels forced to step into the breach and select one of its own approaches, which complicates the decision process. Moreover, the confusion over energy policy goals at the highest levels of the executive branch means that congressional involvement will be episodic, uncoordinated, and inconsistent.

The energy issue is comparable to foreign affairs in its ability to exhaust the political power and public support of U.S. presidents. They are criticized for taking advantage of the powers given to them by Congress to launch policies in opposition to Congress's wishes. (Presidents Johnson and Nixon were particular targets of this criticism as was Ford when he tried to impose his oil import tax.) At the same time they are accused of *not* using these powers to defend the public interest as mandated by Congress. (President Reagan's lack of protection for energy consumers and independent refiners is an often-cited example, as is Carter's inaction during the 1979 gasoline shortage.)

As was pointed out, the short-term energy policy is essentially a zero-sum or negative-sum game; for each winner there is at least one loser and often more. Therefore, any action is bound to displease a significant segment of the public and, more important in its political consequences, the public's organized interest representatives. Energy decisions attract attention from across a broad spectrum of interests and the resulting pronouncements of opinion affect both the president and Congress. Energy policy has become a bottomless morass, a veritable black hole absorbing the efforts, power, and ambition of the politically potent.

Independent Legislative Initiatives

Examples of Congress's independent initiatives, created wholecloth out of individual congressmen's interests in response to executive actions, have been detailed in earlier chapters. These initiatives forced the executive branch to alter its own proposals in the direction of congressional priorities.

In a sense, Congress and the executive branch have been playing their constitutional roles. Whereas the president tries (or should try) to represent a single national perspective, members of Congress represent a collection of diverse and competing local viewpoints. Congress forms its policies to pla-

cate local constituent interests and the short term. A president who calls for
real sacrifices is likely to be overruled by Congress. He may respond by
vetoing Congress's more lenient alternative, but a veto is not constructive
policy nor does it promote the unity necessary for making sacrifices. The
president may also try to mobilize the public, to turn local constituent opinion
in his favor; he can then apply pressure to the hundreds of lifelines that run
between members' offices and their districts or states. All recent presidents
have used this tactic, with varying degrees of success. In terms of the
conservation/energetics perspectives discussed in the previous chapter, which
require some sacrifice and altered living style, of the few presidents that have
tried, none has yet succeeded in creating a national constituency for sacrifices, and none is likely to.

Establishment of Commitments

Although Congress has been bold and imaginative in establishing energy
goals, it has not been able to provide the programs and intellectual coherence
necessary to achieve them. For example, while the Energy Policy and Conservation Act was a commitment to conserve fuels, it ended up encouraging
fuel consumption. The Energy Research and Development Act of 1974 (PL
93-577) set national goals for the use and funding of alternative energy
sources to alleviate the concern that too much effort and money was being
devoted to nuclear energy alone. By simply making a public commitment to
support "free" energy sources, such as solar energy is imagined to be, Congress members obtain valuable publicity without actually having to spend any
money or offend any interest group. Such facile but unfulfilled commitments
direct attention away from national energy policy inadequacies and permits
Congress (or, in the case of Project Independence, the president) to escape
responsibility for the situation. Nevertheless, commitments can be substan-
tively valuable, as when the Energy Research and Development Act enabled
Congress to gather and utilize coherent data on energy resources.

Although Congress has surrendered control over certain policy matters to
the president that cannot be recovered without protracted effort,[7] it has also
restricted the president's freedom to create energy policy. There are times
when such restrictions become politically useful—to the president by allowing
him to use his lack of control as an excuse for inaction and to Congress by
permitting it to make a scapegoat of the president.

Energy Policy Sources

There is a tendency to underestimate Congress's role in shaping energy
legislation, partly because of the greater visibility of proposals made by the
president and the administration's spokesmen in Congress. The executive
branch's salience tends to obscure or oversimplify the critical role that is

played by less prominent Congress members and their crucial oversight and control functions.

While innovative ideas and policy can emanate from the president and prominent members of Congress, their ultimate fate is affected by myriad sources. When energy legislation is finally approved, it contains an admixture of concepts and procedures derived from both branches of government and an array of interest groups. To fully trace even one of the tortuous paths from idea to law would require an entire book.

Although Congress's initiative and imagination have indisputably contributed to the solution of energy problems, it remains an open question whether it has moved quickly or far enough on energy policy. It is certain, however, that Congress's preference for slow movement and caution when dealing with the nation's resources and institutions has forced administration officials to do much more thorough analyses of proposals and their implications. It has also served to build a public record, permit wider interests to be included in the debates, and utilize independent specialists. There have been many programs resolutely supported by presidents and their experts which, if adopted, would have hurt the nation severely.

Problems with Congressional Assertiveness in Energy Policy

The notion of Congress as a "blunt instrument" acting on the basis of political considerations, and its decentralized nature, causes concern that it will impede policy coordination. Congress can veto or at least paralyze energy policy at the very moment when far-reaching steps are most needed.

Energy policy problems are also created by the somewhat artificial distinction between policymaking and implementation. Because of the conflicts between many energy goals and values, Congress is required not only to take on new problems but also to modify and oversee the consequences of its earlier actions, thus remaining constantly involved in all stages of the policy process, from generation to evaluation. Critics of congressional assertiveness would allow Congress merely to set the general direction of energy policy, leaving details and specifics of its implementation to the executive branch. In general, they prefer energy policy to be handled quietly by administrators, experts, and technocrats rather than subjected to the vagaries of Congress. While it is unlikely that Congress will in principle relinquish its prerogatives over policy, the pressure of new business may force it to do so in practice.

Factors Promoting Congressional Assertiveness

Several factors favor an expanded role for Congress in energy policymaking. Because it seems the only path to stability, there has been a strong and consistent urge toward long-range planning in the United States. Such plans, when they involve national security, environmental quality, and economic growth, also include energy as an inextricable part of global or domestic agenda setting. Devising long-range plans involves extended commitments, for which the executive branch must engage the support of Congress, and in so doing, give it greater power over policy.

It has been asserted that the democratic system can be maintained only in an atmosphere of abundance, in which competition and conflict over goals and decisions are generally based upon humane rather than economic consider-ations. However, an emerging major U.S. problem is the "cacophony of eq-uity demands against the shrinking resource bases." As Horowitz has pointed out, "it is no longer reasonable to expect other nations to permit the United States of America to resolve its own domestic tensions in the world at large with resources supplied by them."[8] Some have argued that these pressures will require adjustments in the ideology of democracy as well as in the me-chanics of distribution and redistribution of wealth and privilege in the United States. Congress would quite likely play a role in the response to these pres-sures. Energy policy creation will remain crucial during any economic change.

Due to necessity, presidents have often called for a more dynamic and meaningful role for Congress in energy policy, although the role they have envisioned is to advance their own personal goals rather than to serve up independent policies. Presidents from Nixon to Reagan have with varying degrees of enthusiasm encouraged Congress to take specific steps to solve energy problems and to assist in creating a unified policy approach. Some have even favored forceful legislative intrusion in energy matters, despite routine complaints of congressional restrictions on the president and other authorities—complaints which, as we have seen, often camouflage political expedience.

Congressional assertiveness in energy issues has been reinforced by its pos-itive effect on executive policy pronouncements and program modifications. Congress has often rethought and improved presidential proposals, building a consensus for action to overcome the divisiveness and anarchy surrounding energy policy. Congress has also been successful in broadening energy policy bases and the energy policymaking process by demanding that legislative and public opinion be effective in an early stage of policy formulation rather than at a time of crisis or when an administration seeks post hoc legitimization for a unilateral decision. Because of congressional efforts, in contrast to centralized nations such as France, public opinion plays a crucial and continuing role in the thrust and content of national energy policy. This congressional contribu-tion is vital if American energy policies are to be compatible with mainstream American values and long-range national goals rather than being stop-gap measures based on the ephemeral personal interests of a particular political leader or party.

A final factor that encourages congressional assertiveness and activity in energy matters is the growth of staff resources. Stronger staffs are able to monitor the energy situation and direct Congress's attention to specific aspects of it. Because staff members must justify their existence, they are attentive and eager to discover issues to engage their time, and since many are energy specialists, energy policy will tend to rise on the list of congressional priorities. As staff size increases—resulting in greater specialization, breadth of coverage, and the emergence of experts comparable to those of the executive agencies—Congress will be able to handle energy aspects of issues more thoroughly. (This subject is dealt with at length in chapter 13.)

Factors Promoting Restraint

There are also factors which make it difficult for Congress to sustain a major role in U.S. energy policy. The decline in legislative activism since the 1973-74 oil embargo suggests that the process of governing in a technological era discourages legislative activism and independence. Unlike Congress, whose power and freedom is unique, the national legislatures of most modern governments either work closely with the executive branch or have been losing power to them. In Great Britain, France, West Germany, and Japan, for example, energy policy is almost entirely controlled by executive officials. It appears, therefore, that factors within industrial democracies actually work against strong legislatures. Perhaps a highwater mark has been reached in congressional activism before a falling back to passivity in both national and energy affairs. It is noteworthy that the number and substance of the bills passed dropped sharply during the Ninety-seventh Congress.

Because the energy problem in the United States is intimately related to every other important national issue, it is difficult to construct an institutional situation for the separate handling of energy. Centrifugal movement and fragmentation have characterized the treatment of energy problems, so far as they have been related to functional areas (e.g. agriculture, housing, taxation) and economic sectors (e.g. steel, utility, and auto industries). Differentiation and specialization, while ubiquitous in modern society, have a unique effect on broad energy issues, namely to increase their diffuseness as they are grappled with by the political system (as discussed in chapters 14 and 15). Congress tends to divide energy along sectoral lines which have regularized interests and participants. As a result, committees or individual Congress members can increase their power through the traditional operation of the "cozy triangle" or the now more common "sloppy hexagon," while Congress as a whole loses control over broad energy legislation as its focus wanes and its grasp of the energy problem's complexity diminishes. (See preceding chapter.)

Congress's agenda constantly changes, often in response to the latest public crisis, rather than adjusting itself to long-range national goals. Energy is thus dealt with episodically, without the general evaluation or institutional support that would permit it to remain consistently high on the national agenda. The new proverb—"no one worries about energy when the gas tank is full"—can be applied to the congressman as well as to the consumer. As long as we have a strategic petroleum reserve and a loose regulatory environment, many believe—as the Reagan administration does—that no national energy policy is needed; the free market can substitute for it. Similar conclusions expressed in 1977[9] seemed embarassingly premature in the wake of the Iranian shortfalls; and whether temporary gluts appear or not, there seem to be constant threats to vital oil supplies.

The systematic forces discussed earlier also oppose congressional involvement in energy by preventing consultation and coordination between the executive and the legislative branches. Congressmen find themselves isolated from the White House and deluged with conflicting, unverifiable facts, often fed to them by staffs who were supposedly hired to explicate and organize energy matters and by experts who may be in basic disagreement with each other. Congress has no systematic or orderly means to organize its overwhelming energy information. When there is a plethora of opinions and little certainty about complex subjects, interested parties choose the expert who can most convincingly present their side of the issue. The highly technical nature of many energy issues and disagreement among equally qualified experts combine to paralyze congressional action in energy affairs.

The public's attitude about Congress itself also affects the form and degree of congressional assertiveness. Congress is still viewed much as it was when Mark Twain teased that there was no criminal class save Congress. Revelations resulting from influence peddling, drug use, Abscam, and Koreagate, among other scandals, have damaged the public's confidence, as have accusations of obstructionism (especially on energy policy issues). Congress's eroded public support reduces the legitimacy necessary to sustain an activist orientation in energy affairs.

The public's attitudes about energy itself also restrain congressional activism in energy policy. Energy has attracted the public's eye as a result of recent events, but the public's eye is a roving one. When there are no gasoline lines or brown-outs, people may grumble about prices but their attention soon turns elsewhere. Lack of knowledge is partly responsible for this fickleness. Surveys show that public knowledge about energy affairs is generally abysmally low and that even the "attentive public"—that 15 percent who are reasonably interested in and informed about governmental activity—are often overwhelmed by the mass of detail involved in energy programs and the cacophony of contradictory opinions and clashing expert testimony. The attitudes of many in Congress reflect public indifference and ignorance, while overall congressional interest in energy matters ebbs and flows with that of the public at large.

Constituent demands can also inhibit a dynamic and sustained role by Congress in energy policy. Constituency-related business claims a large portion of most legislators' time and attention and, even with a greatly enlarged staff, they find it difficult to meet their constituents' demands. As suggested earlier, legislators do not have the time or inclination to acquire expert knowledge of more than a few, if any, of the many complex energy policy questions. Because those in Congress must choose a fraction of the plethora of facts, figures, and reports on energy for their perusal, a "natural selection" takes place favoring interpretations that fit an ideological position.

The congressional approach to energy is strongly influenced by local and special interest consideration, while attempts to understand issues or concern about the national interest play a less important role. Evidence from case material offers support for those who assert that Congress is deeply divided, preoccupied with personal, local or state interest, and indifferent to its own leadership. In general, Congress's involvement in energy policy tends to be intermittent, short-lived, and influenced by the newsworthiness of an energy policy issue. During an energy crisis, legislators' attention enthusiastically turns to energy problems and their causes, but when public interest dies and the crisis subsides, only a handful of senators and congressmen are left to monitor the energy situation and encourage farseeing action.

Future Directions

Looking ahead, it seems clear that there will be continuing conflict about national energy program goals and the appropriate methods for achieving them. Since the 1973 embargo, the executive and legislative branches have faced parallel problems fulfilling their roles in the energy policy process. Schisms, turf battles, competing interests, and centrifugal forces militate against either branch achieving a sound position on major energy issues, even though each has made significant and distinctive contributions to the substance and process of energy policy.

In the event of another energy crisis the executive will be disoriented and will have to scramble for control over energy issues, just as it did during the 1973-74 embargo. Despite organizational improvements, Congress would be similarly beset in an energy crisis. Congress is better equipped for routine energy policy matters and can moderate conflicting group demands. Although it has now established an influential presence in energy policy and can be expected to maintain it, Congress is poorly equipped for this responsibility, despite advances made in the integration of its operations. Thus far, few congressmen have tackled the organizational and procedural changes required to fully participate in the setting and evaluating of the nation's energy policy.

As Congress gradually wrestles with immensely complex and interrelated problems, it appears to be more decentralized, fragmented, and resistant to unifying influences than in any other recent period, and thus ill-prepared to adapt its organizational policy structure and internal procedures to the demands of an active energy policy role.

Despite all these shortcomings, Congress's resistance to presidential energy proposals, and to those of its own leadership, has a positive side. If some of these proposals had been adopted *in toto*, our nation would be worse off than it is now with its patchwork of inconsistent energy programs.

Notes

1. David Potter, *People of Plenty* (Chicago: University of Chicago Press, 1954); Kai Erikson, *The Wayward Puritans* (New York: Wiley, 1966); Clayton Brown, *Electricity for America: The Fight for the REA* (Westport, Conn.: Greenwood Press, 1980); Laura Nader and Stephen Beckman, "Energy as It Relates to the Quality and Style of Life," in *Annual Review of Energy, Volume 3* (Palo Alto, Calif.: Annual Review, 1978); Gunter Schramm and Stuart Bruchey, eds., *The Role of Low-Cost Power in Economic Development: The Case of Alaska* (New York: Arno, 1976); George W. Pierson, "The M-Factor in American History," *American Quarterly* 14, no. 2, pt. 2 (1962): 275-89. An especially interesting case is presented in Phillip Selznick, *T.V.A. and the Grass Roots* (Berkeley: University of California Press, 1949).
2. Lester Thurow, *The Zero-Sum Society* (New York: Penguin, 1979); Irving Louis Horowitz, *Equity, Income and Policy: Comparative Studies in Three Worlds of Development* (New York: Praeger, 1977).
3. Brown, Electricity for America; Steven DelSesto, *Science, Politics and Controversy: Civilian Nuclear Power in the United States, 1946-1974* (Boulder, Colo.: Westview, 1981); John Waltrip and Stuart Burchey, eds., *Public Power during the Truman Administration* (New York: Arno, 1979); Barry R. Weingast, "Congress, Regulation and the Decline of Nuclear Power," *Public Policy* 28 (Spring 1980): 231-55; Craufurd Goodwin, ed., *Energy Policy in Perspective* (Washington, D.C.: Brookings, 1981).
4. James E. Katz, *Presidential Politics and Science Policy* (New York: Praeger, 1978).
5. See chapter 12. See also Samuel P. Huntington, "Congressional Responses to the Twentieth Century," in David B. Truman, ed., *The Congress and America's Future,* 2nd ed. (Englewood Cliffs, N.J.: Prentice-Hall, 1973); and Harvey C. Mansfield, Sr., "The Dispersion of Authority in Congress," in Harvey C. Mansfield, Sr., ed., *Congress Against the President* (New York: Praeger, 1975). These are two representative pieces of the vast literature.
6. A General Accounting Office report found in fiscal year 1981 that federal agencies had over 82 liaison offices employing more than 1,100 staff. The liaison staff

budgets exceeded $12,000,000. *Washington Post*, June 4, 1982, p. A 21.
7. Harvey G. Zeidenstein, "The Reassertion of Congressional Power: New Curbs on the President," *Political Science Quarterly* 93 (Fall 1978): 393-411; Thomas E. Cronin, "A Resurgent Congress and the Imperial Presidency," *Political Science Quarterly* 95 (Summer 1980): 209-37.
8. Horowitz, *Equity, Income and Policy*
9. David Stockman, "The Wrong War? The Case Against a National Energy Policy," *Public Interest* (Spring 1977): 3-44.

12
The Impact of Congressional Reorganization on Energy Policy

The major wave of reform in the House of Representatives initiated by the liberally-oriented Democratic Study Group (DSG) in 1969 was already four years underway when the world energy crisis reached America. Arriving in such close proximity, the reform movement and the realization of energy scarcity helped make the 1970s one of the most tumultuous decades of Congress's history. As demonstrated in chapter 2, Congress's initially confused and chaotic reaction to the 1973-74 oil shortages and embargo indicated a structural unpreparedness for dealing with energy crises. The executive branch faced the energy shortage similarly unprepared. Confronting the problem thus meant creating new organizational structures and procedures within both branches of the government. Because this effort occurred simultaneously with the original House reform—an independent reorganizational scheme with different, often conflicting, goals—both reform movements were undermined.

The House Democratic reformers' goals were a committee structure more responsible to the Democratic Caucus and party leadership, and a House more responsive to its constituents' wishes. The mechanisms for altering the entrenched structures were: (1) relaxing the seniority rule; (2) diminishing the committee chairman's powers and that of certain committees, especially Ways and Means; and (3) opening to public scrutiny the congressional process from committee room to the floor. These aims and methods in themselves could conflict with the separate objective of making Congress function more smoothly as a policymaking body, particularly in energy policy. There were, however, other less overtly stated goals, such as securing passage of liberal legislation and "spreading the action" down to the subcommittee level, where the reformers were beginning to attain to chairmanships.[1]

These last two goals coincided because the DSG spearheading the reforms was led by liberals who had entered Congress in the 1950s. In the early 1960s they began opposing the traditional seniority system and powerful committee chairmen. They identified these House traditions with the obstructionism of conservative chairmen like Howard "Judge" Smith of the Rules Committee (who served from 1931 to 1967). By the 1970s, as junior committee members, they became impatient over the eight- to ten-year-wait before they might secure chairmanships. Their impatience was expressed primarily in complaints about the chairmen's inactivity, although policy differences were undoubtedly involved.

The impatience for reform was encouraged by the crisis mentality that pervaded the early 1970s. The country, awakened to the problem of diminishing resources, demanded some solution, and Congress was not equal to the challenge. The more junior members reacted with frustration and, believing that action was crucial, finally seized the initiative and overturned the existing power structure, both within individual committees and in the House as a whole.

It may be questioned why a similar reform movement was not initiated in the Senate. Possibly it was because there was less dissatisfaction with existing structures there, where a relatively unchallenged seniority continued to inhibit not only ambition but also ideological and generational conflicts, thereby reinforcing consensus. As evidenced by the handling of energy legislation, there appears to be less overt conflict over jurisdiction in the Senate than in the House.

In some respects, Congress's response to the energy crisis was an attempt to establish new structures and procedures that would allow the legislative body to exist in "equilibrium" with its environment through the creation of energy policy. House reforms were an important part of these changes. Yet, the upheavals and power shifts during this period have still not been completely played out. (The chapter's final section examines Congress's policy relationships still requiring further adjustment.)

The Energy Policy Breakdown

Pre-1973 energy policy lacked coordination and coherence and, at times, was misdirected. Confronted by an energy crisis, Congress reacted by holding hearings—the usual procedure when members need more information, are too confused to act, or want to appear decisive. The hearings so proliferated that little was really accomplished. Congress did not want the executive to assume policy dominance or allow new cozy clientelistic relationships to grow up between producers and executive agencies; but in the heat of Watergate, it may have guarded its prerogatives too zealously.[2] The extensive hearings, without a functioning federal energy-policy-structure, interfered with the executive branch's efforts to organize its energy decision making. (As noted earlier, William Simon and his successors spent much of their stints testifying to Congress.) The hearings have been justly called an "unseemly scramble" for jurisdictional advantage,[3] but they preceded the turf fighting that followed immediately afterward.

Reforms Great and Small, and Their Aftermath

In the fall of 1973 the House Select Committee on Committees—called the Bolling Committee after its chairman, Richard Bolling (D-Mo.)—began formulating its draft plan for committee reorganization in the House.[4] This reform effort was separate from that of the DSG, and although there was some overlap between supporters of both movements, the direction of the Bolling Committee's proposals antagonized many important DSG reformers. A major realignment of the House committee structure, though it might have reduced the power of seniority and the authority of committee chairmen, might have also jeopardized some DSG reformers' goals to advance liberal legislation and legislators.

The two most adamant opponents of the Bolling plan were Phillip Burton (D-Calif.), the DSG's chairman, and John Dingell (D-Mich.), later to become the House's "Mr. Energy," but at the time highly concerned about Select Committee attempts to eliminate the Merchant Marine and Fisheries Committee, the subcommittee which he chaired. Dingell's second concern, as a Commerce Committee member, was the Bolling proposal to transfer energy jurisdiction out of that committee (and several others) and into a new Energy and Environment Committee, likely to be based on the existing Interior and Insular Affairs Committee. Dingell and Burton enlisted the aid of Ralph Nader and various environmental groups to resist this proposal, arguing that the new committee would favor the energy industry to the environment's detriment. Thus, outside liberal interests were recruited to defend liberal legislators' interests. The Bolling Committee's work was ruined by conflict over areas of authority, especially in energy, where the jurisdictional lines had never been clearly drawn. The Bolling Committee heard from so many claimants for energy jurisdiction that they became leary of even trying to settle the question. Bolling at one point suggested that the contenders negotiate among themselves. The committee's draft plan, while removing some energy authority from many committees, still gave them a voice in energy matters. But the plan concentrated most jurisdiction over energy resources and regulation in the proposed Energy and Environment Committee. Most "losers" of energy jurisdiction supported the substitute amendment offered by Congresswoman Julia Butler Hansen (D-Wash.), whose Steering and Policy Committee had been commissioned by the Democractic Caucus to produce a more acceptable plan. Because to Caucus members (more than half of whom were committee or subcommittee chairmen) "more acceptable" meant closer to the status quo, the Hansen Committee left energy jurisdiction in its then fragmented form. With 75 percent of the voting subcommittee chairmen and thirteen out of fifteen voting committee chairmen supporting it, the Hansen substitute passed 203-165. While Hansen described her victory one way—"Too many of us have put too many years into this institution to have it all torn apart and upset by so-called reformers," House Speaker "Tip" O'Neill said it differently: "The name of the game is power, the boys [sic] don't want to give it up."[5]

Since reforms are supposed to disturb—if not break up—"subgovernments" or "cozy little triangles," it is remarkable that energy producers did not lobby on either side of the Bolling reforms. Only environmentalists entered the debate on energy jurisdiction, while subgovernment clients in other areas mobilized against the Bolling reforms. Hence the maritime industry fought to save the Merchant Marine and Fisheries Committee and organized labor campaigned against splitting-up the Education and Labor Committee. Possible reasons for the absence of producers' lobbies are: (1) energy producers wanted low visibility to reduce unfavorable public and congressional attention they had been receiving; (2) the energy policy structures of both the executive branch and Congress were in such disarray that new clientelistic relationships had not had a chance to develop; (3) producers were content to watch and wait for the outcome; (4) they were distracted by other matters. However, even if energy producers had supported the idea of a single energy committee, generally the strongest lobbying occurs against a proposal which hurts a lobby's interest, however marginally, rather than for a proposal that offers marginal benefits. The "inside-outside" coalitions most evident in opposition to Bolling's energy proposals were not composed of the usual producer and client arrangement but instead displayed the new teaming of "public interest" group clients with liberal legislators.

The jurisdictional tangles which the Bolling Committee was not allowed to resolve were left to be fought out in: (1) intracommittee disputes; (2) intercommittee disputes; and (3) the Democrats' Caucus (which was large enough from 1975 to 1978 to prevail over the whole House). The reform process deeply affected energy policymaking structures and policy outcomes at each of these levels, largely because the reforms allowed policymaking to be conducted at all levels simultaneously, without the existence of a coordinating body or centralizing force.

Rise of Subcommittees

Although it was recognized by 1973 that the DSG reform movement was pushing Congress ever further toward a subcommittee system, the Bolling Committee sidestepped the delicate and complicated issue of subcommittee proliferation and power. However, this move was "a fundamental conceptual miscalculation."[6] Not surprisingly, major opponents of the Bolling reforms had been, or would become, the authors and beneficiaries of revolts against the chairmen of their full committees. Phil Burton, a Bolling Committee opponent, led the 1973 uprising against Wayne Aspinall (D-Colo.) on the Interior and Insular Affairs Committee. A more spectacular revolt, in the wake of the Bolling Committee's defeat, was led by Commerce Committee members John Dingell and John Moss (D-Calif.) against its chairman, Harley Staggers. In both committees, power devolved to the subcommittee level, but the Commerce Committee rebels went beyond even the reforms passed by the caucus. They not only took away Staggers's single subcommittee chairmanship on Oversight and Investigations, but also gave budgeting and staffing control to subcommittee chairmen.[7]

The Commerce Committee shakedown precipitated a dramatic realignment in energy policy structure within the House. It created a policy focus in the Energy and Power Subcommittee and its chairman, John Dingell, whose domain was now as large as some full committees.[8] Although Dingell was required by the reforms to relinquish his Environment Subcommittee chairmanship, his move toward control of energy jurisdiction more than compensated for the loss. John Moss, on the other hand, had his interests split between two of his favorite areas, energy and health care. Under his chairmanship, the Oversight and Investigations Subcommittee devoted itself almost exclusively to energy for the next several years, especially to investigating alleged industry withholding of natural gas. Although designated an oversight body, Moss's subcommittee aimed at affecting legislation and was used by Moss as a platform for opposing energy deregulation. His policymaking interests impeded Dingell's subcommittee's legislative responsibilities and generated friction between him and Moss, notwithstanding their twenty-eight year association.

There were also differences of opinion between Dingell's subcommittee and the full committee, but it is unclear whether this conflict resulted from the deep philosophical divisions displayed in the energy debate, or whether it merely contributed to them. During its deliberation on the Energy Policy and Conservation Act in 1975, the subcommittee by a one-vote margin approved Bob Krueger's (D-Tex.) four-year decontrol plan with windfall tax provisions, while the full committee rejected the plan by a similar margin. Harley Staggers, defending the full committee's position, finally prevailed on the House floor after a prolonged battle. The incident demonstrates that with sufficient consensus, subcommittee dominance in the full committee and the whole House could be effectively checked.[9]

The Ways and Means energy tax bill of the same year represents a less favorable outcome for energy policy resulting from reformed committees losing control of their legislative products between the committee room and the floor. Ways and Means, a principal reform target, was the most weakened. Its authority was seriously damaged by the abolition of the "closed rule" on Ways and Means bills, as occurred with the 1975 energy tax bill. Another cause of its losing control of that bill was the element of internal revolt which it shared with other reformed committees. When the energy tax bill came up, the committee had been "packed" with the addition of twelve new members (four of them freshmen), and, as caucus rules required, subcommittees had been added. Previously, Wilbur Mills (D-Ark.), who resigned his chair under a cloud of scandal in the midst of the reforms, had seldom taken on members with fewer than three terms, and never freshmen, and had maintained auto-cratic control by refusing to have subcommittees to which he would have to delegate power, budgets, and staff. Rather than representing a solid voting bloc behind an indivisible tax package, as before, Ways and Means in 1975 could not win a majority of its members' support for three out of six of its energy tax provisions. Some committee members even led the floor fight against portions of Ways and Means energy tax bill and others changed posi-tions between committee and the floor. The main issue was a proposed 20¢ per gallon gasoline tax, on which the committee had managed to agree after bitter dispute, but for which there was no support on the floor. It may only be speculated whether a more disciplined Ways and Means under a closed rule could have pushed the gasoline tax through, or whether opposition to such a tax was simply too strong. In any case, this Ways and Means failure illustrates the extremes to which both the reforms and energy policy differences pushed the committee system. Yet, if committees were not permitted to function as filtering and consensus-building mechanisms, then legislation must be by a committee of the whole (i.e. by the entire House meeting at once), where building consensus would be practically impossible because of its unmanage-able size.

Slicing Up Turf

An important factor contributing to the committees' difficulties with energy legislation was their continued jurisdictional feuding. Exemplifying this was the three-way struggle within the House to produce a Democratic energy plan in response to President Ford's proposals in early 1975. (Also affecting policy development were the diverse proposals advanced by various members and committees.) In an attempt to unify the House and eliminate jurisdictional battles, Speaker Carl Albert (D-Okla.) asked the Democrats' Domestic Steer-ing and Policy Committee to produce the energy plan which, after consulta-tion with the Senate, became the Wright-Pastore Plan described earlier. How-ever, most committee chairmen expressed little interest in this plan.[10] Al Ullman, the new Ways and Means chairman, came out shortly afterward with his own plan. Meanwhile, Bob Krueger and other members of the Energy and Power Subcommittee developed decontrol and windfall tax proposals similar to Ford's. Speaker Albert set a ninety-day deadline for committee consideration of the Ford plan and the Wright-Pastore alternative and used his newly granted power of joint and sequential referral to send pieces of the proposals to appropriate committees. Nonetheless, he had no means of enforcing his deadline or of preventing committee and subcommittee chairmen from substituting their own programs for the party's.[11]

The melee which ensued was depicted by analyst Elizabeth Drew as an "energy bazaar" where public and private interests were traded. By contrast, Bruce Oppenheimer, a political scientist, saw it as largely a contest between the Commerce and Ways and Means Committees, with intracommittee intrigues adding to the confusion.[12] Oppenheimer claims that because Ullman was jealously guarding Ways and Means' jurisdiction against further encroachments, his committee's antidecontrol members managed to turn him against Krueger's plan by arguing that it infringed on Ways and Means' tax jurisdiction. Ullman then set out to best the Commerce Committee bill in a "race to Rules," and decontrol opponents on the Energy and Power Subcommittee of Commerce obliged him by stalling until he got the bill cleared for floor action.

Still, Commerce Committee members were among those who added scores of floor amendments (see below) to gut the Ways and Means energy tax bills. One of those which carried, a substitute for the auto fuel efficiency tax, was proposed by Ways and Means and submitted by freshman Phillip Sharp (D-Ind.), a Commerce Committee member. Mileage standards were a matter of particular concern to Dingell because he came from Michigan and both the auto manufacturers and the unions had opposed tough standards. Their position was that if emissions were to be limited, it was preferable that the Commerce Committee write and control legislation which would limit emissions by regulation instead of by taxes, as would be the case if Ways and Means controlled the legislation. Revenue measures are more difficult to alter. If, therefore, Dingell did not visibly challenge Ways and Means while it drew up its bill, it may simply have been for tactical reasons, so that he could ambush it later on the House floor.

There were other minor feuds over energy jurisdiction in 1975: both the Armed Services and Interior Committees developed Strategic Petroleum Reserve bills, and three committees—Interior, Judiciary, and Merchant Marine and Fisheries—had to settle their claims to outer continental shelf jurisdiction through an ad hoc committee.[13] All these flare-ups, major and minor, might have been avoided if a formalized mechanism for allocating jurisdiction and settling disputes had been set up; instead, committees were forced to use informal mechanisms which led to conflict and Byzantine intrigue. There can be no question that this gap in the reforms had an adverse, disjunctive effect on energy policy formulation.

The Caucus Gets into the Act, and Out

The reforms that revitalized the Democratic Caucus and gave it power to override committee chairmen further decentralized authority in the House (the "sunshine" provisions would theoretically be even more decentralizing by including *everybody* in the decision-making process). Because a reform aim was increased party responsibility, partisan leadership also received powers. But these did not tip the balance of power, which was heavily on the side of the Democratic Caucus. Both the Speaker and the caucus, for example, could pressure the Rules Committee to report out a bill, but only the caucus could issue binding instructions against a "closed" rule that allowed no amendments on the floor. This "closed rule reform" was another of those targeted at the Ways and Means Committee, which traditionally requested a closed rule for its bills.

Ironically, as it later turned out, Ways and Means chairman Al Ullman at one point pressed Speaker Albert to require that the Rules Committee report out Ullman's 1975 energy tax bill without waiting for it to be combined with the tardy Commerce Committee bill, as the Speaker wished.[14] Ullman's request was granted, but he received more than he had bargained for: under an "orderly open rule," over 200 amendments were offered (although fewer were actually considered on the floor) and his bill was gutted, with every title substantially amended. Ways and Means had already been burned once that year by an open rule when a committee Democrat, William Green (D-Pa.), asked the caucus to issue binding instructions to the Rules Committee to report an open rule for the Tax Reduction Act, to which Green hoped to add an amendment to eliminate the oil depletion allowance. In 1974 Green had managed to obtain a similar rule through the caucus but at that time Chairman Mills had simply refused to send the bill on to Rules Committee. In 1975, however, Green succeeded in having the bill reported under an open rule, and the amendment was accepted.[15] This was an extreme case of "spreading the action" and was, perhaps fortunately, the only case in which the caucus played a direct role legislating energy policy. After it had unseated three committee chairmen and issued binding instructions not only on the oil depletion allowance but also against any further funding for U.S. involvement in Southeast Asia, the caucus found itself quickly losing force because more senior members saw it as exceeding its limits.

Much has been made of the phenomenal increase in new members of Congress, particularly during the arrival of the "Watergate babies" in the Ninety-fourth Congress. Although their election further deranged energy policymaking, such freshmen as Bob Krueger and Joseph Fisher made valuable contributions, due partly to their energy affairs experience before coming to

Congress. Still, the large influx of new members in the 1970s created a vote pool in committees supporting structural and procedural changes. (The Commerce and Ways and Means Committees' upheavals, for example, resulted directly from adding new members.) Moreover, the caucus could not have become an aggressive activist body in 1975 without the influx of the freshmen "class of 74."

New Quasi-formal Organizations

The multiplication of quasi-formal caucuses and groupings, called Legislative Service Organizations (LSOs), in the last ten years has been another decentralizing innovation, if not a reform. Now numbering about seventy, some, like the Democratic Study Group, the House Wednesday Group, and the Conservative Democratic Forum, represent a particular political viewpoint. Others, such as the Congressional Rural Caucus, the Port Caucus, the Steel Caucus, and the Textile Caucus, represent sectoral interests, while still others, like the New England Caucus, the Northeast-Midwest Coalition, and state delegations, represent regional or state interests. Many are bipartisan efforts centered on an issue-area, like the Energy and Environmental Study Conference, the Members of Congress for Peace through Law, and the Congressional Clearinghouse on the Future. Together, these LSOs constitute an independent network of congressional information and decision-making structures. Their impact on an issue-area such as energy is usually to reinforce ideological or regional cleavages, or more rarely, to promote partial consensus within party or factional limits.

After House attempts to improve its own energy decision-making process by establishing formalized structures and procedures failed, infighting and the rule of numbers prevailed, supplemented by quasi-formal organizations. These informal attempts at control, combined with some ongoing reforms, produced an environment within the House hostile toward coordinating energy policymaking. By the end of 1975, however, the informal arrangements had assumed some stability. The Energy and Power Subcommittee emerged as the House's primary focus for energy legislation, while both the Ways and Means Committee and the caucus retreated from the energy field. The leadership learned the limits of its powers in relation to the caucus and the committee and subcommittee chairmen, and various ad hoc arrangements were applied to settle jurisdictional disputes. The next phase for the House, which began in 1977 (little was done in the energy area in 1976), was characterized by finer adjustments. Meanwhile, the Senate, where energy policymaking had stabilized much earlier, focused on Senator Jackson's Interior Committee. However, formalizing Jackson's energy jurisdiction did not foreclose the possibility of a major jurisdictional battle, which, in fact, took place in 1977-78.

A Partial Stabilization

The Senate Side

The House revolt against seniority was not repeated in the Senate during this time, but two important reforms did occur there. Republicans were the first to provide for election of ranking members without regard to seniority, and in 1975 the Senate Democrats decided that a vote of one-fifth of the caucus could request secret-ballot election of committee chairmen. The second reform came about in a more dramatic way when prominent Democrats resigned from the Interior and Insular Affairs Committee, accusing chairman Henry Jackson of absolute control over committee staff. With the support of senior senators from both parties, the junior members secured the passage of Senate Resolution 60, allowing senators to hire up to three committee staff directly responsible to them.

In 1976, the Senate also formed a Temporary Select Committee to Study the Senate Committee, also called the Stevenson Committee after its chairman, Adlai Stevenson (D-Ill). Its goals were more modest than the House reorganization committee's. Political scientist Roger Davidson, who served on that and the Bolling Committee staffs, observed: "We didn't do very much. We managed to preserve Senator Jackson's domain, calling it the Environment and Public Works Committee. It was more cosmetic than anything else. We were advised to be careful about the jurisdiction of major senators."[16]

The Senate's informal mechanisms of seniority and collegiality smoothed out many jurisdictional conflicts, though the National Energy Plan (NEP) battle, as recounted in chapter 6, represented an occasional exception. Senator Russell Long's Finance Committee, whose energy tax jurisdiction was left intact by the Stevenson Committee, substantially altered Carter's energy tax proposals, exchanging conservation and redistributive energy taxes for producer and business-oriented tax credits and incentives. Long and Jackson, the NEP's chief Senate defender, were appointed to the conference on the bill, and the many months of wrangling which followed were due as much to their disagreements about natural gas pricing and taxes as to conflicts between the House and Senate versions of the bill. Their dispute recalls the feud between the tax-writing and energy legislation committees in the House two years earlier. But it also illustrates the deadlock that can result when two different committees serve as platforms for competing energy philosophies, as well as how powerful personalities impact on congressional structures and policies.

The Ad Hoc Select Committee on Energy

The impact of personality on Congress was exemplified by Speaker "Tip" O'Neill's success coordinating House action on Carter's NEP. Benefitting from Speaker Albert's earlier vain attempts to harness reform efforts and maintain energy policy control, O'Neill designed a temporary coordinating body, the Ad Hoc Committee on Energy, which took into account both the new powers granted the Speaker and their limits. The Speaker defused opposition to his plan from committee and subcommittee chairmen by openly announcing his intentions and by reassuring the chairmen that their jurisdictions would not be violated. Public grousing from the chairmen was thus largely eliminated, although some of them remained apprehensive, as suggested by Al Ullman's remark, "I would hope that we will very jealously guard the prerogatives of the committee."[17] The new procedure did safeguard committee autonomy, while giving the Speaker a means of setting and enforcing deadlines for committee action, as Albert had been unable to do. The NEP would first be sent to the Ad Hoc Committee for two weeks' consideration, then referred to the appropriate standing committees by the Speaker, according to the Ad Hoc Committee's recommendations. If by the end of the period set aside for deliberations, a committee had not reported its portion of the bill back to the Ad Hoc Committee, the latter would assume responsibility for that portion of the legislation. This procedure magnified the Speaker's power.

Because O'Neill had stacked the Select Committee in his favor, he was assured 12 votes out of a total of 40, including that of the chairman, Thomas "Lud" Ashley (D-Ohio), chosen for his reliability. Therefore, the bill went through the committees and passed the House with unprecedented speed. However, much of O'Neill's work was undone in the Senate and the subsequent conference. At this final stage the committees reasserted their preeminence. O'Neill was forced to appoint Harley Staggers, instead of Ashley, to chair the House conferees, probably because of a concession made earlier to secure the Commerce Committee's cooperation with the Ad Hoc Committee exercise. While the Ad Hoc Committee innovation worked well, Congress's decentralizing nature required that it not be an enduring organization. This same nature ultimately led to the powerful Joint Committee on Atomic Energy's demise.

Disbanding the Joint Committee on Atomic Energy: An Era's End

As the Ad Hoc Committee was being formed, the coup de grace was being administered to a severely weakened Joint Committee on Atomic Energy (JCAE). JCAE, a unique congressional institution, was a novel organizational attempt to control a newly unleashed technology that had tremendous potential for benefit and destruction. Congress had specifically created the committee with immense powers to foster and control atomic energy technology.

In 1946, the Atomic Energy Commission (AEC) was created to place civilian control over the management of nuclear power in all its various forms (e.g. civilian nuclear power plants and military weaponry). It formed, with

JCAE and the nuclear industry, the "cozy triangle" mentioned in chapter 11. The powerful JCAE not only was the only permanent joint committee ever created that could develop and report its own legislation, but it could introduce legislation in both houses and serve as a conference committee to resolve House-Senate disputes over nuclear-related legislation.

The committee was given exclusive legislative jurisdiction over all aspects of nuclear energy, and all resolutions, bills, and other matters relating to nuclear energy were by law to be referred to it. This gave the committee a unique status that it zealously protected and used to foster nuclear technology and to dominate congressional and executive branch policy. For most of its life, JCAE's preeminence went largely unchallenged, but opposition eventually began to form in several quarters. JCAE was pressured by "democratic" forces in Congress (described above), by presidential efforts to centralize the energy bureaucracy (see chapter 3), and by a growing antinuclear movement. Opposition also came from those concerned about energy policy balance or who believed that nuclear energy was sufficiently mature to no longer require a congressional committee's special attentions. Common Cause, a "good government" lobby, voiced a general sentiment when it charged that JCAE ignored safety issues and cost overruns, while redirecting lavish federal spending to its members' states and districts, making of itself the "classic special-interest committee." Common Cause also asserted that JCAE operated "in an arbitrary and inequitable manner."[18]

An important setback for JCAE occurred when AEC was split into the Nuclear Regulatory Commission (NRC) and the Energy Research and Development Administration (ERDA). Although JCAE kept jurisdiction over all nuclear programs, ERDA accepted a constituency that extended beyond atomic energy and soon came to represent all energy forms to a varying degree. While this was occurring in 1974-75, Senator Abraham Ribicoff's Government Operations Committee was able to intrude on JCAE jurisdiction over some nuclear matters.

Another serious challenge was mounted when the Bolling Committee advocated retracting JCAE's civilian nuclear authority. The Bolling Committee diplomatically stated that, although JCAE's record had been "highly successful" in fostering nuclear energy, its unbalanced favoritism "short-changed" competing sources, especially coal. Despite the defeat of the Bolling Committee's recommendations, their articulation had accelerated the erosion of JCAE's jurisdiction, first by the House Interior and Insular Affairs Committee and then by the House Science and Technology Committee. Finally, the House itself asserted its right to concur in nuclear export decisions, thus creating a larger role in nuclear policy for the House Foreign Affairs Committee.

Organizational reformers in the Senate also eroded JCAE support. On October 15, 1976, the Senate Temporary Select Committee to Study the Committee System, using organizational streamlining as a rationale, advocated the elimination of all joint committees (such as the Joint Economic Committee), thus adding momentum to the movement against JCAE.

By 1976 JCAE's critics had become shrill, and for the first time were able to defeat its proposals on enrichment, NRC staffing, and research funding. By late 1976 the Atomic Industrial Forum noted that at least eighteen congressional committees, including the budget committees, had jurisdictional interests in civilian nuclear power application.

On the first day of the Ninety-fifth Congress, January 4, 1977, the House formally adopted a cluster of reforms which eliminated JCAE's legislative authority. One month later the Senate concurred with the House decision and reorganized its committee structure, abolishing JCAE. As each house split the JCAE's authority into at least four standing committees, this unique organizational innovation passed into history.

In a sense, JCAE was a victim of its own success. Those concerned with both the environment and with energy shortages in the late 1960s and 1970s felt that nuclear power was being emphasized to the exclusion of other energy sources. New mechanisms were required to balance nuclear energy with other energy forms and larger concepts of social benefit. At the same time, JCAE's awesome power made it an inviting target for those who wished to expand their own domains. When the junior House members "revolted," a natural affinity developed between their interests and those of liberal antinuclear power elements. As these challenges succeeded in encroaching on JCAE jurisdictions, JCAE began devoting more effort to defending its authority and maintaining its existence, and less on promoting nuclear energy. Certainly there was much truth in accusations that JCAE was high-handed in its preference for nuclear energy over other sources (see chapter 3), but its partisanship was mandated by its original legislation. Reacting to the limited knowledge and conventional wisdom of their time, their main concern had been to create an organization powerful enough to nurture nuclear energy against all opposition; and until 1977, they had largely succeeded in their objective.

More Attempts at Fine-Tuning

A few jurisdictional disputes about energy policy control have occurred since 1977, notably between the House Interior and Commerce Committees. Their conflict over the Energy Mobilization Board was mentioned in chapter 8. On this occasion (and over a nuclear waste disposal bill), the Interior Committee went first to the House Parliamentarian to establish that it had primary jurisdiction, and Commerce Committee was given secondary jurisdiction.

Although Commerce and Interior Committees were able to reach an agreement on nuclear waste disposal, the dispute over the board was acrimonious and prolonged. When an attempt to settle the disagreement in the House Legislative Counsel's office failed, each committee presented its own bill on the floor, with the Commerce Committee's version prevailing. Interior Committee, however, ultimately triumphed when the conference bill, after months of work, was recommitted with its encouragement.

There seemed to be only a modicum of interest left in the subject of committee realignment when it surfaced again in the House early in 1979. The new Select Committee on Committees, led by Jerry Patterson (D-Calif.), was approved by the thin margin of 208-200. Its main targets were energy jurisdiction in general and Dingell's Energy and Power Subcommittee in particular. A proposal for a new separate energy committee, made by "Lud" Ashley with O'Neill's support, was taken up by the Patterson Committee.

Unfortunately for its chances of success, the Patterson Committee cut too deeply into existing committees' energy jurisdiction. Mo Udall, for instance, who had supported the Bolling Committee and, initially, the Patterson reforms, turned against them when it was proposed to include NRC oversight in the new committee. Fearing that an energy committee would favor nuclear energy over environmental protection, Udall joined Mike McCormack (D-Wash.), of Science and Technology, and Dingell, in opposing the reforms. These "Cardinals of the House," as Speaker O'Neill called them,[19] united around a much weaker substitute proposal sponsored by Jonathan Bingham (D-N.Y.), which gave some additional nuclear energy jurisdiction to Science and Technology, but otherwise left the status quo intact. The Bingham substitute was accepted by 300-111.

If the outcomes of the Bolling and Patterson reorganization efforts seem strangely similar, it is probably because John Dingell led the fight against both of them. Congressman Dingell found no fault with energy jurisdiction being spread over sixty or seventy committees and subcommittees, because, he explained, "there is one that's really got it and that's the one I chair. And I intend to see to it that this remains so."[20] When the Bingham substitute renamed the Commerce Committee the Energy and Commerce Committee, to take effect when John Dingell succeeded to the full committee chairmanship, he fulfilled his ambition to be the House's "Mr. Energy."

Continuing Problems: Is Everybody Happy?

This survey has viewed the evolution of congressional energy policymaking structures since 1973 in relation to the internal dynamics of Congress. The impact of reform, personalities, and organizational rivalry on the process of organizational consolidation and articulation, and thus on energy policy, has been examined with appropriate examples. The conclusion that logically ensues is that Congress rejected formal plans for organizing energy decision making and was thereby required to take a far more circuitous and hazardous path toward consolidation of that function.

The remaining question concerns the *external* dynamics that influenced Congress in its search for effective energy policy and policy structures. If indeed the drastic reforms and upheavals within the House were partly aimed at severing clientelistic relationships, it would be of great importance to discover what actually became of those "cozy triangles." The classic case of such an "inside-outside coalition" of clients, regulators, and congressional overseers was JCAE during the tenure of Chet Holifield (D-Calif.). Holifield's committee, which initiated the Breeder Reactor program and determined the shape of executive and legislative branch decision-making structures in energy, was a major force in energy policy until it was weakened by Holifield's retirement and—in addition to the reasons discussed above—by Ralph Nader's and environmental groups' revelations that the committee had suppressed information about the potential hazards of nuclear power in the interest of protecting the nuclear industry.

JCAE's disbanding and the division of its jurisdiction followed typical House procedure. First, an "inside-outside coalition" of public interest groups and liberal congressmen succeeded in passing a Democrats' Caucus resolution disbanding the committee (the caucus route, rather than a floor vote, was chosen once again because the caucus was much more liberal than the congressional or committee leadership). Next, the staffs of the interested committees—Commerce, Foreign Relations, Interior, and Science and Astronautics—met to apportion the jurisdiction. The Interior Committee had a prior claim because it had "inadvertently" been given some nuclear power oversight jurisdiction two years earlier; Commerce Committee's claim was based on its Federal Power Commission and electricity utility jurisdiction, and de facto jurisdiction over energy policy in general. These two committees reached an agreement on NRC oversight authority which was formalized by entering their "Memo of Understanding" in the *Congressional Record*. Interior received primary jurisdiction and Commerce secondary, which mainly allowed it to review Interior's annual authorization proposals. The final outcome typifies the House's fragmented jurisdictional approach, for JCAE's fate reflected less a frontal assault on nuclear power as it did an equalization of nuclear power's status with those of other energy sources. Thus, in terms of breaking up cozy triangles, the NRC, and gas, oil, and electrical industries all complain about having to go to many committees to get anything accomplished, this was a new experience for the nuclear industry. Once the industry became mature, and its special relationship abolished, its complaint essentially became that it was treated like everyone else.

The aspects of this case which are typical of House procedure are: (1) there was an "inside-outside coalition" predominating (while in the mid-1970s it was composed of public interest groups and liberal members, at other times it has been energy producers and pro-producer members); (2) the semiformal and collegial procedures were used to divide jurisdiction; (3) the resulting jurisdictional lines were fragmented; and (4) there was philosophical acceptance of that fragmentation. The last point is worthy of discussion because it has been advanced, by John Dingell and some committee staff, as the preferred congressional approach to energy policy. They maintain that organizing committees with criss-crossing energy jurisdictions inhibits the development of protective, clientelistic relationships between committees and particular types of energy producers (or, for that matter, with any group).

On the whole, it would seem that Congress accepted this formula. The trend throughout the 1970s was to increase "access points," which meant decentralizing wherever possible. This direction may have been taken to help Congress in its "facilitator" role as broker for myriad public and private interests (as discussed in chapter 11), but it led to policy breakdown and incoherence in 1975. It was not "big oil" that unravelled that year's tax and conservation package, but snowmobile owners, boat owners, farmers, auto workers, auto makers, and all kinds of "consumer" and "public interest" groups. These and other groups constantly changed sides and alliances as they pursued their interests in a new and unchartered arena.

Because Congress represented the public opinion spectrum across all regional, urban/rural, income, and occupational lines, it reflected the lack of national consensus, which prevented it from building a consensus around a single integrated energy policy. Whether Congress's proper role includes seeking such consensus was discussed in chapter 11, but a broader view was offered by a former staffer who worked on both the Energy Policy and Conservation Act of 1975 and the National Energy Act of 1978:

> If we look back fifty years from now, we'll see that Congress made mistakes in energy policy, but it was the mistake of going too slow, not the mistake of going too fast, and that's simply the nature of Congress as a deliberative body. We as a nation are not agreed on energy policy. Congress has acted as a filter, and has arrived at a common denominator, which has been put into law.[21]

Notes

Robert Reynolds made significant contributions to the preparation of this chapter.
1. David J. Muchow, *The Vanishing Congress: Where Has All the Power Gone?* (Washington, D.C.: North American International, 1976); Leroy N. Rieselbach, *Congressional Reform in the Seventies* (Morristown, N.J.: General Learning Press, 1977).
2. Elder Witt and Tom Arranadale, "Energy Policy: 'Overestimating the Capability of Congress?' " *Congressional Quarterly Weekly Report* 33 (June 28, 1975): 1343-46; Alton Frye, "Congressional Politics and Policy Analysis: Bridging the

Gap," *Policy Analysis* 2 (Spring 1976): 265-81.

3. Roger Davidson and Walter Oleszek, *Congress Against Itself* (Bloomington, Ind.: Indiana University Press, 1977), p. 91. "Every committee of Congress has somebody worrying about energy. . . . We are holding great hearings, I understand, having people come down to tell us about oil production. That is public relations, that is not proper legislative jurisdiction." Congressman Charles Wiggins (R-Calif.), quoted ibid., p. 174.

4. U.S. Congress, House Select Committee on Committees, "Committee Reform Amendments of 1974," hearings, February 4 - March 13, 1974.

5. Davidson and Oleszak, *Congress Against Itself*, pp. 203, 250-54.

6. Ibid., p. 262.

7. Staggers was "outbid" for his subcommittee chairmanship, following a bidding process initiated by a 1973 reform. See David E. Price, "The Impact of Reform: The House Commerce Subcommittee on Oversight and Investigations," in Leroy N. Rieselbach, ed., *Legislative Reform: The Reform: The Policy Impact* (Lexington, Mass.: Heath, 1978), pp. 137-40.

8. By 1978, the subcommittee employed twenty-one staff members and had a budget of $764,460. See Michael J. Malbin, *Unelected Representatives: Congressional Staff and the Future of Representative Government* (New York: Basic Books, 1980), pp. 105-6.

9. Norman Orstein and David Rohde, "Revolt from Within: Congressional Change, Legislation Policy, and the House Commerce Committee," in Susan Welch and John Peters, eds., *Legislative Reform and Public Policy* (New York: Praeger, 1977), pp. 64ff.

10. Charles O. Jones, "Congress and the Making of Energy Policy," in Robert M. Lawrence, ed., *New Dimensions to Energy Policy* (Lexington, Mass.: Heath, 1979), p. 170.

11. Bruce Oppenheimer, "Policy Effects of U.S. House Reform: Decentralizaton and the Capacity to Resolve Energy Issues," *Legislative Studies Quarterly* 5 (February 1980): 10-11.

12. Ibid., pp. 5-30; Elizabeth Drew, "A Reporter at Large: The Energy Bazaar," *The New Yorker*, July 21, 1975, pp. 37-71.

13. Roger H. Davidson, "Breaking Up Those 'Cozy Triangles': An Impossible Dream?" in Welch and Peters, eds., *Legislative Reform and Public Policy*, pp. 44-45.

14. Oppenheimer, "Policy Effects," pp. 11-12.

15. Catherine Rudder, "The Policy Impact of Reform on the Committee on Ways and Means," in Rieselbach, ed., *Legislative Reform*, pp. 82-85.

16. Interview with Roger Davidson, Congressional Research Service, July 28, 1981. See his "Two Avenues of Change: House and Senate Committee Reorganization," in Lawrence Dodd and Bruce Oppenheimer, eds., *Congress Reconsidered* (Washington, D.C.: CQ Press, 1981), pp. 107-33, for a comparison of the Bolling and Stevenson Committees.

17. Oppenheimer, "Policy Effects," p. 20.

18. Common Cause, *Stacking the Deck: A Case Study of Procedural Abuses by the Joint Committee on Atomic Energy* (Washington, D.C.: Common Cause, December 1976), p. 1.

19. Davidson, "Two Avenues of Change," p. 119.

20. *Energy Users Report*, February 14, 1980, p. 7.

21. Interview with House Energy and Power Subcommittee staff member, July 7, 1981.

13
Congressional Staffing
As Policymaking

Because Congress had been rapidly increasing its staff and analytical capacity even before the 1973 energy crisis, it was prepared to begin organizing its energy data collection and analysis, on its own, when the executive branch began similar procedures in 1973. By separating its information-gathering structures from the executive's, Congress was seeking independent control over its external environment.

Congress's attempt before 1973 to strengthen its staff and other support capabilities was partially a response to pressure for general reform and decentralization as described in the preceding chapter. Yet it was also a response to the trend toward a more aggressive presidency, which reached a peak with President Nixon. It became clear that in order to challenge the massive executive branch bureaucracies' policy analyses and actions, Congress would need many more people and machines to process and package information. Accordingly, Congress passed legislation to improve its existing informational capacities and create new ones. The Legislative Reorganization Act of 1970 reshaped the Library of Congress's Legislative Reference Service into the present-day Congressional Research Service (CRS), added new responsibilities to the General Accounting Office's (GAO) traditional audit functions, and permitted the minority party to hire its own committee staff aides. More House committee staffs were added by a 1971 reform, allowing subcommittee chairmen to appoint at least one staff member; the Senate followed suit in 1976, allowing junior committee members to appoint up to three committee staffs each. Congress also created two entirely new support agencies, the Office of Technology Assessment (OTA) in 1972 and the Congressional Budget Office (CBO) in 1974.

Energy was an especially urgent example of the issues and problems which Congress's new auxiliaries were expected to handle. Because Congress only dealt with discrete energy subsystems, rather than with energy in general as a scarce resource, new information was needed. A former Senate committee staffer commented:

> There was no energy organization in the executive branch. . . . People looked for guidance, and there wasn't any. . . . There was no center of competence that knew what . . . was going on. We needed to know how to manipulate the oil industry, which was a large part of energy policy in the early 1970s . . . . how do you move oil, how much oil is there?[1]

Disastrous mistakes were possible as long as government policy makers remained ignorant and inexperienced in energy matters. Some argue that serious mistakes *were* made despite the sincere and prodigious efforts of Congress and the executive to obtain all the energy data available. In fact, it has been claimed that Congress acquired more data than it could effectively manage and that the data was used to support entrenched positions rather than to suggest new solutions.[2] (An organizational change theory, which involves congressional handling of data nad analysis, is presented in the next chapter, Figure 14.2, and serves as a model for interpreting some conclusions of this study.)

Congressional Staff and Support Agencies

Personal and Committee Staff

Since the committee/subcommittee system has emerged as the method of congressional organization for developing legislation and overseeing executive branch actions, the committee staffs have assumed a growing importance in congressional deliberations. Although congressional committees' original purpose was to make each Congress member an expert in a few areas, when it became apparent that the committee members themselves needed help if Congress was to obtain and assimilate necessary information, committee staffs grew in size and importance, a fairly unique development in Western democracies.

Although staff numbers have multiplied rapidly in the ten years since the Legislative Reorganization Act (and not without criticism),[3] personal and committee staff member numbers began to increase at a slower rate and finally to decrease over the last few years, as is shown in Table 13.1.

While their growth rates have slowed, these staffs have become professional and able to take advantage of technological and organizational innovations to enhance their effectiveness. For example, Congress's access to information and ability to transmit it has been considerably enhanced by the use of such machinery as word processors and computer terminals in members' offices and by the establishment of various data bases.

The staffing patterns of the main energy committees influence the formulation of U.S. energy policy. The House Energy and Commerce Committee employs 36 staff members, and the committee's two energy subcommittees—Conservation and Power as well as Fossil and Synthetic Fuels—each have

TABLE 13.1
Size of Congressional Staff by Fiscal Years 1957-1981[4]

Staff Category	FY1957	FY1967	FY1972	FY1976	FY1980	FY1981
House Clerk Hire	2441	4055	5280	6939	7371	7487
House Committees	375	589	783	1548	758	768
Total House	2816	4644	6063	8487	8129	8255
Senate Personnel	1115	1749	2426	3251	*	NA
Senate Committees	558	621	918	1534	*	
Total Senate	1673	2370	3344	4785	3743	
Grand Total	4489	7014	9407	13272	11872	
Percent Change	+56	+34	+29	(−10.5)		

*Senate personnel and committee staff figures aggregated after 1977.

another 11 staff members. The Senate Energy Committee on Energy and Natural Resources has 51 total staff members (Senate Energy Committee staff members are not specifically designated as belonging to the full committee or the subcommittees).

While some other committees with energy jurisdiction have an unusually high number of scientists (e.g. House Science and Technology) or economists (Senate Banking), the two main committees' staffs conform to the average professional mix—mostly lawyers, a few economists, and even fewer members of other professions.

The range of committee staff operations span a continuum beginning with the partisan staff oriented to enhancing the political careers of its employers, and ends with the nonpartisan "professional" staff, whose primary objective is acquiring unbiased information for sound legislative development. Although documentation is sketchy, energy-related committees during the 1970s seem to have been more partisan while the Nixon and Ford energy proposals were being considered than when Congress deliberated over Carter's plans. Under the Carter administration, the committee staffs functioned more as professional advisors with the stated objective of patching up what to some seemed rushed and unprofessional energy legislation.

By broadening its range of professional expertise and lessening its traditional reliance on lawyers, committee staff were able to gather and analyze complex energy data. Energy and Power Subcommittee staff (of the House Interstate and Foreign Commerce Committee) exemplified this trend. During the drafting of the Energy Policy and Conservation Act of 1975 (see chapter 4), the subcommittee depended less on the Ford administration for information and more on its own staff. While its staff relied in part upon information provided by interested parties, it also directly received information being used by the Ford administration and the energy bureaucracy drawn from sources that in the past had often been withheld from Congress. Congress was also conducting its own original research and contracting work to outside experts.[5] In another case, the subcommittee was able to discover from its own sources within the Federal Power Commission that the commission was not releasing information showing that natural gas suppliers were deliberately withholding gas from the interstate market and failing to fulfill their contracts in anticipation of price deregulation.[6]

Although partisan staffs help Congress members use independent information to develop effective and politically attractive legislation (or to hold lively oversight hearings that draw welcome media coverage), they can also create political difficulties for congressmen. For example, during 1974 drafting of legislation on utility coal, the chairman of the responsible committee was encouraging conversion to support the dominant coal industry in his state, West Virginia. But he was presented with a draft drawn up by the Subcommittee on Environmental Pollution's partisan staff, which reflected the staunch environmentalism of its chairman, Senator Edmund Muskie (D-Maine).[7]

Despite committee staffs' growing technical prowess in complex energy issues, there is pressure from legislators for relevant, quick-answer studies that support the legislators' predispositions and at the same time invoke the imprimatur of objective analysis. However, the professional staff are predisposed to heed professional canons of objectivity, caution, and skepticism and will attempt to thoroughly master areas that affect policy issues. Thus, their desire to adhere to professional, academically induced norms can conflict with their allegiances to political bosses. These value differences create a role strain that has implications for the organizational arrangements discussed in the next chapter. Legislators have become increasingly critical of studies which, though technically sound, may lack applicability for drafting particular pieces of partisan legislation—a major congressional function. On the other hand, energy debates increasingly rely on statistics and economic analyses rather than legal principles to support their arguments. Partly in response to these problems, Congress has in recent years been placing greater emphasis on the four congressional agencies mentioned earlier.

Congressional Research Service (CRS)

The reorganization of Congress's "reference service" into a "research service" was an important aspect of the 1970 Legislative Reorganization Act. The change not only enlarged the reference service's staff and expanded its facilities, but also increased its responsibilities. The Reorganization Act added new services for members and committees to the traditional reference function (which included constituent requests passed on by members). Although the new CRS has managed to eliminate some services, consolidate others, and transfer the bulk of requests to reference librarians and computers, it still faces the herculean task of responding to 340,500 requests per year. One former head of the Legislative Reference Service has written that CRS is "defenseless . . . in terms of availability to assume a workload."[8]

Because CRS maintains strict confidentiality, it is impossible to determine how many responses it generates in the energy area. It is known, however, that the House's main energy committee made much greater use of CRS than did the Senate's. CRS's large workload indicates that it is making a serious effort to satisfy committees' needs. However, there are variations in the extent to which energy committees use CRS, and these have implications for energy policy which will be discussed later.

Despite recent CRS growth in size and professionalism, it is still inadequate to deal with the demands made upon it. These demands and a rapid turnover of professional staff prevent sustained analytical policy studies and have thus resulted in a serious decline in CRS's contribution to the national energy policy development. Some flawed energy policy analyses have been submitted to Congress by CRS, including a poorly documented paper which estimated the cost of natural gas deregulation to consumers at more than twice what was indicated by any other researcher at the time.[9] However, CRS has been successful in compiling research done by outside experts and in presenting analytical accounts of congressional action in the energy area. Nevertheless, it is being forced to reconsider its priorities, and even this effort is complicated by Congress's failure to indicate clearly whether CRS's primary function should continue to be providing straightforward information for individual members of Congress or policy analysis for congressional committees.

General Accounting Office (GAO)

Of the congressional support agencies, GAO has the largest staff (5,200) and budget and the longest institutional history, dating back to 1921. GAO was established as Congress's watchdog over federal programs and given the main functions of auditing, evaluation, and financial control. It also assists in congressional oversight activity, a function that has expanded to occupy 39 percent of its time, compared to 7 percent in 1966. Congress has also added to GAO's duties numerous auditing and review responsibilities, particularly in the energy area. During 1981 hearings GAO's director listed 70 legislative requirements that Congress had mandated since 1970. The list includes verifying the validity of Energy Department data; subpoenaing information from energy corporations; monitoring and evaluating programs in the DOE and its Energy Information Agency; and auditing for the Synfuels Corporation, the Solar Energy and Energy Conservation Bank, and the Trans-Alaska Pipeline Liability Fund. He complained of the strain Congress was putting on GAO's budget and time.[10]

GAO has a precise focus for energy issues in its Energy and Minerals Division, as well as precise figures for that division's operations: the division employs 184 full-time staff, of which 127 are assigned to energy. Although GAO claims it has little time for congressional requests, more than half of its staff years expended in the energy area in 1980 went to committee requests alone, while another 38 percent went to member requests, and only 10.5 percent to legislative mandates. Of the 63 staff years devoted to committee requests in energy, 24 were for requests from the House Energy and Power Subcommittee.[11]

Some in Congress see GAO's growing involvement in policy studies and program evaluation weakening its auditing capability.[12] Ethical and practical problems occur when GAO recommends new policies and programs to Congress, since the office might also be responsible for evaluating them if Congress enacts them. GAO's power and its relatively recent mandate to evaluate the executive branch has also provoked hostility. A former Environmental Protection Agency official accused GAO of becoming "a fourth branch of government."[13] On the other hand, many in Congress maintain that GAO's function of providing it with information should be expanded so that Congress can compete with the executive branch in setting national policy. Congressman Elliot H. Levitas (D-Ga.), for example, wants to extend its full subpoena powers from energy to all industries.[14]

Although GAO has frequently helped Congress evaluate presidential proposals, develop energy policy, and oversee its execution by federal bureaucracies, its evaluation of the Department of Energy has been especially harsh. For example, at Senator John A. Durkin's (D-N.H.) request, GAO investigated the Department of Energy's performance in carrying out a 1973 law discouraging price gouging by oil companies. The report alleged that DOE and its predecessor agencies "consistently dragged their feet in sending cases of apparent criminal conduct to the Justice Department, with delays so severe in some instances that they made prosecution impossible." A December 1979 report alleged that DOE was neglecting its "primary responsibility—the audit of crude oil sales"—and thus provided support for those in Congress, such as Senator Durkin, who had called for the resignation of Energy Secretary James Schlesinger.[15] These and other studies indicate that GAO has continued to serve as a valuable auditor of DOE's enforcement procedures, and gives Congress useful leverage over the management and operation of executive agencies.

Congressional Budget Office (CBO)

CBO was a structural response by Congress to an overweaning executive. After President Nixon established the Office of Management and Budget (OMB) in 1970 and began the unprecedented impounding of congressionally appropriated funds, Congress moved to reassert its budget prerogative with the Budget and Impoundment Control Act of 1974. CBO was thus created as an adjunct to the new House and Senate Budget Committees and as a counterweight to OMB; its main functions are assisting in the preparation of annual budget resolutions, providing cost estimates for proposed legislation, and tracking "reconciling" appropriations and authorization bills with the budget resolution. CBO also issues semiannual economic forecasts and, at Congress's request, has assumed the additional duty of analyzing the inflationary impact of bills.

CBO is involved in energy matters mainly through the budget process and bill cost estimates. It has provided cost estimates for about 93 percent of all energy bills reported.[16] Because of staff limitations[17] and its wide mandate, CBO responds only to carefully selected committee requests for studies. Although CBO completed only seven detailed studies on energy in fiscal year 1980, some of these—such as the report on the windfall profits tax, discussed below—had a major impact.

CBO has also proven consistently useful in providing independent analyses of presidential energy policy proposals and rectifying their overly optimistic assessments. For example, in May 1979, the Congressional Budget Office released a study concluding that "decontrol of U.S. oil prices will cost American consumers more and result in smaller increases in oil production than the Carter administration has estimated." The CBO report estimated that the cost of deregulation for an American family would be approximately $135 during the first year of full decontrol in 1981, while the Carter administration had placed the highest possible cost estimate at only $100 per family. The study concluded that decontrol would increase oil production by merely 405,000 barrels a day by 1985, rather than the 750,000 the Carter administration had predicted.[18] The CBO study became an important weapon in the fight to end oil price controls. It underscored Congress's need for independent sources of analyses to end the traditional reliance on biased executive branch figures. However, an unresolved problem of CBO's energy studies is the need to incorporate sound scientific, engineering, and other noneconomic elements in budgetary and policy analyses.

Office of Technology Assessment (OTA)

OTA was created in 1972 to provide Congress with "competent, unbiased information on the potential impact of technological applications"—a mandate that has never been made entirely clear. The OTA is unique among the support agencies in having a congressional board. The board, composed of twelve members (six senators and six congressmen), has often been a source of controversy. Like CBO, OTA accepts only committee requests for reports and information, and the board can filter out those which it deems inappropriate.[19]

Because the board includes members such as Congressmen Dingell and Udall, who can themselves request studies, OTA has become involved in energy issues. In fact, the Energy Program employs 15 of OTA's 130 full-time staff, along with about 5 contract or temporary workers. Since its creation, OTA has completed twenty major energy-related studies and is currently working on five more, some of which will be discussed below. Because OTA studies generally take from six months to two years to complete, and concentrate on future effects of technologies and policies, some in Congress claim that they are untimely and irrelevant for debates on topical issues.

But OTA has often been successful in identifying weaknesses or biases in energy programs. A 1975 OTA study of the Energy Research and Development Administration (ERDA) pinpointed numerous inadequacies of agency management, programs, and goals. On the basis of this study, which was intended to assist both ERDA and Congress, one critic concluded that OTA had "demonstrated its evaluation capacity by exposing major weaknesses in ERDA"; he added, however, that OTA's findings were not "systematically integrated into Congress's consideration of the ERDA budget and program priorities." Instead, congressmen used OTA studies to "substantiate congressional positions on energy policy issues."[20]

As a congressional agency, OTA is affected by practical political considerations and has difficulty creating its own agenda and research topics, though many would like to see it operate as a disinterested fact-finding body. The first chairman of the Technology Assessment Council views OTA as "squandering its energies on routine tasks for congressional committees." Other analysts suggest that the partisan battles that erupt when the congressional board in charge of OTA attempts to set its agenda "threatens to wreck" the floundering agency's effort to establish itself as "an unbiased source of scientific analysis for Congress."[21] These various observations underscore the serious political constraints governing OTA operations, as well as the difficulties involved in attempts to use OTA studies in the policy process.

Unintended Consequences of Structural Change

Since the congressional support agencies' purpose is the rapid provision of accurate and unbiased information and analyses, criticism is usually directed to their failure in this area. More serious problems are bureaucratic biases and clientelistic relationships between support agencies and personal or committee staffs. Also, the support agencies often produce such a great volume of information on certain policy issues that Congress is overwhelmed and the issues are complicated rather than clarified. (This problem has been turned to advantage by the executive, at times.) Other problems are generated by congressional misuse of information during a debate. The more biased the information produced, the more emotional the disagreement; and the more information generated, the more protracted and intractable the debate.

Unintentional duplication of effort between congressional support agencies has been largely eliminated with the institution of the four-agency Research Notification System and through bimonthly meetings of agency representatives. Only when the notification system was introduced in January 1976 did the agencies realize the extent of overlap in their studies, particularly in the energy area.[22] Some duplication intentionally occurs when Congress takes advantage of various analytical approaches, as when all four agencies were called upon to examine Carter's 1977 energy program. For the most part, however, the support agencies are willing to share resources and forward requests to the appropriate agency. (The possibility of support agencies duplicating executive functions will be discussed later.)

Schedules and Agencies: Conflicts over Control

Decision makers react to the pressure of deadlines by forcing agencies to produce complex studies within strict time limits. Lacking the resources to handle new assignments, the agencies can only respond by interrupting work in progress, displeasing both the professional who must abandon a project and those who requested it. Personal and committee staff members complain about the slow response to queries about policy issues or the quality of information produced under pressure. There have also been complaints about inappropriateness of approach and materials used in policy studies. Rejection of an agency's work can also be due to the unrealistic expectations of the decision makers. OTA's energy program director Richard Rowberg, although he wishes he "could get stuff out more quickly," insists that the OTA wants to conduct studies in a rigorous and objective manner, "the way we are supposed to do it." He asserts that "if Congress wants solid scientific studies" it should be "willing to wait for them," but agrees that the situation is "frustrating for all parties."[23]

These and other comments suggest that analysts face not only conflict caused by external limitations on the task, such as time and manpower, but also conflict between diverging expectations, between desires for solid "scientific" analysis and quick answers of dubious reliability or validity. That internalized professional norms of many agency members are in opposition to the norms of politically attuned legislators and their personal staff can prevent agencies from producing necessary information at crucial decision points. Important analyses may be held up indefinitely or delayed until their usefulness for guiding policy decisions has ended.

The congressional agencies have generally responded to criticism of their work by pointing out that an increased congressional assignment has not been adequately balanced by increased funding. Clearly, if staff size and budgets were increased, more projects on more topics could be produced more quickly. But while these tactics may prove temporarily effective, they eventually become counterproductive by further bureaucratizing the agencies. The result is more administrative problems (and a displacement of resources to handle them), greater diffusion of responsibility, longer response periods, and a bifurcation of the staff's institutional loyalty, identity, and goals.

Besides asking for more resources, the agencies have generally attempted to solve their problems by instituting incremental, often stopgap, measures which lack the foundation of an overall strategy. For instance, OTA has responded to demands for greater policy relevance and accelerated preparation of studies by establishing a new category of short-term studies and farming out studies to other agencies. While these measures may silence some critics, they do not resolve the basic problems of unresponsiveness, delay, and irrelevance.

Similar problems beset CRS, whose staff members complain of deadlines that prevent meaningful and valid studies and superficial reference work that has included writing term papers for congressmen's children. CRS's tendency to substitute reference work for research undermines the capacity and reputation for in-depth studies it wants and needs to cultivate.[24] An inability to pursue the professionally prescribed approaches to a policy question due to time and subject matter limitations, erodes CRS's morale and impedes it from attracting and retaining the highest quality specialists.

Another problem that faces the agencies is determining how time is to be used. While OTA has its board, the other agencies are governed only by their legislative mandates and the ability to answer for themselves at appropriations time. Regardless of the priorities of GAO outlined above, GAO's Energy and Minerals Division has a reputation for pursuing self-initiated studies to the exclusion of congressional requests. Indeed, a 1976 list of major GAO energy reports shows nineteen congressional requests versus twenty-four "self-initiated or anticipatory" studies.[25] The question can be reduced to one of external versus internal setting of agendas, and who is being served by the agencies in the final analysis. It has been charged that the agencies often serve themselves.

Abuse of Information by Congress

The foregoing complaints about the support agencies and Congress's use of them seem mild when viewed in relation to various theories about the ultimate impact of large staffs. Such theories assume that every attempt to improve matters eventually fails, leaving Congress in a worse state for having increased its staff and information-gathering facilities. (A graphic depiction of this process is presented in the next chapter, Figure 14.2.)

The most extreme of such theories is presented by Michael J. Malbin.[26] He asserts that committee staff, who direct congressional activities, are not motivated by the "good government" concerns of traditional career civil servants, but rather by partisan concerns, primarily the promotion of the committee chairman and his political program. Support agencies have been coopted into feeding partisan staffs precisely the information they desire, a situation Malbin saw in the clientelistic relationship between a CRS staffer and the staff director of the House Oversight and Investigation Subcommittee. The staffs themselves ignore or even suppress information that runs contrary to the arguments they wish to advance. Information and analysis thus become ammunition used in debates that no longer concern the merits of the case in question but are governed by ideologists or interests. Such misuse of information, Malbin concludes, is inevitable: "Congress as an institution cannot be an intelligent consumer of analysis, able to sift the good from the bad," first, because the majority of staffers are lawyers accustomed to tailoring their arguments to their clients' needs and using information in an adversarial process, and second, because there is simply too much information and too much business for Congress to transact.

Interviews with congressional staff members supported Malbin's contentions in particular instances. When questioned about which information sources were relied upon, the following response was both typical and revealing:

> It depends on what one wants. One is usually looking for support for a position, so one perceives the suppliers of information as a sympathetic or unsympathetic to one's position. . . . CRS can produce statistics for *anybody*. I can call CRS and ask for an estimate of how much each barrel of additional oil produced by decontrol will cost, and I'll get my figures: $300 a barrel. Then someone who advocates decontrol can call and ask them how many more barrels of oil it will produce, and he'll get the figures *he* wants. You just have to ask the right question.[27]

Asked if this were true, a CRS staffer admitted:

> We do try to please both parties. Dingell could call one day and Broyhill the next, but we don't have to tell the second caller, "We gave the opposite numbers out yesterday to so and so."[28]

This confession reflects more evenhanded clientelism than bias. There have been other charges, however, that were more serious. For example, a former Senate staffer's criticism of GAO's Energy and Minerals Division was harsh and explicit. He called it:

. . . a disaster. They write controversial reports for colorful congressmen who want to get into Jack Anderson's column. They write the press release before the study, and then bring out this big goddamned study the day the vote takes place on the floor. . . . GAO's energy policy program was started at just the wrong time, with a bad cast of characters. They were out to make a name for themselves. Visibility is everything in this town, and the best way to make yourself visible is to start some fights, which they did. . . . Their studies are frequently timed to come after the useful debate, and dropped like a bombshell at the last minute.[29]

The debate over the Clinch River Breeder Reactor was cited many times in interviews as typical of emotionally based conflicts over energy issues that cannot be resolved by analysis. However, when asked why GAO and not OTA had studied the Clinch River Breeder Reactor, OTA's Energy Program director Richard Rowberg answered:

GAO can take a look at things on its own initiative. . . . It should have been something we looked at in the very beginning, and exactly the kind of thing OTA was organized to do; but once there's so much momentum behind a project that's hard to do—there are interests on either side. Even if we could prove that the breeder reactor is a worthless device, or that building it could wait fifty years, it wouldn't change much.[30]

Rowberg was echoed by Dan Dreyfus, who served fifteen years on Senator Henry Jackson's personal and committee staff:

Clinch River is a good example of an emotional debate. . . . There's no more technical information available . . . and the adversaries have drawn the line in the dust. Even if the thing blew up, some people would still insist it was a good project. The technical answer doesn't matter.[31]

Clinch River exemplifies a contention of Dreyfus's which complements Malbin's thesis about how analyses should be performed. Dreyfus argues that Congress makes two primary types of decisions: those involving technical issues that have already been settled by specialists, and large political decisions. The former are small, pro forma decisions, and are usually Congress legitimizing technocratically agreed upon interpretations of how to solve an empirical problem; the latter are decisions that when they reach Congress have already become part of a national debate involving a multitude of interested parties deluging Congress with analyses, argument, and opinion. In making this type of decision, Dreyfus maintains, "the last thing Congress needs is more information, because the lines are already drawn, and more information is not going to change anybody's mind."

In general, Dreyfus believes that Congress is sidetracked from its real purpose, which he defines as "redirecting fundamental policy" by pursuing analytical and budget functions that properly belong to the executive branch.

Dreyfus argues that analyses, assessments, and trade-offs should be performed at the earliest stages of policy development, as an issue moves through executive branch bureaucracy. According to this orderly, technocratic view, political and value considerations belong at the end of the decision process when all the facts are in (and when, of course, it is too late to influence the architectonic policy). When asked about the feasibility of the executive evaluating a program it is promoting, Dreyfus responded, "There are a lot of ways to have an independent body within the executive. . . . Congress should come in on the end to introduce the political considerations; that's a bad time to consider the long-term implications." When Congress encounters difficulty in obtaining accurate information from the executive, Dreyfus insists, "The problem should be fixed there. Congress should move analysis back where it belongs." However, the assumption inherent in this view—that technical, political, and value judgments must somehow always be separated—is unrealistic and interferes with the effective utilization of staff resources by creating expectations that cannot be fulfilled. The result of staff work cannot always be neat, indisputable technical answers that will resolve all political and value questions.

Another theory about the impact of large staffs on congressional activity and information handling is presented in James Carroll's study of CRS. He sees a confluence of "fact" with "opinion," of "data and findings" with "values and interpretations," in expert advice provided to Congress. While Malbin and Dreyfus insist that the distinctions between analysis and advocacy should be made, Carroll finds their fusion necessary and even desirable. Noting that "political considerations often do prevail," Carroll accepts the inevitability of "decision-justifying" research and information as well as "decision-conditioning" and "decision-making" research and information. Because congressional relationships are based on loyalty and trust, staff aides look for information that is "objective on our side" and approach agency specialists with that consideration in mind. Therefore, attempts to neutralize bias in a study to enhance an agency's credibility are bound to fail, for facts and predictions cannot be separated from values and perceptions. Carroll concludes:

> Information and analysis are often thought of as the refuge and hope of those who do not understand the calculations of passion, position and power seeming to characterize congressional activities and decision-making. [But] in the congressional context, analysis is the continuation of politics by other means.[32]

Beneficial Results from Congress's Increased Analytical Capability

Even Congress's harshest critics concede that some intracongressional analyses have been successful. When Congress's analytical capacities are applied as they were intended, they contribute to Congress's basic understanding of an issue and, by bringing either executive or congressional projections and proposals into line with reality by challenging incorrect conclusions, they facilitate the congressional function of redirecting policy. All four support agencies, in addition to several committee staffs, examined the major energy bills of the Ford and Carter administrations. While their analyses may have retarded the decision-making process, they uncovered substantial flaws in the presidential proposals (e.g. see chapter 6, Table 6.2). In another instance, OTA and CBO deflected congressional enthusiasm for synfuels from the original ethanol-based approach to other more promising sources. An OTA oil shale study, used especially by the Senate Banking Committee, was claimed to be "instrumental" in Congress's decision to scale down an $80 billion synfuels program to $20 billion. For its part, GAO touts all the savings it achieves in federal programs through auditing, financial control, and evaluation activities.[33]

Still, the agencies themselves recognize the limitations the political process imposes on the acceptance of analysis. They have found that some members are more susceptible to "decision-conditioning" analysis than others and that timing is a crucial factor. Dr. Raymond Scheppach, director of CBO's Natural Resources and Commerce Division, sees two key periods when the potential impact of analysis is greatest. The first is early in the policy formation stages, when the analytical experts meet with the committee staff. At this point, he explained, "The staff is open, the members are open, the committee chairman is open, and we discuss, 'How should we draft this bill?' " The result of these meetings rarely goes beyond informal discussion, or the drafting of a memo highlighting the issue and any relevant conclusions. The second point where analysis can have an important impact is when members are preparing for a floor vote and have not yet made their decisions. Scheppach admits that while many will vote according to their political constituencies' interest, undecided members, "The ones who will look at the reports," often hold the margin of victory.[34]

Senator Jackson and Congressman Dingell and their staffs have a reputation among the support agencies for accepting and publicizing analyses with conclusions that do not always support their positions. Former Jackson staffer Dreyfus attributes this receptiveness to the wide margin Jackson and Dingell have always received at the polls; holding "safe seats," they can afford to look beyond parochial or district impact. Dreyfus adds, "If you see an issue is not of much interest to your state, you can think a little more about the national interest; you can ask, 'What are the facts?' "

However, not all committee chairmen or staff are interested in unbiased analysis, as CBO's Scheppach makes clear:

> We upset a lot of people, no question about it. Some committees won't request analysis from us for that reason, because we're an uncontrolled cannon—

they've told us so. Sometimes a staff will ask "If we request a study from you, how are you going to come out?" We answer, "We'll come out with a study; and we won't change it."

It is never clear whether Congress wants unbiased expert analysis of policy recommendations that will necessarily become politicized. According to OTA's Richard Rowberg, the Congress suffers as much as the support agencies from this ambiguity:

> . . . in fact, we do our best not to get in anybody's way. We give both sides of the issues, and we make no recommendations. Every question in Congress is decided on the basis of political values, which we don't deal with because we're not authorized to or prepared to, so we don't. It's frustrating for members, because we tell both sides.

It appears that support agencies can have a substantial impact on policy and that analysis can be useful in refining and rejecting proposals, notwithstanding the inevitability of political constraints and members' conflicting expectations.

Facilitation

The perception of a need for an independent analytical capability shifts according to legislative-executive branch relations. An appropriate analytical framework for determining this need in the realm of energy policy has already been provided by Charles O. Jones. Jones defines Congress's potential roles in energy policy as "silent partner" to the executive, "initiator," and "facilitator," and describes modes of organization appropriate to each role. The first two roles share a "technocratic bias" that relies heavily on policy analysis. Those who want Congress to act as silent partner will locate the analytical capacity in the executive, while those who view it as initiator—usually of alternatives to administration policy—will locate it in the legislative branch.[35]

Congressional history in the 1970s was marked by the legislative body's attempts to take on the initiator role in energy policy. Congress refused to be an entirely silent partner even for Democratic President Jimmy Carter, and will probably continue to reject this role even if executive analysis and initiation of policy were shown to increase efficiency.

Moreover, Congress has not been very successful in the initiator role with energy policy, probably because of an unwillingness to relinquish the facilitator role—that of providing access to all particular interests. As was shown in relation to decentralizing reforms, Congress's propensity for the facilitator role has often proved stronger than opposing tendencies over the past decade. Those who favor this role usually reject technocratic solutions, just as technocrats reject facilitation, for the logic of one position excludes the other. While a technocrat believes that only objective analysis will yield facts and that consideration of uninformed public opinion, ideologies, or values merely attenuates or vitiates optimal decision making, a facilitator serves his clients through an ideological or value perspective which is unassailable by scientism and cost/benefit analyses. For a facilitator analyses can only support or threaten an ideology or belief system, never determine it.

While many criticisms of Congress are caused by the perceived bifurcation of planning and policy, there is no pure model involved here. Not all politicians are repelled by "academic" studies, nor are all technical experts disdainful of the political process. OTA's Richard Rowberg opts for a "mixed model," in which analytical components would be separated from value components but political choices would be based on technical analyses: "I don't think it's useful for questions to be decided on even the basis of a 'definitive study.' . . . The best [service of an analytical staff] is to provide a knowledge of the consequences of technology." Rowberg argues that "value judgments are not a part of that process," but that once a base of information is established "you can put value judgments on it. That is a job best done by members. They got elected to represent the people in their districts and those same people can un-elect them, as they have in several cases, if their value judgments don't suit them. No bunch of people sitting off in a building somewhere can make those decisions."

Rowberg's statement suggests that even those who advocate a "mixed model" of analysis and value can advocate an essentially "value-free" analysis by technocrats, leaving the messy fighting over economic and political interests to the "unscientific" politicians. Thus, even those who subscribe to a fairly liberal interpretation of Congress's professional staff's obligations and analytical responsibilities distinguish between fact and opinion. A central premise of this chapter is that this distinction, while it may simplify matters, does not fully explain the purpose and use of advice in the policy process.

Conclusion

Most critics cite a lack of authoritative information as a major weakness in congressional responses to the energy crisis. Although Congress is beginning to obtain its information with less reliance on the executive branch, energy industries, and other special interest groups, it is still questionable whether this information is being used effectively in the development of national energy policy. In determining this, the contradictory and inconclusive nature of the available information must be allowed for. As a result of these considerations and a general lack of consensus about the parameters of the energy crisis, there is a continuing debate on what should be done about it. This confusion and the likelihood that most members of Congress vote less on the basis of intrinsic information than on political and other considerations leads to the conclusion that valid appraisals of Congress's response to the energy crisis can only be made on the basis of traditional political science criteria and not on any "scientific" analysis of the correlation between available information and congressional action or legislation. Moreover, attempts to create an analytical technocracy that can objectively solve political and value issues raised by empirical policy questions such as energy are not only bound to fail, but can also exacerbate the inevitable problems involved in selecting policies based on competing political and value orientations by raising false expectations and engendering unproductive frustrations.

That notwithstanding, there is much evidence that staffs and support agencies generally try to provide objective and thorough analyses under what is an admittedly difficult situation. The goals of those providing advice are usually far more modest than fundamental changes in major policies (although, at times, this is attempted). Rather they seek to improve the basis upon which the decisions are made, despite parochial interests. The alternative—not to provide objective advice—would force the Congress to stumble along even more blindly than is presently the case. Nonetheless, there are prospects that Congress can make better use of information, and these are discussed in the last two chapters.

NOTES

I thank Robert Reynolds for his valuable contributions in the preparation of this chapter.
1. Interview with Senate staff member, August 4, 1981.
2. This argument is best presented in Michael J. Malbin, *Unelected Representatives* (New York: Basic Books, 1980).
3. Representative criticisms may be found in Samuel Patterson, "The Professional Staffs of Congressional Committees," *Administrative Science Quarterly* 15 (March, 1970): 22-37; Milton Gwirtzman, "The Bloated Branch," *New York Times Magazine*, November 10, 1974, pp. 3077; Stephen Isaacs, "The Capitol Game," *Washington Post*, February 16-24, 1975; Walter Pincus, "Hill of Ill Repute," *New Republic* 172 (March 8, 1975): 16-18; "The Scandalous Senate," *New Republic* 172 (February 22, 1975): 16-19.
4. Figures for the table are from Harrison W. Fox and Susan Hammond, *Congressional Staffs* (New York: Free Press, 1977); U.S. Congress, House Appropriations Committee, "Legislative Branch Appropriations for Fiscal Year 1982: Part 2," hearings, February 3 - March 7, 1981 (hereafter referred to as "House Hearings"), p. 252; "Legislative Branch Appropriations for Fiscal Year 1983," hearings, February 13 - March 7, 1982. U.S. Congress, Senate Appropriations Committee, "Legislative Branch Appropriations for Fiscal Year 1982," hearings, March 9-12, 1981 (hereafter referred to as "Senate Hearings"), p. 253.
5. Thomas Tietenberg, *Energy Policy and Planning* (Lexington, Mass.: Heath, 1976).
6. Michael J. Malbin, "Congressional Committee Staffs: Who's in Charge Here?" *Public Interest* 47 (Spring 1977): 16-40.

7. Ibid., p. 19.
8. House Hearings, v. 2, p. 139; Ernest Griffith, "Four Agencies Comparative Study," in U. S. Congress, Commission on the Operation of the Senate, *Congressional Support Agencies*, committee print (1977), p. 102.
9. *National Journal* 8 (December 12, 1976): 1731-37.
10. House Hearings, v. 2., pp. 582-92.
11. Ibid., v. 1, p. 716; v. 2, pp. 628ff., 651-52. Senate Hearings gives no figures for Senate committees.
12. Alton Frye, "Congressional Politics and Policy Analysis: Bridging the Gap," *Policy Analysis* 2 (Spring 1976): 265-81.
13. John T. Rourke, "The GAO: An Evolving Role," *Public Administration* 38 (September-October 1978): 453-57.
14. *Business Week*, July 9, 1979, pp. 62-63.
15. *Washington Star*, December 19, 1979, p. 7.
16. House Hearings, v. 1, pp. 165, 203-4; v. 2, p. 202.
17. CBO's staff size has remained fixed at 208 since 1976, except 10 new positions requested by Congress for inflation analysis. Ibid.
18. U.S. Congress, Congressional Budget Office, "Analysis of the Impact of Crude Oil Price Decontrol," May 1979.
19. "Because of this Board's unique role, I have not had to take undue heat, although sometimes I have to sign the letter." OTA director John Gibbons, quoted in House Hearings, v. 2, p. 495. Energy projects comprised 20 percent of OTA's workload in 1982—down from 27 percent in the previous year. U.S. Congress, House Appropriations Committee, ibid., 1982.
20. Stephen G. Burns, "Congress and the Office of Technology Assessment," *George Washington Law Review* 45 (August 1977): 1123-50.
21. *Science* 193 (July 16, 1976): 213-15.
22. Griffith, "Four Agencies Comparative Study," pp. 109-110.
23. Interview with Richard Rowberg, August 11, 1981.
24. James D. Carroll, "Policy Analysis for Congress: A Review of the Congressional Research Service," in *Congressional Support Agencies*, p. 14.
25. Griffith, "Four Agencies Comparative Study," p. 139.
26. Malbin, "Congressional Committee Staffs," p. 35. See also note 3 above.
27. Interview with anonymous congressional staff member, August 4, 1981.
28. Interview with anonymous CRS staff member, June 30, 1981.
29. Ibid.
30. Rowberg interview, op. cit.
31. Interview with Mr. Dan Dreyfus, August 20, 1981.
32. Carroll, *Policy Analysis*, pp. 15-17, 29.
33. *House Hearings*, v. 2, pp. 200ff., 486ff., 605, 607, 618.
34. Interview with Dr. Raymond Scheppach, June 30, 1981.
35. Charles O. Jones, "Congress and the Making of Energy Policy," in Robert M. Lawrence, ed., *New Dimensions to Energy Policy* (Lexington, Mass.: Heath, 1979), pp. 162ff.

14
An Organizational Theory of Congress and Its Application to Energy Policy

Studies of Congress by political scientists have seldom viewed the legislative branch as simply one formal organization among others. Yet the body of knowledge that has been established concerning business and manufacturing firms, among other organizations, is useful for understanding Congress. It can help in understanding structure and operations as formed by the legislative body itself and its response to the external environment.[1] (The reader may want to refer to the propositions in Table 14.1 while going through the first part of this chapter.)

Theoretical Lacunae

While the studies of Congress on its own terms, as a unique political institution, are undoubtedly valuable, they have not led to generalizations about the functioning of social systems as a whole and therefore have not generated broader social scientific perspectives. They offer a rich body of descriptive data, but their significance has been largely substantive. All the analytical information acquired about congressional voting patterns, committee structure, pressures on Congress members, rules and procedures, has produced little theory applicable across institutions or time. Functional analyses drawing conclusions from these findings have been rare, and causal explanations are still rarer.[2]

However, in order to explain certain salient features of Congress, the findings must be subsumed under more general hypotheses. This in turn requires viewing Congress as a particular of a general phenomenon, as a formal organization among others. The study of formal organizations has produced a rich body of theory that can be usefully applied to Congress for two reasons. First, it should allow the theories of formal organizations to become more generalized, i.e. not only to include business organizations but all formal organizations including legislatures. Second, it allows a firmer foundation upon which to base reforms. In what follows, no attempt will be made to develop a general organization theory of Congress, which is beyond the scope of this book,[3] but rather the nexus of the organization and its changing environment will be theoretically examined. This is the area that has been neglected by organizational theorists of Congress, and is most valuable for explaining changes in congressional activities and for extending a general understanding of structural change. A specific model of social change that can be used for Congress and organizations generally can fill an important gap in the understanding of organizational change.

Contingency Theory

Contingency theory can be applied to interpreting congressional organization. Contingency theorists (like systems theorists, from whom they have branched off) emphasize the interface between the organization and its task environment.[4] Their central premise is that an organization's attempts to adapt to the opportunities and constraints presented by its nature (its size, technology, markets, etc.) will be reflected in its structure. They maintain that organizations change their structures as they respond appropriately to various contexts or situations. Following a functionalist orientation, the contingency theorists have identified variables that strongly affect overall organizational design and thus allow predictions about an organization's structure and functioning.[5]

While Woodward, Burns and Stalker, Perrow, and others have made important contributions to contingency theory, the most important writers for our purposes are Lawrence, Lorsch, and Thompson. Thompson sees coping with uncertainty as the essence of the administrative process and the fundamental problem of complex organizations.[6] For example, because of the 1973-74 oil embargo, governments and businesses faced a future in which the embargo may or may not be lifted, oil may or may not be available or reach too high a price, foreign policies may be changed, war may break out, and economies may be ruined. Thompson maintains that because of their destablizing and disruptive effects, organizations seek to control sources of persistent or critical uncertainty.[7]

Toward this end many firms, especially oil companies, tend to integrate vertically, while Congress has extended its oversight and law-passing activities (which include executive branch report requirements) in order to reduce uncertainty or regulate and control the area of activity which causes the uncertainty. Organizations learn to anticipate contingencies and in the process acquire components with excess capacity that in themselves may bring about new contingencies.

Thompson classifies organizational environments in terms of their stability (highly stable to highly unstable) and their variability (homogeneous to heterogeneous), in order to find how these qualities affect organizational structure. One of his conclusions is that "organizations facing heterogeneous task environments seek to identify homogeneous segments and establish structural units to deal with each.''[8] Thus Congress has attempted to control energy policy by setting up separate units to deal with it in the House and Senate and specialized units within the budget and technology assessment staffs. Congress's own committee structure—a form of divisionalization—reflects the diversified nature and the substantive content of its task environment. In accord with Thompson's theory that ''components facing homogeneous segments of the task environment are further subdivided to match surveillance capacity with environmental action,'' congressional subcommittees are set up to deal with various problems within the energy rubric or to parallel fuel sources and uses. Thompson observes that when ''the range of task-environment variations is large or unpredictable, the responsible organization must achieve the necessary adaptation by monitoring and planning responses, and this calls for localized units.''[9] Decentralized decision making and planning, perhaps Congress's most salient characteristics, are typical of organizations facing unpredictable, highly variable, and contingency-rich environments.[10] Thompson's view is that the most significant responses of organizations to heterogeneous and unstable environments are:

- divisionalization,
- the creation of uncertainty-absorbing (monitoring) mechanisms,
- contingency planning, and
- decentralized decision making.

This view is shared by the systems theorists in general and especially by March and Simon, who posit that organizations develop structures because the capabilities of their human members for processing information and solving problems are limited.[11] Ultimately both contingency and systems theorists seem reform oriented: organizational solutions must be found to problems created by human limitations (see Table 14.1).

Yet a major shortcoming of contingency theorists is their failure to give sufficient attention to the processes by which an organization adapts to its surroundings. In their concentration on the final results of these processes, they create a view of organizations as passively responding to environmental changes rather than actively or aggressively seeking to control them.

Understanding Organizational Power

In order to function and achieve its goals, an organization must actively control its environment, which includes its employees and its customers (or constituents). To accomplish them, organizations use strategies ranging from cooperation to various forms of coercion.[12] While most large organizations display some mixture of these two extremes, mainstream sociological research has generally concentrated on adaptation rather than domination as an organizational response to change. However, Weber emphasized domination in analyses using a methodological approach, which, although mainly applied in studies of organizations' internal functions, are useful for analyzing how organizations attempt to dominate their external environment. Weber also explored the consequences of attempts by organizations to dominate in the larger environmental context, including political sources of control.

Weber's theories are especially useful in analyzing Congress as an organization attempting to control its external environment. Congress members face considerable uncertainty in their relationship to their internal and external environments. Congressmen, for example, must be reelected every two years, and senators every six, while the turnover rate among members of both Houses has been increasing. In addition, Congress members face uncertainty in the enactment of their legislative measures and in their future influence. Equally fluid and fluctuating are congressmen's relationships with lobbyists, special interest groups and constituencies, the White House and president, the executive bureaucracy, and the courts and foreign governments. The interplay of abstract factors such as ideology, public opinion, and leadership also adds uncertainty to Congress's relationship with its external environment. This uncertainty can cause subgovernments or the formation of "cozy triangles" as concerned groups reciprocally attempt to exert maximal control. The dynamics of these subgovernments are explained by Weber's theory that a system of power relationships develops among the actors within an organization and between organizations, as efforts are made to develop an "efficiency of control"[13] in order to exert power over reluctant parties both within and outside the organization.

Bureaucratization

To a limited extent, Congress can govern its external environment by drawing on its power resources; these power resources can be created internally through rules, socialization, incentives, and bureaucratization, and externally by developing formalized laws and regulations over other organizations, launching inquiries, or through informal accommodation with other groups or organizations. However, this attempt to assure calculability in an unstable, ever-changing environment is based upon a contradiction that can never be fully resolved. As Weber has shown, no one organization is capable of entirely controlling or determining the nature of its environment, because of all environments' inherent complexity. An organization is always in danger of responding inadequately or passively to modifications in the environment and thus of becoming subject to external direction or control. Even bureaucratization merely stabilizes the operations of an organization temporarily, without necessarily helping it favorably reconstruct the environment or exert a positive control over it. In fact, it may impede these processes. Internal bureaucratization is adopted as appropriate managerial procedure, the path of least resistance, or the most expedient means of maintaining at least a foothold in a changing environment.[14]

Clearly, a degree of bureaucratization has occurred in Congress, although it has not been studied per se. Increasing automation, staffs, expert resources, and less emphasis on seniority are Congress's functional equivalents of bureaucratization and enable it to handle its proliferating duties. The recorded votes in a session of Congress have increased in the last fifteen years from around 100 to 700, not including votes for the tremendous number of measures passed in the recently expanded "suspension calendar."[15] Demands upon a congressman's time have grown as a result of an expanded coterie of lobbyists and also because of the increasingly complex nature of the problems faced by Congress. The energy problem, for example, involves issues of health, taxation, economy, national security, chemistry, physics, and geology, as well as the more traditional issues of politics and group interests. As a result of the increasing complexity and size of Congress's workload, congressional staffs have grown in number, have become more professional in training and background, and are subjected to greater scrutiny in terms of personnel practices, rules, and regulations. There are now over 28,000 professional staff members assisting Congress and newly generated specialized agencies such as the Office of Technology Assessment (1972) and the General Accounting Office's division for program evaluation (1974). (This phenomenon is discussed in chapter 13.)

This particular type of increased bureaucratization has enabled Congress to cope more successfully, in a formalistic and managerial sense, with changes in its external environment, although the effectiveness of congressional agencies, especially those dealing with energy, has been questioned.

Integrating Differentiated Units

Another strategy used as an internal response to environmental change is the differentiation-integration process, the importance of which has been established by Lawrence and Lorsch.[16] According to their study, those organizations which are highly differentiated and integrated in a complex or highly uncertain environment are the most successful. Variables used in the study include formalized unit structure, interpersonal orientation—either task or social—and time orientation—either long- or short-term. (Differentiation can be interpreted as the differences among the formal structures within a goal-oriented unit, that is, the prevalence of specialized units in an organization, and integration as the state of collaboration among units necessary to achieve unity of effort against the environment, that is, the degree of cooperation among those units.) The study revealed that effective organizations in a given environment achieve more differentiation and more integration at the same time, because differentiation forces the creation of new and more complex mechanisms for achieving integration. In complex environments the traditional mechanism for achieving integration—authority or management hierarchy—must be supplemented by other integrating devices such as special coordinators, long-range planning, and cross-disciplinary teams. These factors in turn are supplemented by a second set of special organizational mechanisms to deal with conflict on both the structural and interpersonal levels. The study concludes that centralization and coordination seem to be natural consequences when organizations handle complex tasks in a complex environment; such as is the case with Congress.

Exercising Power

Another means used by organizations in their attempt to control the external environment is "environmental regulation": coercion or negotiation for the purpose of rendering the environment more predictable. Regulatory agencies are designed by Congress to control relations between the United States and other nations and a broad spectrum of life within the United States itself, and certain executive agencies are created to give Congress an identifiable "handle" on government operations. For example, the Office of Science and Technology Policy was created as a central point through which Congress could monitor, investigate, and make recommendations concerning science and technology policies of the federal government. (This office is frequently involved in energy issues.)

Environmental regulation is usually studied as an attempt by business organizations to increase internal bureaucratization or to coerce governmental agencies to pass laws and create regulations favorable to them. Few scholarly studies have examined attempts by governmental organizations to induce private organizations, especially businesses, to bend their goals to help meet government goals. Presidents Nixon, Ford, and Carter all attempted to check oil price rises by voluntary restraints, backed-up by threats of drastic coercion. The state uses its monopoly on the legitimate use of violence and various positive and negative sanctions, to force compliance by nongovernmental organizations. While states are seldom the unwilling victims of manipulative business enterprises, the reverse is often true. (Of course governments also manipulate other governments, and branches or agencies within a government manipulate each other.)

Organizational Impact of the External Environment

An organization's external environment can be classified by variables that affect the organization's structure. Among these is the degree of turbulence in the environment, that is, the degree to which it is dynamic, unpredictable, fluctuating, or expanding. The opposite of turbulence—stability—denotes a predictable and orderly environment. Environmental turbulence is often related to technological or sociocultural change in the environment and attracts personalities characterized by flexibility and entrepreneurial inclinations who are able to exploit the turbulence to advance their own goals.[17] Organizations sharing a turbulent environment are often in vigorous competition.

The importance to an organization of mechanisms that assist in the absorption or avoidance of uncertainty is in direct proportion to environmental turbulence. Structures and operations that anticipate and/or counteract events that could negatively affect an organization become means of insulating the organization, its goals and personnel against turbulence. Producing forecasts, assessments, and information are major activities of these units.

Turbulence can promote vertical integration since it induces organizations to try to increase their area of control. For example, Congress attempted to control policy concerning the entire range of energy, from its extraction and production to its ultimate utilization. Congress succeeded in expanding its influence over the energy bureaucracy by establishing precise bureaucratic arrangements throughout the spectrum of energy management. As organizations learn that their control over one area depends upon controlling an impinging area, the expansion of integrated control becomes difficult to limit. (This is discussed further in the section on complex environments.)

At the same time, the increase in vertically-integrated control and administrative flexibility generates interpersonal conflict, both within an organization (interdepartmental or intercommittee conflict) and between the organization and the entities it controls. In response to an environment considered hostile (risky, dominating, antagonistic as opposed to safe, rich, encouraging), an organization centralizes power, demanding greater coordination and clearance from higher authorities.[18] The executive's attempt to increase its control over the energy crisis in the United States by creating new agencies in the White House was such a response to supposed hostility in the environment; a similar situation occurred more slowly with the establishment of a specialized federal bureaucracy to handle energy problems exclusively. As hostility increases, the first response of leadership is to become more demanding, more coercive, and more authoritarian toward those within the organization and to individuals from other organizations. Such a response by Nixon and his staff during the energy crisis resulted in a changed relationship between the administration and Congress. When the initial authoritarian response provokes hostility and antagonism in its targets, a more conciliatory and cooperative attitude is assumed by the aggressors. The softened response is then reflected in the attitudes of everyone involved, behavior changes, and damaged relationships improve.

The perception of environmental hostility also stimulates increased information gathering and processing activities, especially those that require sophisticated knowledge and techniques, and increases long-range planning. The threatened organization reacts by augmenting its means of understanding the environment and thus its ability to anticipate or manipulate it to its own advantage.

Heterogeneity is another category in this classification, used to designate the relative number of dissimilar characteristics displayed by an environment. Organizations react to heterogeneity by increasing their structural differentiation. Separate but homogeneous structures are developed to deal with each major distinctive element in the environment, resulting in lack of coordination and duplication of effort. To cope with these factors, organizations establish links between units to coordinate their operations and integrate their functions. (These integrating mechanisms often create unique opportunities for mutual influence by members of the organizations.) In the drive for integration, sophisticated control and information systems are introduced, regularized problem-solving methods are sought, and participation from all levels of decision making is encouraged.

Another external environment characteristic—complexity— differs from heterogeneity in that it indicates interrelationships among environmental elements and their diverseness. An increase in environmental complexity causes organizations to emphasize long-range planning and develop mechanisms and systems that will enhance their planning capabilities. Environmental complexity therefore stimulates an interest in information management and control techniques to handle the data required for planning, and in technocratic-scientific management approaches to decision-making and administrative processes. At the same time there is increased reliance on professional staffs to support planning and information management functions. The U.S. government's reaction to the environmental complexity caused by the energy shortage followed this pattern. For any organization dealing with contemporary energy problems, all elements in the environment or social system become increasingly interrelated. For example, a decision about building nuclear reactors affects decisions about importing of oil, and thus about foreign relations, economic growth, and national security, and affects environmental quality, public attitudes, employment levels, taxes, economic concentration, public demonstrations, and bond ratings.

The external environment can also affect organizations more directly. For example, a highly ambitious and competitive environment will demand similar characteristics in an organization by heightening performance aspirations and providing a negative response if these aspirations are not fulfilled. Congress's activities in the energy area, which gained crucial significance during the energy crisis, disappointed the public, for the greater the challenge provided by the environment, the more severely the response is judged by the public.

Organizational Impact of the Internal Environment

The structures, goals, degree of centralization, and leadership mode of organizations are affected not only by the external environment, but also by their internal environments. When a variety of tasks must be performed by an organization, creating cross-pressures on the subsystems within it, the organization is said to have a differentiated task environment. As has been pointed out, organizations with differentiated internal structures require complex means of integration such as special liaison or linking mechanisms, if efficiency is to be maintained. Therefore, the more differentiated the task environment of an organization's various subsystems, the more it must resort to complex modes of maintaining coordination and integration in its operations. Lawrence and Lorsch hold that an organization with a differentiated task environment is likely to show differentiation in its internal attributes, especially in its goals and normative criteria about member behavior.

Cyert and March [19] have demonstrated, however, that goal conflict among various groups in an organization is a general condition of organizations and that their operating goals (as opposed to those that are formally stated) emerge from this conflict. While to some extent operating goals are set by the ruling coalition (whose strength is supplemented by various "side payments" or "logrolling"), these coalitions are relatively unstable and, therefore, are the organization's operating goals. The stability of operating goals is maintained in large part by reference to unquestioned precedents and by the continuation of past practices through inertia. Thus, the actual goals that an organization pursues are both products of the past and aspirations of the currently ruling coalition.

However, because organizational members usually devote their time principally to particular tasks rather than general goals, their organizations can pursue conflicting goals simultaneously. Such conflict has been typical of organizations involved with national energy policies, especially of Congress when dealing with the Ford administration energy initiatives and in creating the Energy Policy and Conservation Act. Cyert and March conclude that although there is widespread conflict over organizational goals among key factions of any organization, most organizations continue to function effectively because conflict is defused through such processes as coalition building, respect for precedents, side payments, limited or sequential attention to goals, task segmentation, and organizational slack. Consequently, there is usually consistency in following one general direction in the pursuit of goals, although the goals are constantly subjected to marginal adjustments. (This process is applicable to the discussion of ideology shifts in chapter 10.)

An organization can also reduce conflict over goals by preselecting its members, and the less diversity there is in the ideological views of its membership, the more agreement on goals it will exhibit. This option is closed to

Congress, of course, although it can select its leadership and the incumbents for key positions. Also, the less specialization by members (which would include the subject and area specialization that many Congress members pursue) and the smaller the organization (these two aspects are usually correlated), the less goal conflict is to be expected. Finally, integrating mechanisms can compensate for the centrifugal forces of differentiation while decentralization may prevent opportunities and weaken incentives for individuals and units of an organization to pursue secondary goals.

As the internal environment influences the structure of an organization, a reverse process also occurs. The internal and external environments are affected by the visible structures of organizations—their visible superstructure or formal arrangements—as well as the less visible network of controls, procedures, authority relationships, specialization, and so on, which constitutes an organization's infrastructure. Organizational structure reduces external and internal uncertainty produced by unpredictable events and behavior within the organization. It also enables an organization to undertake a wide variety of activities through devices such as departmentalization, specialization, division of labor, and delegation of authority. An organization can coordinate its activities, pursue goals, and maintain a focus in the midst of diversity through the structural elements of hierarchy, formal committees, and information systems that facilitate the integration of organizational activities.

Formal Structure Types and Their Determinants

Formal structure is usually classified as functional, divisional, or matrix—a hybridized form. Functional structure's governing principle is the location in one area of all personnel that can contribute to the accomplishment of a specific function. Divisionalization is an alternative way of grouping organizational members by aggregating all the specialists needed to produce a given service or product. The matrix form involves interdepartmentalization, committees or task forces, and, typically, personnel's membership in two of the organization's units or more at the same time. This is the form followed by Congress. In a matrix structure the ability to work as a team member is extremely important, yet its heterogeneity can induce interpersonal conflict within the team. Consequently, issues must be constantly delineated and recast to prevent interpersonal dynamics from paralyzing committee work. Flexibility is also necessary to free each committee from administrative details so that it may function effectively. At the same time, the diverse activities associated with the matrix form must finally be integrated into coherent policy. This need for diversity and coordination has frustrated many attempts to establish a broad and integrated energy plan. The great variety of projects usually handled by a matrix organization makes an organic management ideology and style necessary, as well as a leadership that is oriented toward human relations and greater participation by members.[20]

A key finding of contingency theorists, and one that fits nicely with the differentiation/integration approach, is that each form—functional, divisional, and matrix—is appropriate in different task environments. But in the present organizational environment there is pressure to move toward divisionalization, because diverse product lines (material, informational, and political) make it difficult for those with authority to be knowledgeable in all relevant areas. Functional specialization, which occurs because of the need to make efficient use of the variegated and high quality staff that this form allows, has also become an attractive option. Galbraith points out that the faster the rate at which new information, products, or services are introduced, the more unfamiliar tasks become.[21] Thus, the number of bills and expanded coverage activities that Congress now faces require even higher levels of expertise, sophistication, and knowledge. Pressure increases for both divisionalization and functional specialization to deal with the growing complexity. However, the final structural form that is likely to result from the cross-pressures to which Congress and other similarly situated organizations are subjected is the matrix form (unless this is prevented by economies of scale, as is the case with massive steel or aluminum plants). The pressure Congress is under for customized outputs also reinforces its need for a matrix form.

The degree to which power and responsibility are centralized also affects organizational structure, although there is disagreement about whether the effect is positive or negative. Some argue that decentralization encourages meaningful and responsible work and flexibility in that it allows more rapid response to local contingencies. Opponents of decentralization claim that it creates vested interests and causes resistance to change and insensitivity to broader interests.[22] The general agreement is that large organizations such as Congress are more decentralized than small ones.[23] The prevalence of professionals among Congress members and their staffs also encourages decentralization of power, as in other organizations composed of professionals such as hospitals, research labs, and educational institutions. Being a member of Congress also confers professional status upon the incumbent, who has independent bases of power and authority along with special prescribed norms of behavior. Thus a professional ethos and milieu reinforce the decentralization that already exists in Congress as a result of its standardized, variable, and custom-tailored tasks.

Propositions

This analysis—covering a few areas where general knowledge of organizational behavior can elucidate Congress's performance on energy issues—suggests an organizational theory significant to events described in earlier chapters. The propositions presented next in this chapter may also prove useful to the development of a robust and useful theory of organizations with theories of legislatures as a subset. Toward this end, the following theoretical propositions in Table 14.1 are offered.

Table 14.1 Selected Propositions Governing Organizational Structure and Behavior

1. As turbulence in the external environment increases
   a. more reliance is placed by an organization on uncertainty absorption and avoidance mechanisms, such as forecasting, analytical techniques, and vertical integration;
   b. administration procedures become more flexible; and
   c. intra-organizational conflict among units increases.
2. As hostility increases in the external environment
   a. the coercive-authoritarian orientation of leadership in an organization first increases, then decreases; and
   b. investment of resources in staff-based, sophisticated information-generating and -processing activities increases.
3. As heterogeneity in the external environment increases
   a. organizational structure and differentiation increases; and
   b. integration (e.g. sophisticated control and information systems, regularized procedures and rules, or participatory styles of leadership) increases.
4. The more differentiated the task environment of an organization's various subsystems, that is, the greater the difference in the task environments of the major parts of the organization
   a. the more internally differentiated is the organization; and
   b. the more it must resort to complex modes for maintaining coordination and integration in its operations.
5. The more technologically complex the external environment
   a. the more an organization and its leadership emphasize planning;
   b. the more sophisticated and complex its control and information system becomes; and
   c. the more reliance it places on subject specialists and scientific and technological experts.
6. The larger an organization and the more differentiated its activities
   a. the greater the conflict within it concerning operating goals.
7. The more differentiated and decentralized an organization is
   a. the more secondary goals it pursues.
8. The more competitive and challenging the environment
   a. the higher the organization's performance aspirations with respect to operating goals.

9. The more intense, diverse, and shifting the pressures on the leadership of an organization
   a. the greater its need for flexibility and an organic style of leadership.
10. The more an organization's superstructure resembles a matrix organization
    a. the more organic, participatory, and human relations-oriented the management style at the operating levels of the organization.
11. The more individualized or variegated the products or services provided by an organization to its clients
    a. the faster the rate of innovation or introduction of new products, projects, or services by the organization; and
    b. the closer the organization will move toward a matrix project structure provided its economies of scale are not large.
12. The more an organization demonstrates professional norms
    a. the more decentralized authority responsible for making operating decisions becomes, especially if the tasks to be performed are relatively variable and nonstandard.

The propositions predict only associations between certain factors. They do not indicate how particular outcomes are generated by the social system. The conceptually simple input-output model of organizations, which is frequently used in constructing theories of formal organizations (especially by the contingency theory school), will be used here only as it applies to Congress's handling of energy policy. The implications of this theoretical perspective will then be used to demonstrate that, while organizational modifications can solve some problems, they can also create or exacerbate others.

Applications of Propositions to Congress

There may be some doubt whether the general organization theory from which the foregoing propositions have been deduced is applicable to Congress and U.S. energy policy. To demonstrate that such an application has merit, each of the propositions (identified by bracketed numbers) in Table 14.1 will be sequentially related to Congress and the energy issue, albeit recognizing that the examples given are merely illustrative and the propositions' validity and applicability require further research.

Proposition (1.a): Unquestionably, the increase of Congress's professional staffs and support agencies (e.g. Office of Technology Assessment) was in response to a need to understand the external environment which, as has been repeatedly pointed out, was becoming increasingly turbulent at an increasing rate. Chapter 3 demonstrates the importance of staff for dealing with uncertainty and for providing analyses and predictions related to the problems facing the nation. Congressional staffs are becoming increasingly sophisticated in their ability to use and produce analyses that further the understanding of problems or suggest tactics to resolve conflict over policy. As indicated, Congress has also expanded its vertical integration and control over the external environment, thereby controlling all phases of policy process. For example, Congress has instructed the General Accounting Office to oversee and evaluate the Energy Department's data collection to assure its validity and timeliness. Congress has also instructed the executive branch to prepare certain regulations and programs (such as rationing programs), while retaining control over such programs not only through its traditional role of formulating legislation, but also by including review and veto provisions in the legislation. Congress also monitors and criticizes the implementation of energy programs and pressures the executive branch for the satisfaction of specific interests concerning various issues. These activities have as their objective the expansion of congressional control over more areas and aspects of energy in order to reduce uncertainty and increase organizational control over the external environment.

Proposition (1.b) manifests Congress's evolutionary changes during the 1970s which led to decentralization, internal democratization, and the relaxation of strict procedural norms. By giving more power to the subcommittee chairman, the responsibility for various legislative matters has been delegated to a greater number of people able to exercise a higher level of decision autonomy. The increase in staffs' number and power often results in greater adaptability and discretion in performing the necessary tasks.

Proposition (1.c) partially explains the conflict that arose during the energy shortages of the early and late 1970s. As discussed in earlier chapters, the conflict was pandemic, affecting relations among committees, subcommittees, between Congress and the executive branch, and among special interest groups. Environmental turbulence dictated that conflict would often characterize interaction over policy.

Although evidence for (2.a) is more elusive, it is supported by the tenor of the debate over energy policy in Congress and its chastizing of the executive branch and the oil companies and by punitive measures written into legislation that was enacted or merely proposed. For example, the initial reactions by committee and subcommittee leadership toward the oil companies after the embargo were coercive to the point of causing oil companies to alter their behavior (even accepting smaller profits).[24] Congressional leadership, at the same time, denounced the administration's attempts to deal with energy shortages and drove staffs to greater efforts in their pursuit of solutions to the energy problem. This coercive-authoritarian behavior became less pronounced as more effective, conciliatory modes of leadership were sought by congressional committee members and their leaders.

Evidence for (2.b) is presented in chapter 3, which traces the growth of analytical staffs and information-handling capabilities in response to perceived threats to congressional autonomy and control posed by an overweaning executive, and also due to various economic and national security threats posed by the energy shortages.

Proposition (3.a) is demonstrated by the increasing internal differentiation of Congress, as evidenced by proliferating subcommittees, specialized and analytical agencies, and operational units within those agencies, all of which developed in response to the increasing diversity of the external environment. Proposition (3.b) refers to the qualities of integrative mechanisms that reduce uncertainty and increase control in order to coordinate and make more effective the newly created units and specialized interests referred to in (3.a), as well as those created in response to environmental turbulence discussed in (1.a). However, the increasing sophistication of analytical outputs (1.a, 2.b, and 3.b) and their increased consumption should not necessarily lead to a conclusion that Congress has become either a systematic or a highly rational planner of policy, especially energy policy.

Propositions (4.a) and (4.b) are related to (3.a) and (3.b) but emphasize differentiation in the external environment. While Congress further differentiates its own structure through a multiplication or rearrangement of subcommittees and jurisdictions, integrating mechanisms are developed to control this differentiation.

Proposition (5.a) is exemplified in the requirements by Congress that reports be filed by the executive presenting and analyzing governmental energy plans and programs and evaluating progress toward energy goals. Congress itself has often dictated goals for the nation and launched programs to discover how the nation could achieve these goals. Once again, however, it must not be concluded on the basis of these attempts to increase planning that Congress has become a technocratic organization pursuing a set of sequential, rationally determined goals. The legislative body has continued to reveal its inherently political nature.

Proposition (5.b) is demonstrated by the proliferation of data-handling specialists, computer systems, data bases, and information access processes available to Congress and discussed in chapter 13. Proposition (5.c) is supported by evidence of the increasingly professional nature of congressional staffs and by the use of specialists in the legislative process. Energy experts are now used in every phase of legislation: for preparing and testifying on proposed legislation, in analyses of its anticipated impacts, and in assessments of program implementation and effectiveness.

Because of Congress's differentiated activities, especially when tackling a novel area, proposition (6.a) has relevance. Congress does not exist simply to make policy but for a variety of purposes that range from venting public sentiment to legitimating governmental decisions; it also enhances national cohesion since it represents all parts of the nation. It was within this framework of criss-crossing functions and goals that Congress approached the new policy area of energy in the early 1970s. The widespread and acrimonious conflicts that accompanied the congressional dealings with the energy crisis were documented in earlier chapters.

Chapter 12 (on congressional structure) begins by noting the conflicts between some of the House reform movement's goals and the need for a coherent, efficient energy policymaking structure. Ambition, party and factional conflict, organizational competition—in short, politics—partially determine the particular organizational and procedural logic that characterizes congressional behavior. One suspects that Congress will not choose the most effective solution to a problem unless it is also politically acceptable. Most representatives probably see pleasing their constituents, securing reelection, and advancing their congressional careers as primary goals and policy formulation as a secondary goal.[25] These factors lead to the pursuit of secondary goals by members of Congress, as indicated by proposition (7.a.).

Proposition (8.a) directly relates to the foregoing. Congress's "performance aspirations" were created by a major audience in its external environment—the public—which demanded a firm, effective energy policy but could not agree about who should sacrifice to achieve this. Criticism of Congress's failure to construct effective energy policy is greatest when the energy problem appears most crucial. Yet it is when there are shortages that congressional action is least likely to have any prompt effect. Congress members become as frustrated as the public because of this situation, and may redouble attempts to end the stalemate. That great challenges have often provoked great accomplishments was recalled by Carter and congressional leadership in 1977 and 1979, when they tried to invoke a sense of emergency about energy. Although this strategy of generating demands for concerted action was temporarily successful, it was markedly less so in fulfilling those demands.

Proposition (9.a) is highly applicable to Congress and helps explain the massive changes that Congress has undergone since the 1970s, when a more mechanistic, authoritarian style of leadership gave way to the current decentralized, free-wheeling, independent style. While Congress has always had an environment of intense, diverse, and shifting pressures that encouraged an organic and flexible type of leadership, in recent years these pressures have increased. Before the 1970s, changes within Congress were slow, partly because they were discouraged by rigid, mechanistic, and quasi-authoritarian procedures; these procedures often made it difficult for change advocates to select leaders and control committee business. Then, mainly as a result of internal pressures, which had been originally created by external pressures, the stranglehold of inertia, tradition, and monopolies of power was finally broken. Once the reforms were realized, those leaders who responded to the need for flexibility—such as Tip O'Neill, John Dingell, and Phil Burton—prospered, while others—like John McCormack and Carl Albert of the old guard—failed to take advantage of the new opportunities, largely due to their lack of organic leadership abilities.

The consensus now is that the reform movement of the 1970s went too far, and that a counterreform movement will begin to centralize and restrict power and streamline organizational procedures. This development follows the pattern of responding to external conditions with differentiated structures to coordinate and facilitate innovations. Congress's response to diverse and shifting pressures is evidenced in the flexible and organic style of leadership that has shepherded controversial energy measures through both houses of Congress. While the interplay between personality and policy in this process has been complex, it is likely that if the leadership could not have fulfilled the demands placed on the organization by its external environment, the organization's power (i.e. ability to control and manipulate the external environment) would have decreased and internal pressure would have been applied to replace the old leadership.

As noted, congressional organization often follows the matrix mode with its "organic" and participatory styles of leadership, and its human relations style of interaction. This is in accord with proposition (10.a). A typical manifestation of the matrix style was the "spreading of the action" that accompanied the emergence of "subcommittee government" and was responsible for democratization within the Congress. The human relations style of interaction has typified the negotiations surrounding energy policy deliberations, and examples of the influence of personality have been offered throughout the preceding chapters.

The energy crisis provoked a flood of new legislative proposals, as predicted by (11.a). Congress itself has apparently become more "project-oriented" in the 1970s as a result of decentralization, evidenced by the increase in bills, hearings, studies, press releases, and publicity. For example, after the reforms that replaced Harley Staggers with John Moss as chairman of the House Commerce Oversight and Investigation Subcommittee, frequency of hearings increased tremendously.[26] Whether or not this added work of Congress has actually produced true innovations and, if so, whether these have served a purpose in any area other than public relations remains to be answered. One thing is certain—the number of bills produced by Congress on energy and every other imaginable subject increased during the 1970s. While the budget battles of the 1980s reduced the variety of legislative initiatives, the scope of legislation has continued to increase. Despite their highly touted emphasis on deregulation, even the Ninety-seventh and Ninety-eighth Congresses have shown remarkable willingness to regulate an ever-increasing number of aspects of national life, from controlling teenage promiscuity to monitoring domestic political behavior.

Proposition (11.b) characterizes Congress. Each member as an individual has multiple responsibilities and also belongs to several committees, each of which has a different area of responsibility and task definition. The resulting organizational design, called matrix style, appears to be a satisfactory response to the disjunctive demands placed on members of Congress.

Proposition (12.a) is applicable to Congress, especially in the Senate, where collegiality is a byword. While some Congress members are more powerful than others, partly because their authority is usually confined to a particular area (making them open to retaliation in areas where other members are more powerful), congressional authority is not hierarchical, and it is becoming increasingly evident that the control of party leaders in both houses is limited.

Dysfunctional Aspects of Organizational Change

As noted, uncertainty reduction, or in the functionally equivalent administrative term, achieving accountability, is a prime organizational task undertaken by an organization as a means of controlling its external environment. "Surprises" that embarrass or threaten an organization can motivate it to undertake uncertainty reduction. The 1973-74 oil embargo, the Shah's fall, and the subsequent oil shortages were such surprises for Congress. In response to surprises, organizations initiate a series of modifications, most common of which is to expand their internal and external areas of control. This expansion leads to a series of intended and unintended consequences that increase the need for control but not necessarily organizational efficiency. Therefore, as changes are produced in the internal arrangements of an organization and its relationship with the external environment, the organization continues its attempts to extend control mechanisms in order to reduce the additional uncertainty.

Following this pattern, Congress attempts to increase the reliability and responsiveness of organizations within its ambit. The legislative branch possesses manifold mechanisms for exerting control over the executive branch, many of which are elaborations of the checks and balances implicit and explicit in the Constitution. These include influencing the selection of members of an external organization through, for example, confirmation hearings of presidential appointees. Other mechanisms permit the setting of regulations, reporting requirements, and goals for both agencies and the government as a whole. While Congress's most successful means of control over the executive branch is its budget-setting powers, it can also pressure agencies with some important sanctions in the form of oversight operations, inquiries, and hearings. However, while Congress's supervision of the executive branch furthers its intended purpose, it can also have unintended consequences that inhibit congressional control. Some of these potential consequences are diagrammed in Figure 14.1.

Attempts to increase the efficiency of control, especially through increased supervision, reveal the disequilibria of power resources. The organizations that are the objects of congressional attempts at control often try to protect their own freedom of action and autonomy and even to reverse the situation by trying to control Congress. As the instruments of authority relations are revealed, hostility and conflict usually increase. Previously undiscerned differences in perceptions, goals, and strategies become visible and informal adjustments that previously eased strain may break down. Personalized behavior can decrease, and actors of the competing organizations perceive each other and act according to the specified rights and duties of role incumbents rather than with a consideration of competing actors as "unique individuals."

Inflexibility in the supervisory agency complicates attempts to control. As Merton has suggested in another context,[27] the rules set down by supervisory organizations become internalized insofar as adherence is a valued response, even when they no longer serve the purpose for which they were originally intended. This rigidity results in a need to rationalize the actions of the supervisory agency, which causes further rigidity. Such a process has resulted in the inflexible attitude toward rules exhibited by the Federal Energy Administration and the Department of Energy, which has caused them to be characterized as abusive and arrogant by the organizations subject to their control.

Some subjects of congressional attempts to control may refuse even superficial compliance. If Congress does not then abandon its attempts, a confrontation may ensue, which, whatever its outcome, will lead to a draining of organizational resources. If the resisting party wins the contest, the resources have been wasted, and the outcome may be highly counterproductive for Congress. But even if overt resistance is temporarily overcome, it is likely that it will continue, latently or through various methods of subterfuge, subtle or otherwise. Such methods of resistance—categorized under the rubric of management of relations—include fulfilling the form but not the content of requirements (or violating the spirit but not the letter of the law), supplying so much information to congressional personnel that important items are lost in a mass of detail, delaying compliance with requests or demands, intentionally misunderstanding directives or instructions, and feigning deference to the point of obsequiousness to deflect congressional attention.

A progression of unintended consequences similar to that which results from attempts to control the external environment also follows attempts to organize internal staff resources. How some of these consequences may occur is illustrated in Figure 14.2. Congress's effort to understand and control

Figure 14.1

Congressional Organization: Consequences of Extending External Control

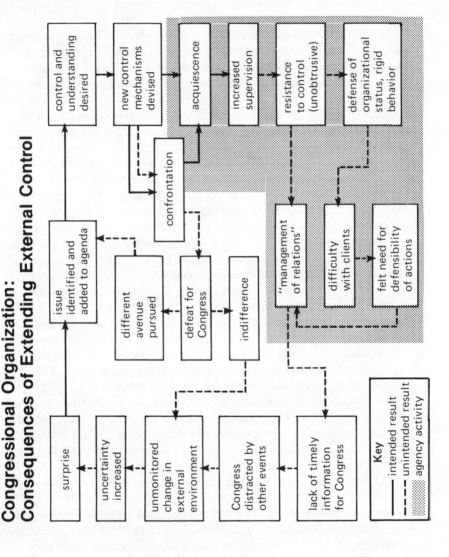

Figure 14.2

Congressional Organization:
Consequences of Extending Internal Control

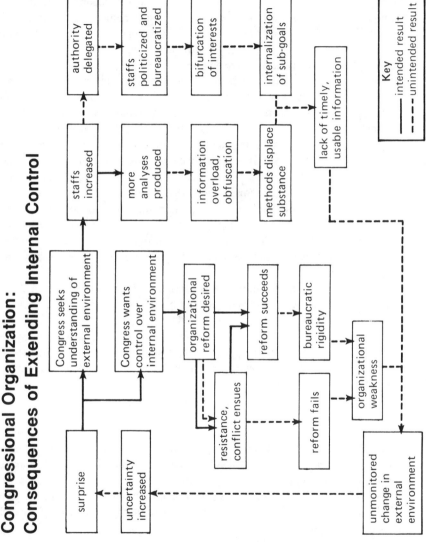

policy-related information and activities and to offset policy "surprises" has led to an increased emphasis on the size and professionalism of congressional staff. While the staffs were created to analyze data and events, monitor agency activity, and assist Congress members, their expanded authority and responsibility are also control mechanisms. Staff members are able to get directly involved in the intimate workings of an agency, if they should desire and if it can at least be superficially justified. As pointed out, staffs are called upon to be politically responsive in their analyses, act on unexamined assumptions, and serve their members' political needs rather than a higher goal. They are often members of a political party themselves or subscribe to an ideological orientation, and their analyses and activities can exhibit this bias. The bureaucratic demands of the analytical agencies can also displace the original purposes for which the agencies were formed as they struggle for preeminence or merely survival. This process is observable in the rapid leadership changes at the Office of Technology Assessment and the politically inspired attacks on the Congressional Budget Office.[28]

As reliance upon the staffs increases, their functional, if not managerial, control can be lost due to goal displacement. The net result might be that the proper information and advice does not reach Congress, which becomes distracted by other events and remains open to unpleasant surprises from its internal environment.

While many of the consequences appearing in Figures 14.1 and 14.2 are negative, Congress is now much better prepared for dealing with energy issues than it was in the early 1970s. Its internal organization has specialized units for dealing with energy issues, and it has available a wide array of experts on committee and personal staffs and among its support agencies. These developments contribute to Congress's ability to respond effectively and rapidly to new energy issues.

Conclusion

Congress has adjusted to its external environment through internal changes which help it to control external forces. However, not all the changes have had their intended consequence. As Figures 14.1 and 14.2 indicate, organizational solutions do not always work well, even though they may be the best available option. The limits to organizational solutions are discussed further in the next chapter.

Notes

1. For example, see Lewis Anthony Dexter, *The Sociology and Politics of Congress* (Chicago: Rand McNally, 1969).

2. Lewis Froman, Jr., "Organization Theory and the Explanation of Important Characteristics of Congress," *American Political Science Review* 62 (1968): 518-27.
3. Joseph D. Cooper, "Congress in Organizational Perspective," in L. Dodd and B. Oppenheimer, eds., *Congress Reconsidered* (New York: Praeger, 1977).
4. Daniel Katz and Robert Kahn, *The Social Psychology of Organizations*, 2nd ed., (New York: Wiley, 1973).
5. Paul Lawrence and Jay Lorsch, *Organization and Its Environment* (Cambridge: Harvard University Press, 1967).
6. J. D. Thompson, *Organization in Action* (New York: McGraw-Hill, 1967).
7. Ibid., p. 159.
8. Ibid., p. 39.
9. Ibid., p. 70.
10. Samuel Huntington, "Congressional Responses to the Twentieth Century," in David Truman, ed., *The Congress and America's Future*, 2nd. ed. (Englewood Cliffs, N.J.: Prentice-Hall, 1973).
11. James March and Herbert Simon, *Organizations* (New York: Wiley, 1958).
12. Kenneth McNeil, "Understanding Organizational Power," *Administrative Science Quarterly* 23 (March 1978): 65-90; Max Weber, *The Methodology of the Social Sciences* (New York: Free Press, 1949); Hans Gerth and C. Wright Mills, eds., *From Max Weber* (New York: Oxford University Press, 1946), esp. pp. 196-244.
13. George Bennello, "Wasteland culture," in H. P. Drietzel, ed., *Recent Sociology No. 1* (London: Macmillan, 1969). See also Max Weber, *Wirtschaft und Gesellschaft* (Tubingen: J.C.B. Mohr Verlag, 1925), esp. ch. 1.
14. Robert K. Merton, *Social Theory and Social Structure*, rev. ed. (Glencoe, Ill.: Free Press, 1957), pp. 195-206.
15. Elizabeth Drew, "Suspension Calendar," *New Yorker* (June 24, 1979), pp. 43ff.
16. Lawrence and Lorsch, *Organization and Its Environment*.
17. An example is Jackson's involvement with energy affairs, which was used to further his presidential bid in 1976.
18. The evidence for this proposition can also be found in a study of the military's response to a crisis. See Morris Janowitz, *Sociology and the Military Establishment* (New York: Russell Sage Foundation, 1959).
19. R. M. Cyert and James G. March, *A Behavioral Theory of the Firm* (Englewood Cliffs, NJ: Prentice-Hall, 1972), ch. 3.
20. Burns and Stalker have identified two radically opposite management styles—organic and mechanistic—based on Durkheim's seminal formulation. Organic style is characterized by flexibility, informality, and easy, frequent vertical and horizontal communication; formal authority is less important than situational authority. The mechanistic management style has highly structured communication channels, a highly formalized authority heirarchy, and strictly defined responsibilities; decision making is centralized and status rankings are rigidly defined. Tom Burns and G. M. Stalker, *The Management of Innovation* (London: Tavistock, 1961).
21. Jay Galbraith, *Designing Complex Organizations* (Reading, Mass.: Addison-Wesley, 1973); "Matrix Organization Designs," *Business Horizons* 14 (1971): 29-40.
22. Heflebower's argument that a decentralized organization is more vulnerable in a crisis is relevant to understanding Congress's unresponsiveness to the energy cri-

sis. See Richard Heflebower, "Observations on Decentralization in Large Enterprises," *Journal of Industrial Economics* (November 1960): 7-22.

23. D.S. Pugh et al., "The Context of Organizational Structures," *Administrative Science Quarterly* 14 (1969): 91-114; John Child and Roger Mansfield, "Technology, Size and Organization Structure," *Sociology* 6 (1971): 368-93.
24. U. S. Federal Trade Commission, "Activities of Oil Companies," 1981.
25. The image of 435 members of Congress scrambling to satisfy the desires of 335 widely diverse districts and 50 variegated states hardly suggests the possibility of agreement on anything as unpalatable as a gasoline tax. The wonder is rather that enough integrating structures and exchanges can be devised to overcome the centrifugal forces and interests sufficiently to gain passage of any of the many controversial measures on energy. A valuable perspective on congressional decision making is John Kingdon, *Congressional Voting Decisions* (New York: Harper and Row, 1973).
26. David E. Price, "Impact of Reform: House Commerce Subcommittee on Oversight and Investigations," in Leroy Riselbach, *Legislative Reform* (Lexington, Mass.: Heath, 1978).
27. Merton, *Social Theory.*
28. For example, see *Science* 203 (February 23, 1979): 729; *National Journal* (September 8, 1979): 1484-88; *New York Times*, December 2, 1979, p. E6.

15
Organizational Limits of Energy Policy Processes

All energy strategy, whether it involves contingency planning, research, administration, or resource management, suffers from limitations imposed by human inadequacies and the essentially political and incremental nature of energy policy decision making. Yet recommendations for improving the energy policy system, especially following a crisis, accident, or emergency, usually concern data collection and analysis or organizational structure and procedures while ignoring the inherent limitations of the system itself and its policy makers. Analytical and theoretical literature that does discuss these limitations is considered hopelessly abstruse or niggling by most of the practical realists who make our energy policy decisions.

An increased understanding of the psychology of decision making as it relates to U.S. energy policy and of the fundamental inadequacies of the system that produces this policy will help to break the present pattern of often creating ineffectual energy policy.

The old conception of organizations—as rational, seeking to maximize goal achievement, and arriving by experimentation at the most beneficial course of action—is being replaced by a less idealistic image. Indeed, recent empirical research indicates that organizations have biases, limitations, and drives for actualization similar to those of individuals.[1] They also behave like human beings in that they design ideal plans to maximize power, wealth, security, or other factors, and, when these prove too costly or ambitious, settle for less exigent or more easily attainable goals.

Organizations are also easily stymied by internal conflict. Even when a strategy involves correcting an ill that is universally recognized, it may be abandoned because of disagreement over the appropriate remedy. For example, the difficulties encountered by Congress in deciding how to alleviate the universally recognized problem of gasoline shortages in 1974 made its actual solution practically impossible. Congress members found it easier to agree on the need for action than on the specific nature of that action. Just as members of a business organization may agree about what factors are inhibiting the organization's growth but not be able to decide on a single plan for boosting productivity, so Congress members can agree that the United States must receive more oil without endangering national security or hurting the economy, yet disagree on the method for accomplishing this.

Organizational Strategies

Strategies used by Congress in addressing national energy policy, both in substance and in terms of federal organization for its implementation, are incremental. Incrementalism—gradual modification of policies rather than their total restructuring—allows a mutual adjustment between an organization and its environment. Many of these strategies, designed to control and manipulate the external environment, are shared with most other organizations.

One strategy is correctability—choosing a course that would enable a reapproximation of the original status quo, if subsequent contingencies should demonstrate that the decision was a mistake. In recognition of the ever-present possibility of error or failure, this strategy attempts to avoid irreparable damage to a necessary or useful part of an organization. To the extent possible, a second chance is thus built into a decision in order to mitigate its consequences if it proves erroneous. This partly accounts for congressional resistance to various sweeping presidential plans for restructuring energy markets, bureaucracies, and consumption patterns.

The correctability strategy is linked with the strategy of seriality, which envisions policy as an ongoing process of sequential decisions and adjustments. No step is seen as the final solution to a problem but rather as one of a series that will become increasingly judicious as further relevant knowledge and experience are gained. Thus, not only policies but objectives may be continually revised in response to changing situations. This step-by-step approach allows flexibility and resilience but results in change which appears significant only in retrospect. This strategy's gradual nature precludes an "all or nothing" approach.

Most strategies used by organizations for the accomplishment of goals in a changing environment are aimed at critical areas or trouble spots and seldom include overarching plans providing for all contingencies. When they have, as with Carter's first National Energy Plan or Nixon's Project Independence, they have encountered serious problems. When a component that is necessary to action or production is missing or malfunctioning—a common occurrence with complex processes and environments—a bottleneck-breaking strategy is usually advanced as the most direct means of adjusting policy to deal with outside pressures.

All the foregoing strategies for goal achievement depend upon feedback from the external environment on their impact and the adjustments required by their implementation. Often a small decision or proposal serves as a trial balloon to generate feedback, informing the organization of the likely result if the direction is pursued in future decision making.

Another advantage of incremental strategies is that it incorporates the cognitive and psychological limits of the humans that run organizations by using incrementalism:

1. Policy makers' analysis is concentrated on areas in which they have more experience.
2. The range of possible alternative policies is greatly reduced, allowing each area to be analyzed more thoroughly.
3. The number and complexity of factors to be analyzed is significantly decreased.[2]

Human nature itself precludes a smooth handling of energy policy and imposes informational and organizational limits to sound policy design. Attempts to change the realities by which organizations operate encounter adamant human and organizational opposition, as will be demonstrated. Indeed, although a large part of the previous chapter dealt with organizational responses to the challenges of the energy situation, the U.S. government has directed little systematic attention to preventing "surprises" like an oil embargo or supply disruption. Rather, such emergencies set off a mad scramble to disinter outmoded contingency plans, allocate blame, reorganize the governmental mechanisms for energy security, and only later assess the lesson learned in the often futile attempt to avoid making similar mistakes in the future.

Such assessments have given rise to arguments advocating the reliance upon technically literate "philosopher kings" to guide society around the dangers of political intrigue and technological or economic mishap.[3] Usually, the concern for future security is translated into recommendations for improved data analysis and methods of prediction, and an enhanced role for scientific advice. While on the surface these notions seem attractive, and it is obvious that societies should try to avoid repeating their past mistakes, corrective measures that depend solely on organizational changes to avoid costly surprises, or even disasters, are bound to disappoint. Organizations in a complex, uncertain environment are destined to be unhappily surprised by unanticipated problems. In order to respond effectively to a problem, an organization must be able to understand it in its total context without distortions imposed by past experience and perceptions. However, confronted with overwhelming uncertainty, the natural tendency is to fall back on intuition, predispositions, and experience as guides to action.

Accurate Predictions Are Difficult to Make

Noll neatly illustrates the fundamental problem when he muses about what, if any, predictions an expert group could have made in 1965 concerning the approaching energy crisis.[4] Given our heavy reliance on oil from the highly unstable Middle East and OPEC's significance in the situation, the experts could have been somewhat alerted to future problems. But because at that time oil was cheap and plentiful, national oil companies dominated the oil trade, the United States was the world's largest oil producer, and OPEC seemed passive and weak, their concern would probably have been mild. On the other hand, they may well have been alarmed about our nearly total dependence on copper imports—another vital resource. The major copper exporters—Chile, Zambia, and Zaire—were all politically volatile and prospects were good for their developing an effective cartel. The experts would likely have agreed on the advisability of stockpiling both oil and copper, but if forced to choose one or the other, would have opted for copper, because while the United States has large domestic oil reserves, there is little indigenous copper production. This decision, if made and acted upon, would be viewed as a typical example of government miscalculation, waste, and bureaucratic bungling (especially considering depressed copper prices), while the stockpiling of oil would be lauded as a stroke of genius.

The fact is that the information base today, as much as in 1965, is inadequate to determine with much certainty whether copper, oil, or some other key commodity is likely to be cartelized and if so, for how long. Therefore, no amount of expertise is likely to improve significantly policy makers' ability to predict future energy conditions, although there are several elaborate, and a few inexpensive, precautions that may afford some protection against surprises in this area. Uncertainty is largely irreducible, anticipatory policy contingencies ineffective, and conclusions and recommendations conjectural. The future occurrence of any event and its possible outcome can be assigned a probability but the effectiveness of each response to the event and counterresponse will remain uncertain. The net result of multiplying contingencies and branching possibilities makes any prediction about energy highly uncertain, even for relatively simple problems.

While the policy system's failures are obvious, its successes are not always observable. Disasters that are avoided are seldom acknowledged, and if a problem is predicted and avoided, the prediction is considered inaccurate. It is practically impossible to determine a cause and effect relationship where energy policy is involved. For example, the oil industry took credit for the plentiful supplies in the decades following World War II, but blamed the U.S. government for the shortages of the 1970s. It is also impossible to know whether CIA involvement in the restoration of the Shah in 1954 had a detrimental or positive effect on long-run U.S. interests. The eventual net effect of continually complying with the wishes of the Saudis is equally unknowable. There is no information about the ratio of successes to failures in prediction; the principles of social causality are so poorly understood that most rationales and explanations for outcomes are of dubious validity (especially those that are patently self-serving).

The failure of organizations to anticipate problems and respond to them is not merely the result of coincidences that can be corrected or accidents that can be anticipated, but often inhere in the organizations' processes themselves. Particularly problematical are: (1) the perspectives used by analysts who provide information to decision makers and those used by decision makers themselves, which blind them to important information and useful approaches; (2) the pathologies of communication, such as breakdowns in the collecting and timely processing of information, in communicating analyses to policy makers, and in impressing the latter with the correctness and importance of the analyses; and (3) the organizational structure itself, which involves unresolvable tradeoffs and dilemmas.

Information and Position

While valuable insights into ongoing situations and operations are gained by low-level personnel in direct contact with problems, the higher echelons of the decision hierarchy are often glutted with interpretive data and analyses from varying sources and usually exclude the direct "raw" observations of the lowest level. From this mass of information, much of which is ambiguous, analysts from operational agencies generally select that which legitimates their agencies' performance and allows the policy makers' perspective to be optimistic. Problems are thus ignored.

On the other hand, analyses from nonoperational units, usually autonomous staffs (e.g. congressional committee or investigatory staffs such as the General Accounting Office) often evaluate an organization's ability pessimistically. Both analysts and policy makers seize upon fragmentary reports or other inadequate indicators of success to rationalize their actions and downplay more general, comprehensive assessments. At the same time, warnings generated by attempts to anticipate emergencies are ignored until they finally desensitize policy makers. Those who continue to disagree with policy makers who use only that information that supports their policies are removed from the decision process by deed, if not by letter.

The usefulness of information in energy planning is also limited by subjectivity. Ideally, planning for energy contingencies would involve estimating future system capabilities, likely behavior by relevant parties, and possible threats to supplies. In practice it is exceedingly difficult to distinguish between policy-relevant analysis of information and policy advocacy, largely because any choices about data interpretation are based on normative criteria.

In planning, organizational roles are reversed from their positions in operational evaluation. Operational agencies need to see important roles for themselves in meeting future contingencies and therefore are inclined toward pessimistic interpretations and assessments. This proclivity is geared toward guaranteeing a substantial role for the agency and enhanced prestige and power for its members in the future. Galbraith argues that an organizational imperative is to prolong its survival even if at great short-run cost.[5] Autonomous staff analysts, who do not stand to benefit from budget increases, are influenced by the natural conservatism and debunking tendencies of the general intellectual and policy community and thus are less alarmist. They will ignore warnings, resist allocating more resources to the solution of a problem, and expect a stable, predictable environment in the future. A second factor working against contingency planning is the natural tendency to place future-oriented priorities beneath immediate, politically expedient ones.

Structural Problems

Failures of information handling are inseparable from failures of policy. Despite claims that collection, analysis, and decision should be separate functions, they are in practice tightly interwoven and operationally, if not conceptually, indistinguishable. Decision and analysis are interactive, not sequential, processes. Hence although inadequate data has contributed to energy policy failures, it is not in itself an underlying cause for failure. The blame more accurately falls on structural problems such as the ignoring of professional analysis and counterintuitive warnings, and the continuous pressure of special interests and energy industries in pushing their own perspectives.

These structural inadequacies result from characteristics inherent in most organizations: hierarchy, and centralization of information flows. Wilensky maintains that efficient use of information in organizations is interfered with most frequently by these characteristics.[6] Policy organizations make varying efforts to prevent misuse of information by leveling hierarchical structure, decreasing centralization, and increasing specialization and internal differentiation. Nonetheless, there are limits to the extent a formal organization can modify itself and still maintain its basic integration. Other structural characteristics that obviously constrain optimal processing of energy information include limitations of time and resources and gaps in an organization's vertical and horizontal linkages.

Another factor related to organizational failure in information processing is the predominant position that managers hold over staff workers when it comes to advising policy makers. Policy makers often are more swayed by managers' anecdotally-based reports than staffs' systematic analyses, even when the former may have been shaped by self-interest in the success of unit operations.[7] The higher the level of the policy makers, the more likely they are to prefer operational advice and inputs over those of autonomous staffs. Moreover, since these high-level policy makers feel they have a wider viewpoint and need greater autonomy because they serve a broader community of interests, they are uninterested in listening to advisors assigned by someone else, and will subvert any attempts at dictation about procedures.

The dynamics of the decision process itself militate against analytic refinements. During a crisis, both the data inflow and demand for policy decisions exceeds analytic capability; careful and comprehensive information gathering and staff work become impossible. When there is no time pressure on decisions, bureaucratic inertia and other forms of institutional interference become more prominent. Under most decision circumstances, there is a call for more evidence and analyses, without an attempt to assess whether an incremental addition to the data base of a decision is worth the additional resource costs. The demand for more data and new mechanisms to produce it are persistent, and at times become ends in themselves, without regard to improvements in the final product.

Human error also complicates the use of information in the policy process, resulting in the essential ambiguity which characterizes all evidence about energy situations and policies. Obviously a goal of energy data collection and analysis is to reduce uncertainty, but very often, even after a thorough analysis has been performed and estimates have been developed, as much uncertainty remains as before the analysis was undertaken. Expert energy advice and analysis—supposed to extract certainty from an uncertain environment and to promote a coherent policy in a fluctuating and cross-pressured situation—is in great part accomplished by extrapolating from data that is highly ambiguous, with the result that reality is oversimplified and policy makers are misled. Analysts who attempt to include caveats and qualifications in their assessments usually yield not more accurate but more ambiguous advice, which is dismissed by policy makers who contend that the expert analysts have failed in their role. Moreover, a policy maker's conundrum is that data's precision and accuracy is inversely related to its importance and policy relevance.

Preparing for the Worst

The ambiguity of the environment can also be worsened by an *excess* of information. It is difficult to distinguish the occasional crucial piece of information from the torrent of insignificant items, observations, and comments. The sheer volume of energy information generated by public and private groups dwarfs the ability of a policy organization to sort, study, and absorb them. Hence, when policy makers are pressed for a decision and at the same time inundated with data that is highly ambiguous, intuition takes over and an analysis is selected to legitimate or disguise it.

Crises and disasters stimulate demands for organizational changes that will prevent repetition of mistakes. Many times, however, such changes are fa- cades over old patterns which continue unimpeded. Standard practices often persist because they adequately serve an organization's real intentions rather than its publicly stated ones. If reforms invoked in the wake of a crisis do not serve organizational needs, if they complicate operations or strain organiza- tional resources, they will either become token practices or simply fall into disuse. Thus the reporting to Congress that is required of many energy units becomes a meaningless form,[8] the congressional oversight function becomes a publicity gimmick or headline-attracting "window dressing." The rapid de- generation of organizational reform serves the hidden purposes of preserving the target organization's control over resources and maintaining its latent goals.

One way of coping with ambiguity and ambivalence is by adapting the most pessimistic interpretation to data and constructing worst-case scenarios out of them. Among the disadvantages in assuming the worst are the exhausting costs that must be accepted. For example, the Nixon administration's initial reaction to the 1973-74 embargo was to seek energy autarky—Project Independence—which would have cost billions of dollars with little recom- pense. Similarly, the concern about nuclear safety, heightened by the accident at Three Mile Island in Pennsylvania, led to demands that all nuclear power plants be closed or that so many safety features be added that their operation would be practically impossible. While these steps might have "solved" the initial problem, their monetary costs would have been exorbitant and the ac- companying social dislocation massive.

This worst-case position, if not reasonable, is always defensible. A disaster or crisis can always be attributed later to a mistaken calculation of probabili- ties and a failure to take into account some shred of evidence hinting at the disaster. But the total threat response is a useless guide to normal procedures; in practical terms it is seldom realizable, especially since most predicted prob- lems never materialize, and preparing for the worst eventuality requires a considerable expenditure of resources that might otherwise be devoted to more beneficial ends. Further, since most dire contingencies do not befall the policy system, routinization of warnings would quickly render them meaning- less. Too many false alarms dull the reaction capabilities of the system.

Difficulty of Reform

Another approach to solving energy policy problems is multiple advocacy. Academic observers have proposed that multiple advocacy sources would al- leviate the problems of unexamined premises, reliance on institutional author- ity, and irrelevant analyses—problems that have arisen from policy makers ignoring unpopular viewpoints.

Still, it is doubtful whether multiple advocacy would resolve the fundamental problems of data overload, time constraints, and ambiguity. The problem of uncertainty could be aggravated by the addition of yet more diverging opinions and interpretations of policy needs and implications. New viewpoints would receive a patina of empirical validity while the policy maker continued to follow his or her predispositions as before. It is also likely that if ambivalence increased, conservatism or paralysis on the part of policy makers would be the consequence. Further, most nonexpert policy makers have problems arbitrating intellectually between experts who disagree with one another; they also have difficulties extracting the vital decisional component from the academic and methodological accoutrements. Moreover, the multiple advocacy model depends essentially upon equal distribution of power, influence, competence, analytic resources, and bargaining skills, an extraordinarily difficult accomplishment. And if equal weight in an argument is given to each viewpoint, erroneous or misleading viewpoints will receive as much salience as sound ones, thus compounding the problems of uncertainty and policy inefficacy.

Those who argue for multiple advocacy or redundancy—and who assume that more analysis and discussion is always better—are countered by those who recommend consolidating and streamlining information flows. Emphasizing constraints on policy makers, including limitations of time and attention, the consolidationists maintain that too much analysis by too many parties results only in confusion. They advocate fewer and superior evaluations. To accomplish this—and to increase the clarity, analytical sharpness, and timeliness of decisions—they would centralize and focus the energy policy hierarchy.

An opposing argument contends that centralization creates pressure to compromise views in order to gain agreement, while individual reservations and the limitations of the analysis become blurred by the necessity of reducing the complex world to an abbreviated form. Further, bureaucratic dynamics come to the fore, limiting the utility of the policy information and recommendations. Those processing information may become insulated from the larger world and thus find their products diverging ever more widely from the policy makers' needs and the reality of events in the external environment. On the other hand, the group may be captured, either by an outside interest group (as was the case with the Department of Interior's oil and gas unit during the 1950s), or by the department within which it exists; in either case, the group serves an entity other than the policy maker. Finally, with such a narrowly focused agency, and with such a reduction of staff involved in collecting and processing energy information, new gaps and holes appear in the agency's range of coverage.

Reorganization is limited in its ability to address major problems, since many reforms are mere box-shuffling or impression management exercises, even though reforms can fail to prevent a resurgence of the same organizational features that contributed to the original problem. Moreover, initially extreme changes have often been quickly moderated to avoid the new problems they entail. Compensating for inadequacy is usually interpreted to mean increasing organizational size rather than reducing it, causing new structural problems. However, attempts to streamline an organization through reducing its size, inertia, or complexity opens up new gaps in its coverage and new problems in its operation.

A final problem inheres in the nature of information. Information does not exist abstractly but is created by humans and is shaped to serve specific needs. Therefore, the data creation process is influenced reflexively and interactively by social processes, and despite theoretical conjecturing, the necessary information about energy resources and future conditions is always unavailable. No amount of additional data collection can eliminate this fact. The plausible futures cannot be sufficiently limited or homogenized so that a single policy can predominate.

A common strategy for solving energy policy problems has been to enlist the aid of experts. As indicated in earlier chapters, limitations of time and expertise force policy makers to delegate investigative and analytical tasks, and even many decisions, to experts. The configurations of this model varies, but the essence remains the same: objective, neutral specialists are retained, and they collect data on an area of concern, set down the most likely implications of various courses of action, and recommend the optimal course, given the policy maker's goals. This model predominates throughout the energy policy process, but is concentrated in the strategic planning, research and development, and regulatory subareas.

Often, policy makers draw their experts from a single discipline (economists, military strategists, nuclear engineers, urban planners). An unrecognized problem with relying on this system is the experts' self-oriented viewpoint that is built in. The economist will seek and propose economic solutions, the military strategist military solutions, and so forth, with the result that policy makers, unaware of their experts' limitations, misallocate resources and fail to perceive the broader picture.

Policy makers receive information in three ways: (1) by purchasing information through research, contracting, and related activities; (2) by generating and processing information within their own organization; and (3) through formal and informal channels that interested organizations and individuals use to provide information at their own expense, such as lobbying or testifying at congressional and regulatory hearings.

Influencing the policy process usually involves decreasing uncertainty for one unit while increasing it for other units in the society. An extreme example of transferring uncertainty to others was provided by the policy of maintaining price controls on gasoline during the 1970s, a practice which guaranteed gasoline price but increased uncertainty over supplies, indirect acquisition costs, and automotive companies' inaccuracies and distortions in reporting estimated reserves.[9]

Reliance on professional skills for information further reduces the protection of unrepresented groups. When the rules of evidence and mechanisms for evaluating the quality of information places responsibility for information in the hands of specialists, established institutions and procedures are favored. Because information about existing policies and operating institutions is more certain, it takes precedence over conjectural assertions about a future state of the world and its unrealized institutions and policies. Thus, implicitly, most of the burden of proof falls on those who argue for a deviation from the status quo and who want to support a policy change toward that end. This is the precise challenge faced by the energetics perspective, outlined in chapter 10.

Any attempts to solve our energy problems by introducing a "devil's advocate" or by adding more participants to the policy process are likely to fail, because they will be either paternalistic or insensitive, depending on the degree to which underrepresented groups are included. In real terms, the addition of heretofore unrepresented groups simply increases policy makers' desire for certainty and their reluctance to consider new options. If they are formally included, their influence in the decision process is limited. Further, adding participants merely preserves the status quo by increasing the information to be processed, the issues to be considered, and the time needed to arrive at decisions. Consequently, the expected net gains from a proposal would be reduced since its enactment would be pushed further into the future and the costs of participating in decisions would increase as additional information was required. The result would be a reduced incentive to propose changes in policy.

Conclusion

Organizational solutions to energy policy problems are hamstrung in three ways: (1) most procedural reforms that address specific problems aggravate them or cause new ones, (2) modifications of analytic processes cannot overcome the inherent ambiguity and uncertainty of reality, and (3) rationalization of information systems cannot overcome the predispositions and perceptual idiosyncracies of policy makers nor the political pressure and time constraints placed upon them.

As a result, the paradoxes of energy policy are not resolvable in any pure sense. Energy problems will continue, despite improvements in organization. But, the energy policy record is encouraging because it has not been worse;

incremental improvements have been made since the early 1970s and their combined impact has been significant. While these changes have added new pathologies to the system, they have also added fairness and rationality. There has been some diversification of interests in the policy process and increased representation in many policy councils. Progress has also been made in counterbalancing the weight given the energy industry, although, as indicated in chapters 9 and 10, more progress is necessary. The coordination of energy policy, information, and administrative processes has been markedly enhanced. Post hoc evaluations and recommendations are less often made by those initially responsible for the problems and more frequently by a relatively more neutral group. Anticipation and response to energy emergencies, both domestic ones involving accidents and international ones involving oil disruptions, have been improved. At times policy makers have been more innovative, experimental, and willing to apply the results of social scientific research. Until the Reagan administration came to power, energy resource statistics had been improved in terms of quality, comprehensiveness, and usefulness. At times policy makers seem more receptive to countervailing opinions and willing to consider alternative interpretations of facts and events.

On the negative side, however, the dangers inherent in the supply perspective have not been explicitly addressed by the public or by top policy makers. In addition, there is no evidence that truly innovative opinions have been systematically incorporated into the policy process, let alone been influential in policy outcomes.

Although the many marginal reforms made since the oil embargo reduce the probability of error, the unresolvable paradoxes and barriers to analytic and decisional accuracy sustain the possibility of energy policy failure. The intractability of the energy problem, the high degree of uncertainty involving most of its aspects, and the ultimate reliance on the predispositions and values of policy makers add to this possibility.

The focus of what little study has been done on energy policy has been on procedural values as ends to themselves. Little attention has been given to the way these procedures affect important substantive areas such as national security and economic growth. Even less attention has been paid to the actual collecting, processing, and applying of data or to the resource and political costs involved. Finally, the relationship between uncertainty and organizational procedures in energy policy has been all but ignored. Problems in these areas are apparently so threatening as to discourage specific policy recommendations for their resolution.

It is hoped that this book is a start toward filling in some of those major gaps. An often repeated contention is that the energy problem is a social problem, not a technical one. It would seem logical, in that case, to undertake research on the larger social consequences of various energy policy options.

Further effort in this area would contribute substantially toward a more stable energy situation in the United States.

In light of the present work on Congress and its response as an organization to energy crises, the principles discussed above indicate several areas that hold promise. Additional sociological research can help Congress to better understand the organizational problems it is facing and suggest ways of circumventing them. This is true for other governmental entities as well. We can build into congressional organizations greater resiliency so that they can respond and reorganize quickly and smoothly in the face of new challenges. Once policy makers understand these potential contributions, they would be more supportive of social science research. They would also be more amenable to applying research findings to energy problems and other fundamental, far-reaching questions with which sociology deals.

Notes

1. Amitai Etzioni, *A Comparative Analysis of Complex Organizations* (New York: Free Press, 1961); Graham Allison, *The Essence of Decision* (Boston, Mass.: Little Brown, 1971); Charles Perrow, *Organizational Analysis* (San Francisco, Calif.: Brooks-Cole, 1970).
2. D. Braybrooke and Charles Lindblom, *A Strategy of Decision* (New York: Free Press, 1963); Richard Cyert and James March, *A Behavioral Theory of the Firm* (Englewood Cliffs, N.J.: Prentice-Hall, 1963); James March and Herbert Simon, *Organizations* (New York: Wiley, 1958).
3. Edward Wenk, "Political Limits in Steering Technology," *Technology in Society* 1 (Spring 1979): 27-36; *Margins for Survival: Overcoming Political Limits in Steering Technology* (New York: Pergamon, 1979).
4. Roger Noll, "Information, Decision-Making Procedures, and Energy Policy," *American Behavioral Scientist* 19 (1976): 267-78.
5. John Kenneth Galbraith, *The New Industrial State*, 3rd rev. ed. (New York, New American Library, 1979), p. 67.
6. Harold L. Wilensky, *Organizational Intelligence* (New York: Basic Books, 1967), pp. 42-62, 126, 179.
7. Cf. Melville Dalton, "Conflicts between Staff and Line Managerial Officers," *American Sociological Review* 15 (1950): 342-51.
8. The executive makes over 1,300 reports annually to Congress, many of which appear to be little used. For a listing, see U.S. Congress, Clerk of the House of Representatives, "Reports to be Made to Congress," *Communication*, January 25, 1982, House document 97-130.
9. Morton A. Elliott, "Many Complex Factors Affect Oil and Gas Reserve Data," *Oil and Gas Journal* 75 (May 30, 1977): 152-56; Aaron Wildavsky and Ellen Tenenbaum, *The Politics of Mistrust: Estimating American Oil and Gas Reserves* (Beverly Hills, Calif.: Sage, 1981).

Index